Living North Country

Living North Country

Edited by
Natalia Rachel Singer
&
Neal Burdick

North Country Books, Inc.
Utica, New York

LIVING NORTH COUNTRY

ISBN 0-925168-82-3

Library of Congress Cataloging-in-Publication Data

Living north country : essays on life and landscape in northern New York / edited by Natalia Rachel Singer & Neal Burdick.
p. cm.
ISBN 0-925168-82-3 — ISBN 0-925168-80-7 (pbk.)
1. Adirondack Mountains Region (N.Y.)—Geography. 2. Adirondack Mountains Region (N.Y.)—History. 3. Adirondack Mountains Region (N.Y.)—Biography. 4. Country life—New York (State)—Adirondack Mountains Region. 5. Natural history—New York (State)—Adirondack Mountains Region. 6. Landscape—New York (State)—Adirondack Mountains Region. 7. Human geography—Adirondack Mountains Region (N.Y.) I. Singer, Natalia Rachel, 1957- II. Burdick, Neal S.
F127.A2 L59 2001
974.7'5—dc21 2001032997

Published by
NORTH COUNTRY BOOKS, INC.
311 Turner Street
Utica, New York 13501

Dedication

In memory of John Van de Water
Writer, Educator, Farmer, Neighbor

Contents

NEIGHBORS

GHOSTS

SKELETONS

LOOKING FOR HOME

Preface
Lighting Out for the North Country

I have a confession to make. When I came to interview for my job at St. Lawrence University in February of 1990, I had to find Canton, New York on a map, and even then, I wasn't sure how I could "get there from here." I was living in the Pioneer Valley of Western Massachusetts and believed that "Upstate New York" was not such a vast and vaguely defined place, or at least, was only a short bus ride away from nearby Albany. When I found out that Greyhound, with layovers, would take over thirteen hours, I realized that I would have to drive. This posed some difficulties, since I possessed neither a car nor a driver's license. Luckily, a friend came to my rescue and we were off.

The drive north from Albany took us something like six hours, stopping as we did now and then to gape at mountains and frozen trees. It was February in the North Country, the coldest time of the year, but I felt warmed by the startling light illuminating the ice-capped High Peaks of the Adirondacks. By the time we got to Blue Mountain Lake, where men were ice fishing on the frozen water, I was ready to tell these St. Lawrence people that I would do anything to be able to stay.

What was it, exactly, that I found so appealing? The forests: those bare birch trees with bony branches like giant X-rays, so startlingly naked beside the shaggy hemlock and white pine? The carved blue bowl of sky so bright I needed sunglasses? The prospect of peaceful, writerly isolation? I kept turning to my friend as we passed empty fields, long stretches of nothing—all that space—and asked him if he'd ever seen so few signs of development anywhere in his life. We were used to Northampton, Massachusetts, where every piece of land on every stretch of road is claimed by *something*—a Victorian house, ornate as wedding cake; brick apartments, boxy and densely peopled; restaurants offering everything from braised arugula to sushi; gorgeous white-pillared farm houses with fields of tobacco, corn, and berries; somewhere to get your hair dyed purple / dog groomed / taxes done / energy channels balanced / nipples pierced.

I had been happy in Northampton, but now I wanted a place where people spent a little less time kowtowing to the tyrannies of hipness and more time in the company of cows. I wanted some more room to move around in. What was underneath all that snow? Cornfields? Grazing land for cows? Weeds? I was curious and humbled by my ignorance. Why was I so surprised to learn that there were still spots on the earth outside the designated wilderness areas where the earth itself lay idle?

And yet there were signs of the human presence everywhere: old stately farmhouses and homes with broad beams and wide porches, red barns and tractors, small churches, and the occasional sign promising maple syrup or cords of wood. And there were signs of the past, of people who had just had enough and left: abandoned houses with sagging porches, trailers heaving behind piles of rusting slush-covered junk. Who lived here now, and how did they make their living? Who had been here, and why did they leave? I felt the mystery of the place as we drove.

I also had the uncanny feeling that I was coming home. I believed that I was somehow *meant* to live here, if not forever, then for a long, long time. I can't honestly say why. Maybe, at 32, I was simply ready to settle down, join a community, become some sort of citizen. But I think it was more than that. Perhaps, in some subtle way, I was still afflicted with the developer's mindset: in a place so cut off from the rest of the world, so wide open, with so much space, I believed that the sky was the limit as to how I could live, who I could be. If I got in my car—yes, I would have to get one right away, I realized—I could drive to one of these empty fields some dark night and howl at the moon like a coyote, and no one could come and arrest me.

It is easy for any reader of American literature to track down the source of my romantic fantasies. Like Huck Finn, I was hoping to "light out for the territories." I was following a distinctly American pattern. A midwestern gal—born in Chicago and raised in Cleveland, the industrial wasteland where a river had once caught fire—I had grown up daydreaming green vistas, mountains, and babbling brooks. I had already lit out for the territories once before—to Seattle after college, where I'd learned to cross-country ski, walk on snowshoes, and carry a full-frame pack weighing half my own weight up and down mountains without hurting myself. But then Seattle got "discovered" and overpopulated, and it was time to move on, to graduate school in Massachusetts, a place I had known from the start would just be a transition zone until I got a "real job" and began my "real life."

With that chapter coming to a close, I was ready to feel rooted, to begin living in the present. If I got hired at St. Lawrence, with a little bit of luck, I would invest in a home, learn the lay of the land, and find out where, exactly, I was.

And so, the idea of this book came to me. I decided that if I got the job, I was going to write about this place and gather a group of writers to help me. And now, over a decade later, this collection of essays, to my astonishment, has finally materialized. I don't know that it completely solves the mystery of exactly where we are and who else has been here before us. But in the long process of putting it together, it has helped all of us who contributed to the book solve the more personal mystery of how it is we came to be here, and what being here means to us.

"If we know where we are," says Wendell Berry, "we know *who* we are." That's an inquiry that demands hefty doses of research and self-reflection. To know where we are, we need to cultivate what Barry Lopez calls "local knowledge"—local social history, natural history, and more. Acquiring local knowledge also means developing one's own philosophy of place, an understanding of what Lopez describes as the "spiritual and psychological dimensions of geography." To get local knowledge, you have to get out of the house. You have to explore the neighborhood.

And so, one of the first things I did after I became a North Country resident was to get myself some wheels. I bought a Toyota the color of the North Country sky I loved so much and learned the geography while I learned to drive. I started close to home: up Route 68 past the horse stables at St. Lawrence, toward

Colton, and over the back roads to Potsdam, where I bought eggs at a diner and eavesdropped on fellow citizens speaking rhapsodically about weekends at their summer camps in the Adirondacks. As time went on, I went farther: to a swimming hole in Parishville. On to Santa Clara, where I climbed Azure Mountain and mistook some turkey vultures for American eagles. To the nature trails of Paul Smiths. To the Thousand Islands for walks around Wellesley Island and days of miniature golf with family and friends. Through the Champlain Valley on my way to Vermont on fall foliage missions. Through Keene Valley to Lake Placid to watch skiers hurl off Olympic jumps.

Through the mountain towns down to Lake George on my way back down to visit old friends in Western Mass. Through Ogdensburg on my way to Canada, and Massena to shop for shoes. And through the small talc-mining town of Gouverneur, home of the giant Lifesaver statue that commemorates the candy's marketing genius E.J. Noble, who was born there.

To acquire local knowledge, you also have to meet the neighbors. A year or so into my new life here, I was ready to begin soliciting manuscripts from local writers for the North Country book. My first step was to invite some potential contributors and active community members for a brainstorming session, and during that one productive afternoon, I made a number of important decisions. The first was the turf itself: the book would, on one hand, attempt, without any rigid borders, to take in the broadest geography, from the Thousand Islands in the west to Lake George in the southeast. It would be a book about place. It would also be a book about people. I wanted to profile some of the groups who have made their home here—the Amish, the back-to-the-landers, the Mohawks of the Akwesasne reservation—as well as some residents from history, including author Frederick Exley, among others.

It would be a book in which the past—the mines in Moriah, the sanitariums of Saranac Lake, the Vaudeville theaters of the Adirondacks, the old train system, the old Canton county fair—would interlock with the present—the rapid growth of federal prisons and shock camps in upstate New York, wide-spread poverty and violence against women and children, among others. While the book would celebrate the North Country, it wouldn't romanticize it, and I welcomed essays that examined our area's skeletons in the closet as well as those that praised our way of life.

Another major decision was that the book be written for a general audience as a collection of creative nonfiction essays, and that the style of writing—vivid, lyrical, often poetic—would be just as important as the content. This meant that some of the contributors to the collection, scholars like the linguist Karen Johnson-Weiner, whom I invited to write an essay about her ethnographic work among the Amish, would be branching out from more scholarly writing to literary memoir. This was true, as well, for Lynn Ekfelt, Peter Van De Water, and many of the other writers I contacted later, like Alice P. Green, director of the Center of Law and Justice in Albany, whose memoirs about growing up African-American in the Adirondacks were her first—but I've since learned, not last—experience in creative writing.

I suppose the most significant decision of all was that in compiling a collection of essays that would be about—first and foremost—community, the *process itself* should reflect community values. Although creative writing privileges voice and individuality, the more original and idiosyncratic the better, I wanted a compelling work in which individual voices were raised in the service of an idea of community and place. I was interested in what Bellah et al, in *Habits of the Heart,* refer to as "civic individualism," a condition in which genuine individuals—nature-enthusiasts, teachers, farmers, poets, prison guards, Amish mothers, college deans, commune-dwellers, you-name-it—exist in relation to a larger whole. I wanted essays that explored the way our sense of place in the North Country affects both our public and private lives.

How to create a book that embodies civic individualism? First off, to stop thinking of myself as an "I." Soon after Neal Burdick had contributed his excellent "North Country Idyll" to the book, I asked him to become a co-editor, and to my great delight, he accepted. Neal brought to this joint enterprise a keen editor's eye, a writer's love and mastery of delicious prose, and, having spent all but four years of his life in the North Country, an impressive depth of "local knowledge." Not only did he know a great deal about the geography, geology, flora and fauna, and social history of the North Country, but he knew just whom to contact when we needed, say, an essay about hunting or about the "shock camps" in the North Country's prison system. He shared my vision that the process of gathering essays be democratic, inclusive, communitarian: that we publish well known writers—people like Bill McKibben, Roger Mitchell, Elizabeth Inness-Brown, Maurice Kenny—as well as new talents like William Gadway, Peter Van de Water, and former students Heather Allison-Jenkins, and Jonathan Mairs.

We were also not the least bit shy about indulging in a little healthy nepotism, for when we discovered that we would have three generations of the Van de Water family represented in this book, we were glad to find some way to demonstrate the importance of family and ancestry to residents of the North Country. (John's death, early in the editing process, saddened us deeply and made us all the more grateful to receive his grandson Tom's lyrical, compelling, and informative essay on the mines of Moriah.)

Although we were glad to invite some academicians to try their hand at creative nonfiction, we also wanted to include a wide range of authors who had no connection to the universities in the North Country. We wanted our writers to reflect the diversity of our various neighborhoods.

One of our top priorities was to discover and nurture previously unknown talent. Once we had committed in principle to an author's essay, we were willing to host peer-editing sessions with some of the writers, so the submission process was not the simple (but often intimidating) yes/no. If we saw potential in someone's manuscript, we brought it to the group, and other contributors had a hand in the revision process.

Therefore, although Neal Burdick and I are the primary editors of what you see before you, many of the authors in this book have had their hands in the whole conception of the book, from initial brain-storming to line-editing. This book has been a big part of the lives and landscapes of our authors for several years, and without their help above and beyond the fine writing itself, there would be no book.

It has now been over eleven years since my first encounter with the North Country on that wintry drive. My love of the spaciousness, the quality of light, the proximity of the Adirondacks, the quiet, has not diminished. But in the process of becoming a citizen, I've also learned about the area's "negatives"—the poverty and domestic violence, the intolerance of a few of our neighbors toward difference, the long, brutal winters, those blood-thirsty blackflies. The delight and freedom I still feel from having lit out for this territory is tempered by this new knowledge. There may be empty fields to enjoy, but I wouldn't want to drive into one all by myself to howl at the moon.

Fortunately, my sense of individuality has also been tempered by my growing awareness of what it is to be a citizen. I see no need to go it alone. While we were working on this book, Northern New York was hit by a devastating ice storm in 1998 that knocked down power lines for over two weeks in some places, and people had to rely on each other for food, wood, generators, plumbing advice, candlelight reading materials, and help milking cows. I was reminded of something I tell my students: that the frontier has been closed for more than one hundred years. And even when the wild west was first being settled, it was not really lone individuals and outlaws who made the place inhabitable, but people sharing resources, talent, labor, affection, their favorite books.

When you light out for the territories, you meet the neighbors.

Welcome, readers, to the neighborhood.

Acknowledgments

We extend thanks to the following for their varied support and assistance in compiling this collection: Varick Chittenden, Laurie Olmstead, Bonnie Enslow, Vickie Perrin, Charlotte Ward, Jennifer Wootton, Joan Potter, and Beth Larrabee. Special accolades to Ken Alger for the map. Thanks also to St. Lawrence University for funding a writing retreat and a workshop for contributors to this book, and to the University's associate dean, the late Betsy Cogger Rezelman, and Associate Vice President Lisa Cania for their encouragement. Thanks to Nathalie Costa, executive director of the Adirondack Center for Writing, whose enthusiasm about this book kept us excited down the last stretch. We are grateful for the encouragement and support of three people associated with North Country Books, who were involved with this project at three different stages of its development: Sheila Orlin, Nick Burns, and Rob Igoe. Finally, we are most appreciative of all who submitted their work, without which there would be no book.

Neal Burdick
Natalia Rachel Singer
Spring 2001

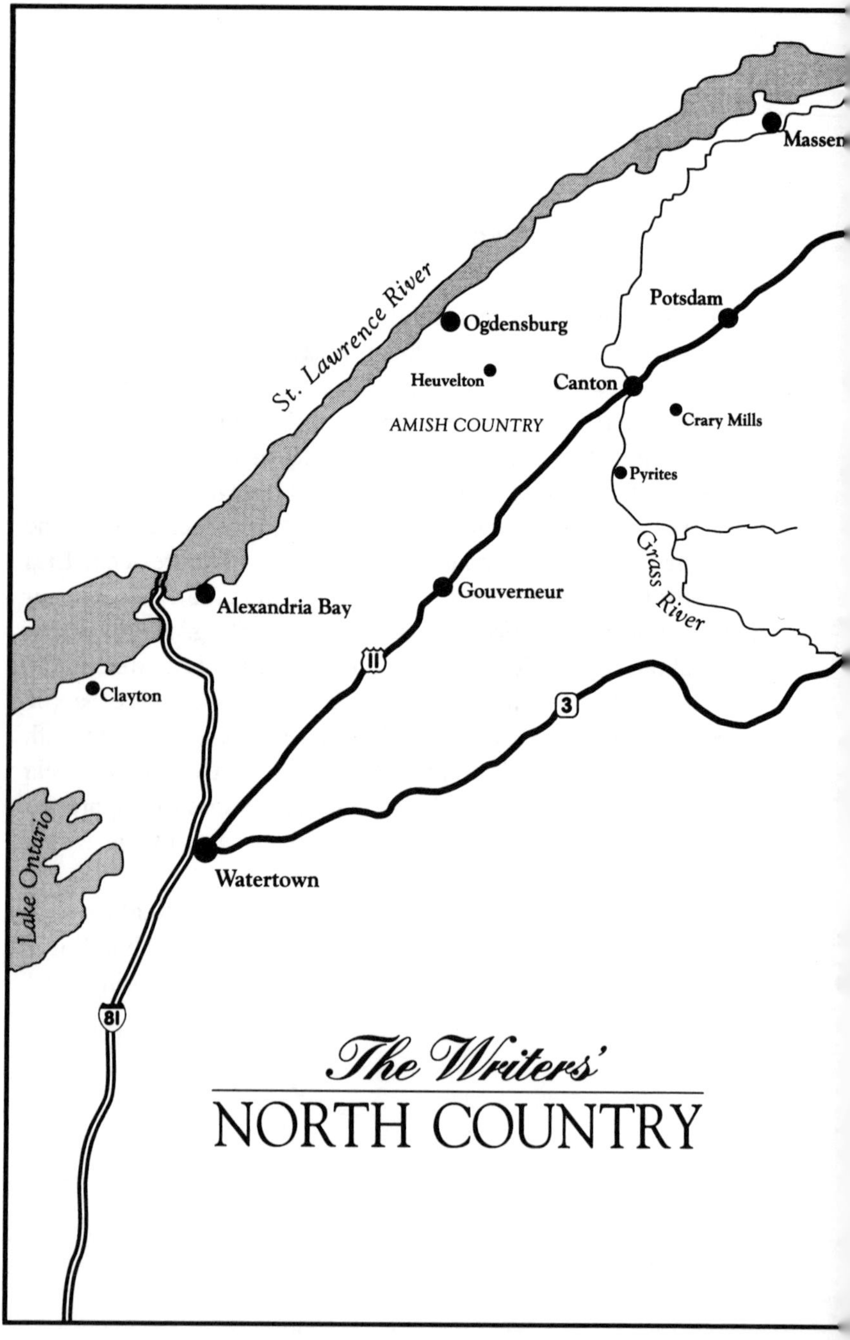
St. Lawrence River
Massen
Ogdensburg
Potsdam
Heuvelton
Canton
AMISH COUNTRY
Crary Mills
Pyrites
Grass River
Alexandria Bay
Gouverneur
11
Clayton
3
Lake Ontario
Watertown
81
The Writers'
NORTH COUNTRY

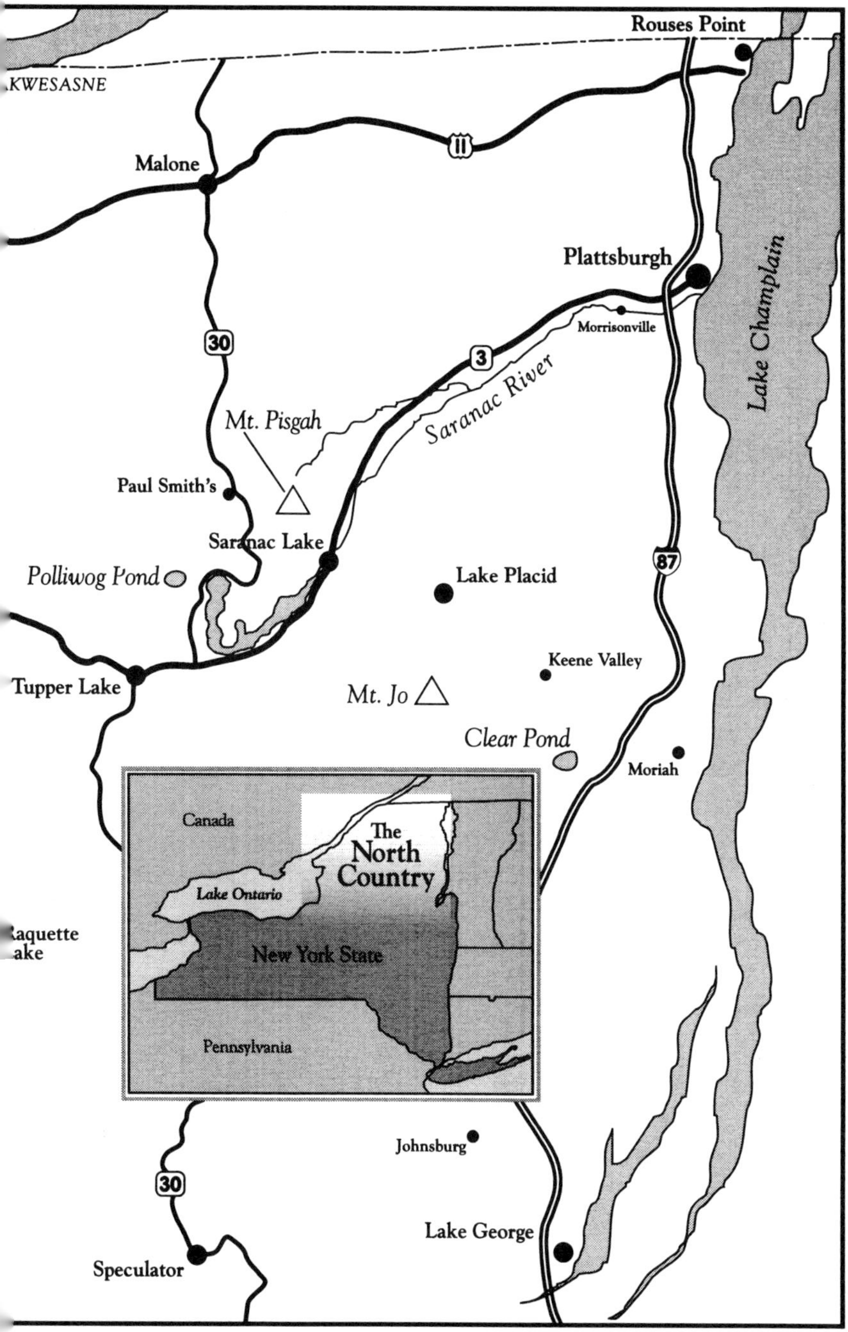

Rouses Point
KWESASNE
Malone
Plattsburgh
Morrisonville
30
3
11
Saranac River
Lake Champlain
Mt. Pisgah
Paul Smith's
Saranac Lake
Polliwog Pond
Lake Placid
87
Tupper Lake
Keene Valley
Mt. Jo
Clear Pond
Moriah
Canada
The North Country
Lake Ontario
New York State
Pennsylvania
Raquette Lake
Johnsburg
30
Lake George
Speculator

Settings

North Country Idyll

Neal Burdick

In early morning's fragile light, a solitary deer browses on frost-laden stubble in a hilly field beside the road. I pull over to watch. She raises her head to glance at me, then returns to her search for food. Thin fog lies across the land, clinging to its contours like a well-worn, homespun quilt. Goldenrod wilts under the weight of frozen dew.

Once again I find myself driving across northern New York, that narrow strip of winter-whipped, north-sloping land between the Adirondacks and St. Lawrence River. I'm heading from my home in Canton to conclude some personal business and visit my parents in their home of over fifty years in Plattsburgh. It's rush hour by the clock, but in the last ten minutes I've seen one school bus, a log truck with Quebec plates, a shiny Kraft tanker proclaiming "Milk Is A Health Kick," two pickup trucks, and a single car. Three hundred miles south, tens of thousands of vehicles are log-jammed at toll booths on bridges and expressways funneling into New York City. The city symbolizes New York, the

Empire State, to many people, but this deer, this fog, this nearly empty two-lane narrow-shouldered road are empire enough for me.

I've made this trip more than two hundred times over the last thirty years, in all kinds of weather, at all times of day and night. Native to this region they've called the North Country for at least a century, descendant of families who settled it over two hundred years ago, I decided to leave it after college. But then, I came back. My roots, I've learned, are deep; it's hard to step aside and analyze this land in which they're fixed. What is there to say in defense of it? The region is so ill-defined that our federal government once built a fort to guard its northern frontier, then discovered it had put the fort in Canada, which magnanimously responded by giving the United States the violated patch of ground. The North Country is framed on the east and west by lakes that seem on maps to buttress it, and on the north by the St. Lawrence River and an arbitrary manmade international border that lies halfway between the Equator and the North Pole and shoots straight through farms, bars, private homes, even somebody's pool table. But on the south, it loses itself like a disoriented hunter somewhere in the Adirondacks, the vast maze of wetlands, woods, and hills that splits the region from the rest of New York State.

Or perhaps it doesn't. Indeed, no one can agree whether "the North Country" includes the Adirondacks, or stops at some hazy boundary where fields finally give way to forest at the mythical edge of what St. Lawrence Valley folk traditionally called "The Great South Woods."

Either way, the region's too big; people in Plattsburgh and Watertown, 170 miles apart and hubs of east and west respectively, know little of each other and don't seem inclined to find out more. When plans for a covered mall were announced in Watertown, that city's newspaper proclaimed it the first in the North Country, even though Plattsburgh had had one for ten years. And when Plattsburgh lost its Air Force Base to politics, civic leaders there lamented the loss of "the North Country's only military installation," ignoring Watertown's massive Fort Drum, bigger than an average county.

The moniker is not unique: Maine, Wisconsin, and Minnesota have North Countries of striking similarity, lightly populated backwaters cut off by a broad tourniquet of woods from the main circulatory systems of their respective states and forced to associate themselves with other states, even Canada. But the very term "North Country" must offend Canadians and reinforce their suspicion that Americans think the civilized world simply ends at their border. To demographers, the region leads the state in unemployment, incest, and illiteracy. It's cold, springless, hobbled by its inhabitants' sense of defeat, stubbornly conservative. But it's home, and I embrace it with an affinity I cannot well explain.

Now, at summer's end, acre upon acre of farmland is obliterated under weeds. Thin gray barns lean as though to mock the thin gray men who try to prop them up another year. Great slumping rolls of hay dot fields like some giant's shredded wheat. Late corn goes from green to tan as golden, gossamer tamaracks shine beside beaver ponds that have overtaken long-abandoned fields. Milkweed spreads its seed to the swirling winds in one last act of faith; sumac leaves blaze deep scarlet. There's a look of grim detachment in the face of a farmer on a rusty, coughing tractor hauling a full manure wagon into a rocky field ahead of me. Poison ivy and morning glory nearly hide an ancient, collapsing stone wall that angles away from the road. Dried-up beech leaves filter down without apparent provocation; some settle on the road in front of me and are torn to pieces by my tires.

Unlike many parts of America, in the North Country the amount of land consumed by housing tracts, industrial parks, and shopping malls has not yet overwhelmed that used for agriculture. But forest and brushland may. There appears to be no future in farming. Failed attempts at price supports, the jaws of agribusiness, and government indifference as farmers have lost their political clout seem to doom the family farm, although it holds out yet in the North Country. It's become the exception to find a farmer who doesn't have some other source of income—a job in one of the mills in Massena or Plattsburgh, maybe a forty-mile drive one way; or at Fort Drum, or in one of the bright new prisons that have sprung from the belief that the way to "correct" criminals is to banish them to alien environments. Or maybe they stay closer to home with a school bus run, or a firewood business on the side.

They say the most successful crop in the North Country is rocks: they come up every spring when the frost goes out, and you don't even have to weed them. It used to be said there were more cows than people in the St. Lawrence Valley. I haven't heard that expression for years; I suspect it's no longer true. Every week, the papers list half a dozen farms for sale or auction. Rarely do they carry a Want Ad from someone seeking to buy such a place. As I ponder how the phrase "bought the farm" came to be synonymous with "died," I consider who acquires these tractors, these tools, these dairy cows, these barns. . . .

Some farms—minus their mechanical appliances—become the new homes of Amish transplants. The Amish resolutely pull these places from the brink of demise, returning them to productive operation while tolerating in silence the high taxes, the Social Service bureaucrats, the threat of proposed county landfills, the dangers drunken drivers pose to their buggies and horses, and the stares of all of us "English."

Other farms become the property of youngish urbanites with fancy diplomas who've decided to quit the proverbial rat race and find—something. They bring innovation, which some traditional North Country farmers seem constitutionally reluctant to embrace. They're willing to raise bison, for example, or manufacture yogurt, or plant wheat. Those few who stick it out may have the future of farming in their hands. If the alternative is to see a farm bequeathed to barn swallows and ragweed, a redefinition of "farming" may be in order.

I pass a farm, unusually tidy by North Country standards. A sign by the driveway declares it a "Dairy of Distinction." The next place is shabbier; it seems to have been unoccupied for some time. It has a sign too, albeit more tattered and less literate: "House and Farm with 57 Acres 4 Sale. Inquir Within." Farther on, there's one whose "For Sale" sign has been standing so long it's as decrepit as the farm. The buildings are uniformly weather-beaten. The house shows signs of having once been gutted by fire. The barn has long since tumbled into kindling. Before it stands a white television satellite dish capable of receiving, I fancy, 200 channels; there's nobody home to surf. A tall metal blue Harvestore silo stands empty and useless, a patient servant awaiting some command from its long-dead master. Attached to the "For Sale" sign is an addendum: "Price Reduced."

A colleague at work once told me about a conversation he'd overheard at a local farm implements dealer's:

"What would you do if you won the lottery?"

"Ohhh, prob'ly keep on farming 'til it ran out. . . ."

North Country roads are lined with abandoned farms, the ones that nobody bought. Swaybacked barns sag a little more each year, lightning rods listing more and more toward sumac tips, until a wind or heavy snow finishes them off, or time and rot complete their work. Woods encroach upon untended fields and pastures, attracting birds and beasts driven off when the land was cleared, as early as 1800. I wonder if two centuries of cultivation have been a blip in the continuum of nature's rule that is over now, as people surrender and wilderness regains its foothold in a place that was never meant to be subdued.

Deserted farmhouses seem huge, with gaping cavities where doors and windows used to be—eye sockets without eyes, mouths without teeth. They slant like their barns. Wind batters them, and they have no help.

A deep-bellied ringer washer sits on the porch of one such deserted house on a back road near Hopkinton, barely visible in late summer through towering Joe Pye weed and mullein. I wonder how many years it has been there, left behind when the last generation to work the place gave up the annual struggle against short growing seasons, summer frosts, rocks in the fields, and declining prices, sold off their cows, auctioned their possessions, and used the cash to move to some not-too-distant city—Syracuse, perhaps, or Utica—in search of steady work. They were latter-day Joads, hoping the truck would hold together. The washer on the porch retains its whiteness, the only man-made thing in sight that hasn't had its color abraded into gray by an endless assault from wind, sun, sleet, snow, wind.

The porch pitches forward a few more inches after each spring's thaw. In some year, at some moment, it will collapse, and the washer will plummet out of sight for good. The house will fall in upon itself. Trees and brush will envelop the site, and it will rest undisturbed until an anthropologist from a local college comes upon it during a field trip with his students from Long Island one gentle spring afternoon, when superannuated lilac trees have struggled into bloom and revealed its location. They will peer into the cellar hole and spy the sunken hulk of washer and wonder what sort of people used to live here, and what they did, and why they left. They will never know.

Some say North Country folk haven't realized that the Great Depression ended well over half a century ago, because nothing's changed. The region has pockets of rural poverty to rival any in the nation. I drive through a couple on this trip. Paintless old houses are patched up as long as they can be, then abandoned in favor of rusty trailers parked in front of them, as if to hide them from public view. They are not torn down; there seems no point. They merely wither, like their owners.

Nor are old cars hauled away. Havens for squirrels and rats and teenage sex, bolt-buckets with fenders wide enough to support elbows and beer cans and an ancient cobbled engine to tinker with on boring summer evenings, they settle and rust in grassless yards beside older ones, beside ancient peeling haybalers and trucks and snowmobiles and school buses—every time I make this trip, I'm astonished at how many places are the final resting spots of derelict school buses. The young are taught discouragement by example. Not many of them stay on. Those who do find their lives narrowly prescribed.

Near East Dickinson, an abandoned church of uncertain denomination sits a few feet back from the road. It's typical of rural churches in the Northeast—a clapboard box, once white, with steep-pitched roof, tall narrow windows, heavy double doors, and precious little else that isn't necessary. I've been watching it for years as I've made this drive. Each time I pass, a little more paint has peeled away, a little more of its steeple and belfry lie crumpled in Queen Anne's lace and blackberry brambles at the feet of its walls, a few more boulders have appeared in the bumpy cow pasture that surrounds it. I wonder when someone last rang its bell, sang a hymn, heard a rousing sermon, mourned a dead child, locked the door and turned away.

Across the road is a small, square cemetery embraced by an iron fence someone has recently given a coat of paint. It's populated by thin lichen-covered stones bearing the names of New Englanders who appropriated this region not long after the Revolutionary War, and of their descendants who built the church and worshipped and married and grieved there: Larkin, Hastings, Clark, Woods, Austin, Potter, Roscoe, Whitman, Rice, Flint, Smith. There's been no burial here in nearly thirty years; the young no longer stay around long enough to grow old and die.

Lining the cemetery are several immense sugar maples, maybe a century old and planted, I imagine, by the farmer-parishioners who had responsibility for this plot so that sap would not be far away each spring. Now, in this time of rapid flux from one season to the next, frost has killed off the colors on the ground—deadened the wild mustard and black-eyed susans, Indian paintbrush, hawkweed, red-berried nightshade and chicory, clover, fireweed, and goldenrod, the marigolds someone planted last Memorial Day and then forgot—and transferred them temporarily to the maple leaves above. The colors in the leaves appear to change hourly, green diminishing as daylight dwindles in the dusk, until the leaves themselves dwindle to brittle scraps and dust.

Beyond the cemetery, in the hazy distance beyond field upon downsloping field, past the smoke plumes of Massena and the amber woods of Akwesasne, the St. Lawrence River is a thin, silver ribbon, flowing on to the sea.

Except in hollows where brooks tumble down from the Adirondacks to the rivers that feed the St. Lawrence, dawn's fog has dissipated without announcement. The land has thrown aside its quilt. The sun shines weakly through streaks of feathery haze, giving off no warmth.

A wedge of Canada geese rises from a cutover field of corn beside my road and slices south against slabs of cloud gray and flat as the bottom of a giant griddle, migrating to their winter range. The gleaners have profited more from the cornfield than its farmer will.

Canada geese (not *Canadian*; they give allegiance to no nation) are said to fly due north or south in formations resembling the letter V, but they almost never do. Always calling in measured cacophony, they rearrange their ranks continuously so the leaders, who've broken trail, can retire to the rear and regain strength while they work their way to the head of the line again. We could learn a lesson in cooperation from them. . . .

My anthropomorphizing is shattered by a shotgun concussion somewhere in a nearby field. A moment later one goose drops from the pack and tailspins to earth like a shot-down plane from Fort Drum.

South of Brainardsville, a county road climbs away from the St. Lawrence-bound Chateaugay River, crosses the northeast shoulder of the Adirondacks, and drifts down 2,000 feet to Lake Champlain. From the summit of this road, I see to the south undulating wind-blown farmland squared up by hedgerows and old stone walls, then woods backdropped by Lyon Mountain, almost four thousand feet high. To the north, the nearly uniform horizon is broken at the foot of Mont Royal by the skyscrapers of downtown Montreal, where three million people live and work.

Suspended between wilderness and city, the North Country is far less isolated than many people, the region's residents included, think it is.

Those who measure the value of a place according to its proximity to a major urban area would no doubt regard the North Country as relatively bereft of value. The fact is that people who live in Richmond, Virginia or Portland, Maine are nearer New York City than we are in the North Country. But thanks to Montreal and Ottawa—each an easy drive across the border into Canada—I'm closer here to world art and theater tours, major league baseball and hockey, and the cosmopolitan shopping typical of urban hubs than I would be in large parts of the United States.

In the early 1950s, Plattsburgh acquired one of the first NBC television stations outside a major urban market. Those who couldn't fathom why didn't realize the city of 17,000, second largest in the North Country, tucked away in the northeast corner of what was then the most populous state in the nation, was in fact within electronic striking range of such an urban market, since it was only sixty miles from Montreal. And so, the first television show I ever watched, as a boy of four or five, was about a clown named Pierrot, and it was in French.

What else erodes our isolation? We have ten colleges and universities, a sprawling Army base whose occupants come from every state, "All Things Considered," MTV, puddle-jumper planes, two interstates, 9-1-1, and Wal-Mart shopping palaces to which we drive for two hours to save a dollar on a shirt, lamenting as we go the crumbling, broken stores in all the weedy hamlets on the way. Isolation has been called a state of mind, and we seem hell-bent on breaking it.

More than once, I've made this trip at night. For miles, there's little artificial illumination other than that produced by my headlights or those of the occasional oncoming vehicle.

The darkness has its own rewards. It provides an arena for unencumbered displays of Northern Lights and meteor showers that have accompanied me across the sparsely populated land like cosmic beacons.

It also puts the North Country's rumored isolation in plainer perspective. On the long stretches of this trip where the land drops tangibly and flattens toward the north, I can see near at hand scattered sprinkles of light that mark the occasional farmyard; in the middle distance, bright islands that locate villages nearer the St. Lawrence; and beyond them, the myriad lights of the Seaway and the towns and cities along it, downriver to Montreal and beyond. Guiding the progress of ships from the nations of the world, as well as the nighttime commerce of millions of people, they cast a glow across the sky that is as bright as that from any metropolis. They tie this region to all of the planet.

The road before me glides steadily down into the Champlain Valley. Apple orchards carpeting the land announce the transition from harsh, scrubby foothills to the more fertile, gentler valley floor. As summer fades to fall, the orchards sprout with tall, tapered wooden ladders, stacks of mammoth crates, and migrant workers from Jamaica who wave but don't smile as I drive by.

I think my roots are those of apple trees. When I was growing up I had an uncle whose name was Earl. A keeper of the family tree would point out that he wasn't actually an uncle, but, as happens in large families closely knit in rural areas, in my family any man older than oneself was "Uncle," any older woman "Aunt." And so, regardless of the nuances of genealogies, he was to me Uncle Earl, and his wife, Aunt Ruth. Earl and Ruth: solid monosyllabic, down-to-earth Scots-Irish Protestant farmers' names. He was an Everett; his ancestors had been cultivating the patch of land he called home since 1788.

Asked what he did for a living, Earl would reply not "I'm an orchardist," but "I grow apples." Everett's Orchard was of modest size, by Champlain Valley standards: a few dozen acres perched partway up Huckleberry Mountain, a northeast Adirondacks foothill, on River Road a little west of Peru. From the wide, gray front porch of his New England-style farmhouse—identifiable as such, I later learned, by its second-story window canted at 45 degrees above the roof of the ell—spread a panorama of silo-studded valley, broad blue lake, and the ragged skyline of Vermont beyond. It is the kind of scene urban dwellers see on insurance company calendars and wish they could move to, if only there were any decent jobs up there.

The kitchen seemed immense, and in its center squatted a dark, boxy kerosene heater from whose top emerged a black stovepipe that elbowed beneath the ceiling and disappeared through a tin thimble in one wall. In winter, that heater chugged like an idling railroad locomotive.

Whenever we visited, Ruth would be in the kitchen, a bare-armed, blue-flowered apron tied eternally around her stout waist. She always offered to cut me up an apple, harelip curled into a gentle, perhaps bemused smile. I wonder if she and Earl ever said "I love you" to each other.

You could set your watch by the status of Earl's apple trees—McIntosh, mostly, with a smattering of Northern Spies. If the orchard were a sea of blossoms, it would always be Memorial Day. Drops signaled the beginning of the end of summer. Picking meant wistful September weekends with the smell of burning maple leaves in my nostrils. Pruning limbs for aromatic firewood took place after the passing of deep winter. Then, at about the time I thought it would never happen again, buds appeared in April, maybe in time for Easter, and with them came the planting of new, young trees. Earl's was a year measured not by school semesters or summer trips, but by the annual turnings of his trees. He worried about late frosts, sudden drops in prices, bears coming down the mountain to raid his back rows. Frosts were of more concern to him than bears; he said he could spare a few apples for a hungry bruin, but a killing cold in May could ruin his year.

He was Peru's official weather recorder. For forty years, he dutifully noted the numbers on the rain gauges, thermometers, barometers, and anemometers that sat beside his barn, mailing them all off to some pale, neck-tied bureaucrats in Washington, until they decided the data coming in from the airport in Burlington, across the lake in Vermont, were close enough and told him they didn't need him anymore. Summer and winter, he wore clodkicker boots, sturdy dark green pants and matching shirt, and lighter green suspenders with a wide grey stripe up the middle. The "X" they made upon his back crossed him out from shoulders to beltline.

Apples, I've learned since those blissful days, were first domesticated centuries ago near present-day Alma Ata in Kazakhstan. Indeed, Alma Ata means "father of apples." The fruit in that harsh region had natural resistance to blights, and so was the seed stock, the common ancestor, for all apples ever to be. Apples still grow wild there, but since the coming of the industrial age, they have been losing ground to pollution and urbanization. This is cause for concern among horticulturists with lots of initials after their names, for once lost, these seed producers can never be replaced, never be genetically duplicated artificially, and, like so many other species that have been destroyed in the name of progress, will never reveal whatever secrets of life they may contain.

I doubt if Earl Everett, tinkering forever with his ancient rustbucket of an International Harvester tractor just outside Peru, New York, knew he had anything in common with Kazakhstanis. I never heard him speak of world affairs. He never went to "ag school" to learn the latest methods of grafting and marketing; he just went home one early summer night with his Peru High School diploma in one hand, laid the diploma on his bedroom dresser, and picked up tending the family's apple trees. Yet I suspect he knew that somewhere, in some time, there was an apple that was the Adam—and Eve—of all the thousands, millions, multiple billions of apples that had been picked for millennia, and would ever be.

Earl eventually passed operation of the orchard on to his only child, David, who brought in cold storage apparatus and some other modern gear. He'd been away to school, but he loved to polish a fresh Mac to a gleaming red against his shirt no less than when he was a boy.

Earl died some years ago, about the time I left home for good; Ruth not long after. The orchard is now in the care of their grandson, the tenth generation on the place. I understand he and his boys still set out new trees and chainsaw old, worry about late frosts, and believe there's enough apples that they can spare a few for the bears that wander down from Huckleberry Mountain. And every year when summer turns to fall, I hope their harvest will be good enough that they can go on another year.

My business in Plattsburgh engaged and concluded, I head home by a different route, past the breathtaking gray prison wall that dominates Dannemora, past the skeletal mine structures and identical company houses in Lyon Mountain, past the closed-up summer camps of Montrealers jostling for space on the Chateaugay Lakes. The sky grows lower, grayer. The forecast on my car radio calls for ". . . rain likely this afternoon, possibly mixed with sleet or snow at higher elevations."

Winter whispers its approach. It descends unexpectedly, surprising us from the south while we watch for it in the north, marching down the mountains to occupy the valleys.

Thirteen storm tracks cross the United States, and ten of them plow through the North Country. We pay the price for being a bull's-eye, all year long. For all the times I've done this drive, in shimmering summer heat and raw fall rain and swirling blizzards that made me feel as though I had my head inside a pillowcase, I can't recall a kind of weather I haven't met. . . .

I've seen rain for days on end in autumn, when the foliage could be at its best but most of it lies in cold, glistening lumps at the feet of rain-streaked tree trunks. Tour buses full of retired teachers from Milwaukee and Toledo splash past on the main roads, but don't stop at craft shops or the North Country's earnest but doomed attempts at tourist attractions; they're on their way to Vermont. A handful of spectators at a high school football game shrink down in yellow slickers and watch their sons lose their identity in a swelling sea of mud. In low-slung government-built senior citizen complexes, dried-up old men and women whose children moved them in when they could no longer work their farms sit scowling for hours and stare at the walls in their apartments.

They say more people die between late fall and midwinter than at any other time.

When the storms of winter slant from the east, you know they're going to be bad—slow to taper off, real school-closers, layering snow inch by inch, hour by hour, from Lake Champlain to Lake Ontario. And when you look at sifting snow against a streetlight or farmyard light and see it coming down in thousands of little X's that remind you of a cross-stitch your grandmother might have made, or the plastic bubbles full of powdered soap that you can shake and make a white Christmas, you know the storm is going to last all night.

North Country people have a love-hate relationship with

snow. TV weather-persons condition us to despise it, yet finish up their segments with shots of beautiful sweeps of virgin snow and a cross-country skier casting shadows from the setting sun on a perfect winter day. Local merchants and boosters organize winter carnivals with broomball games and hayrides and outdoor skating under strings of bare bulbs, and pray it won't rain or be too cold; they decorate their shops with cut-out snowflakes and put on smiles that mask their overpowering sadness at the lack of customers and the weight of all that snow on the roof.

After the holidays are over, the decorations put away and the relatives all gone home, we'd just as soon see the snow disappear, although we know it won't and we'll have to bear the annual stupidity of Groundhog Day, when some fool yanks a half-hibernating woodchuck out of its den somewhere down in Pennsylvania and declares there'll be six more weeks of winter, and we question when in recorded history there *haven't* been six more weeks of winter in the North Country. Yet give us a good fall of a foot or more, and we're on the phone to the neighbors who went to Florida to tell them all about it, as if to say, "You left because you couldn't take it, but we stayed and we survived." We'd love a thaw, but in open winters, with little snow, we growl that something doesn't seem quite right. The siege mentality of "real winter" fails to get its proper test in mild years.

There's little to boast of in the North Country—no great cities, museums, Disney Worlds, moving-and-shaking industries—but there is winter, and our gritty endurance of it, and our memory of "old-fashioned winters," when things were as rough as our current imaginations allow them to be.

It's the late snows that are hardest to take. There's a break in the cold, the snowpack starts to shrink, sugar shacks begin to steam, and maybe a few pussy willows pop out, and everyone decides winter's finished for another year. But if fall has glorious Indian Summer, then spring has hateful Indian Winter, with soupy wet snow flattening crocuses, sticking to the frozen carcasses of remnant snowbanks, piling up on sap bucket lids as if to say it's earned the nickname "sugar snow," blasting people back from premature euphoria. Mud Season will have to wait.

Drifts in the higher country and shaded places often survive well into May.

It's weather such as this that gives rise to the old-timers' saying, "There's two seasons in the North Country: ten months of winter and two of damn poor sleddin'." Even those two months of damn poor sleddin' are not always satisfying in this region, where complaining about the weather is almost required by law. Sirius, the Dog Star, lends its name to the Dog Days of August—when summer's worn out its welcome, pallid stirrings of air stumble ineffectively across limp hedgerows, cricket chirps are muted by humidity that clings to the skin like cobwebs, and lustrous green has been seared out of leaves and lawns. Far to the north, somewhere up in Canada, a spinning storm center kite-tails a cold front hundreds of miles out below it, and when that cold front rakes across the North Country, thunderstorms erupt like upside-down volcanoes.

You can hear them coming on the closest afternoons, muffled grumbles to the west as the air grows suffocating. The sky blackens and roils, then is pierced by torpedoes of lightning, window-cracking thunder, and sabers of rain. From the edge of the foothills, you can look out across the St. Lawrence Valley and see half a dozen storms parading west to east, curtains of rain momentarily blotting out patches of the view like strokes of watercolor on an oil painting. You could almost be in Kansas, on your way to Oz—if the land were just a little flatter.

When the storms have passed and the air clears and cools, and the breeze from the north brushes you by without sticking, you feel relief—the kind you felt when you were a kid and you threw up the morning after Halloween.

Turning up the heat in my car, I realize those Dog Days don't seem so long ago, and yet snow is just ahead. Winter is quick to come and slow to leave in the North Country; the brief periods of transition can sometimes slip by almost unnoticed.

I recall filling out a deposit slip at my bank one frigid winter noon and overhearing an elderly woman and a farmer passing the time.

"How cold was it out to your place?" she asked him, sounding reluctant to have him answer.

"Thirty-one out by the barn," he said slowly, after a pause. He didn't say "below zero." He didn't have to.

I'm nearing home. Dusk descends, and with it, a few huge flakes of wet snow. They splatter on my windshield like mortar shells.

A freight train glides across the overpass between the Adirondack Propane store and Agway bulk feed plant just east of Canton. It's short enough that I can see both ends at once: a single blue and white Conrail diesel locomotive, slightly rusty; a Canadian National boxcar, classic dirty freight car red, yellow door ajar to reveal that it holds no cargo; a grey covered hopper bearing the insignia ALCOA in large black letters; an off-white St. Lawrence Railroad boxcar; a long black tanker with no distinguishing marks; a caboose as blue as the locomotive. I stop to watch its movements as it slows to switch cars on the long siding at the bulk feed plant. . . .

A drive around the North Country will reveal to the sharp-eyed the roadbeds of a web of long-gone railroad lines. They stand out if you know what to look for: flat, straight ridges of uniform width, clearly manmade. They make ideal routes for deer and snowmobiles. Alterations to the landscape when they were built, in their decay, they become part of it.

Before the Depression, railroad routes stitched the North Country tightly. It was possible to travel almost anywhere by train, to come within a healthy shout of even the most remote North Country town. Trains were the farmers' bread and butter, picking up their milk trackside every day and delivering it to dairies in Chateaugay, Gouverneur, Lowville, Champlain, Moira, and dozens of other small towns.

Prosperity after World War II brought more cars. Highways improved to accommodate drivers and their votes, trucks took over the region's commerce, and folks turned their backs on trains. The milk depots closed; they're now just concrete foundations and rubble along weed-choked roadbeds every few miles.

Stations rot before the weather if they haven't been turned into taverns or antique shops. The tracks have long since been pulled up and sold for scrap, except on one line that snakes along Lake Champlain, and this one, on which my tiny train is shunting cars in and out of the Agway plant, as though it were a model controlled by a cosmic hand.

It's rare to see a train with a caboose today. The caboose's function was to carry crews, but the railroads, pleading economic stress, successfully lobbied Congress to cut their crews and laid them off, eliminating any need for a place for them to ride. But a train without a caboose is like an uncut field of hay, an abandoned church, an unplucked apple tree. A caboose provides a finish to a passing piece of business, an announcement that there is some order left, some certainty, some connection to our past, however unlike our present it may have been, however little of the future it may predict.

My train has completed its chores at the Agway plant. It pulls onto the main line, a few cars longer now, and gathers speed toward Canton. Whistling brittly for the crossing behind the shutdown Super Duper, headlight beam diffused by thickening snow, it slides into the night like a half-hearted dream. Its caboose is no longer at the end.

Postcards of My North Country

Homer Mitchell

SO VARIOUS, SO BEAUTIFUL, SO . . . ?

Like it or not, the North Country is that part of upstate New York with which even many upstaters can't identify, can't quite place. For residents of the Big Apple and beyond, the North Country is as remote, as foreign—or if you prefer, as accessible, as appealing—as the Gobi Desert. It is a place where cars are replaced (snicker) by dogsleds. A place devoid of airports, shopping centers-culture, sophistication. But is it really the boondocks?

You bet it is. Love it.

When you get down to it, the North Country is merely an idea, a multi-million-acre notion created and recreated in the eye of every beholder.

My North Country may be similar to your North Country, but I'm sure we would both agree they're not the same. The North Country may contain apple orchards and spinach farms, the highest mountain in New York State and millions of acres of lowlands and swamps, the St. Lawrence River and Six-Mile Creek, Lake Champlain and dozens of Mud Ponds, but it cannot be adequately represented by anyone of these.

Without an overriding image—an iconographic identity—the North Country is a marketer's nightmare. It's not the Grand Canyon, the Great Plains, the Badlands, or Niagara Falls. It's not a big city, a tourist trap, or a national park. Perhaps (if we can be so modest, so unprideful), it is that part of New York State where everything else isn't, a land of vague and disparate histories, a cast-off catch-all in the sticks.

But just where do we enter the North Country, and just where do we leave?

Located in a small roadside park in the St. Lawrence County hamlet of South Colton, a sizeable glacial erratic named Sunday Rock has historically marked an imaginary line between the workday world of the St. Lawrence River valley and the deep woods of the northwestern Adirondacks—a land, traditionally, of loggers and hunters, whiskey and boisterous leisure. A land—they said—of Sundays.

We could do worse than have our rough-hewn land demarked by upended boulders and time thrown slightly out of whack. Perhaps what the North Country needs are more Sunday Rocks, more Sundays.

For many, the reality of the North Country will disappoint. Difficult to get to, austere, provincial, deeply conservative, not the least bit cosmopolitan, the North Country and its unadorned welcome mats are conditioned by rurality and by the bitter acceptance that this neck of the woods is first into recession and last out—always. Up here, poverty is not well hidden: drive through the countryside and you will swear you're in the Appalachians. Pass through the downtowns of not a few villages and hamlets and you'll think bombs have struck.

But move past the dilapidated main streets of these old mining and mill towns with their curious architectural blend of the Wild West and the Victorian; keep on going past the front-yard junk, the snow-crushed outbuildings, the shells of cars, and scavenged snowmobiles. There's more to the North Country; thankfully, there's much more. A half-day excursion into this vast area provides a glimpse of greater geographical diversity than entire countries can offer.

Be careful, though: some of the North Country might quietly take purchase; some of what you see and traverse could grow to become a part of you.

In the St. Lawrence Valley, along a stretch of no-man's land on Route 37 between Redwood and Hammond, a sandstone ridge winds close to the road until it finally buttresses the plateau at South Hammond. Looking south, meadows filled with milkweed and goldenrod surround islands of sumac and stone. There is little human habitation here and no conventional commerce; only the business of survival—the industry of field mice, the casual vigilance of hawks and turkey vultures.

On its surface, nothing is out of the ordinary there, nothing by itself uncommon. Somehow, though, in some way, there is an alchemy at that place, even as the big rigs roar past, even as a chainsaw whines in the distance. It is, perhaps, an ineluctable dancing of light translated through a prism of memory and experience that cannot be escaped; it becomes visceral and moves me with the fervor of love. Here is a location for me that for four decades has been freighted with occasion, embedded with signifiers, a dance seen through veils that both withhold and provoke, a tale whispered to me by a hidden Scheherazade.

Can we not call special places such as these home?

Canoe upstream from the landing called Inlet on the Oswegatchie River. Say goodby to civilization: no boat motors, no highway sounds, no shouts, no chainsaws. Like much of the Chubb and Osgood Rivers in the higher Adirondacks, the Oswegatchie meanders extensively, winding back on itself between eskers like a soft ribbon of molasses.

For the hardy, High Falls beckons, twelve miles distant. Farther up, the river dwindles to creek size and passage becomes problematic. Go as far as you want. Jettison civilization with each paddle stroke. Don't count the miles; count cardinal flowers instead. Measure height by the ancient pines, breadth by the span of an eagle's wing.

If you lose yourself even momentarily on this wild waterway and then find yourself again, you will still be forever changed. As you round a bend for the first time in the North Country, pay heed to the dark water that unspools toward you or in fields or forests that part sometimes reluctantly to let you pass, pay heed to what is revealed. If it is somehow familiar—somehow instantly apart of you—record it as a sighting, if only fleeting, of those delicate strands that bind us to all we have forgotten, to pasts we have never really known, and to the other grand stuff of life from which we have become sadly disassociated.

"GREETINGS FROM THE ADIRONDACKS"

You'll find them today sold as ephemera in used book stores and flea markets. These old postcards were produced from black and white prints often garishly tinted with primary colors. Back then they cost a penny or two in roadside shops where toy birch-bark canoes, maple sugar, and embroidered balsam pillows were sold.

My grandmother loved to go for rides into the woods. Once, when I was about eight, my mother prepared a picnic and our family set out from Ogdensburg in the late morning for the mountains, in our '46 Ford.

I remember that picnic among the trees and the openness of the woods—pioneer hardwoods, no doubt, that considerate blend of beech and birch, maple and cherry that makes walking and seeing a pleasure. The woods sloped away into darker woods, and my grandmother, perhaps on her last walk in the forest, strolled down that park-like slope pointing toward nothing but more trees.

"I'll bet Lake George is right over there," I recall her saying with speculation verging on certainty, but with not a glint of water before her, not a sound of boat motors for evidence, just the great silent woods and hope.

I remember that same day narrow, twisting roads, the birch-lined section of Route 73 that squeezed along two slivery lakes between the rocky cliffs of Pitchoff and Cascade Mountains. I was overwhelmed by the views of peaks, distant vistas where range piled upon range at the ragged horizon. I had to press my face to the car window and crane my neck upward to follow closer watercourses, rock slides, and dark mountainside forests to their summits, to the sky.

My grandmother in her Sunday best, rouged cheeks, fancy hat, eyes glistening, repeated again and again like a mantra, "Beautiful, beautiful, beautiful."

I am familiar with that mantra and still speak variations on its theme whenever I enter the mountains. No matter how frequently I see them, those first glimpses of blue peaks never lose their power. As I crest a hill heading east into Tupper Lake on Route 3, the Seward Range humps along the horizon like an old dragon. Behind it the Great Range masses into one thick multi-topped massif.

On the approach to Saranac Lake village from the north on Route 86, the Sewards again offer their expansive countenance; I can see Mt. Seward's steeply sloped forehead, and a hint of nearby Seymour. Heading again toward Saranac from Onchiota on the Oregon Plains Road, the asphalt aims like a dark arrow into the heart of McKenzie Mountain. Here, north of Bloomingdale, McKenzie is as formal and as dominating as Whiteface, but without the scars of commerce.

On the turn toward Franklin Falls from Vermontville, Whiteface and Esther—the Fuji of the Adirondacks and its wide-hipped consort—claim the east. Whiteface is best viewed from a distance, rising a dozen miles away above fog-filled valleys in the morning, or in the fall, when snow showers powder its upper reaches. From a ridge near Middlebury, Vermont, I can recognize Dix and Rough, and the deep valleys that sweep up Giant-of-the-Valley and Rocky Peak.

From that ridge, the High Peaks seem to occupy the whole state, and they beckon fiercely, jagged row upon row, across the pastoral lowlands of Lake Champlain.

I am not certain what the power of these North Country mountains is. But the thrill of the mountain view is compounded by the idea that we are about to enter that view, that we are at a portal of its kingdom. And when I walk through the hardwoods in that kingdom, and the forest floor slopes invitingly into the unknown, I remember my grandmother's vision of Lake George. And in the vastness of the forest, if I squint my eyes, if I listen carefully, I can see its sparkling water, hear the breaking of its waves upon a hidden shore.

STAR LAKE RELIEF

Studying a relief map is like reading a play rather than attending or acting in it. A relief map is nothing but lines and numbers, names and icons. Nothing but imagination.

Here is a hand-drawn map of the Star Lake area in southern St. Lawrence County—the foothills of the Adirondacks. As a sophomore in high school, I frequently visited my friend Mike's summer cottage on the south shore of Star Lake. The cottage was actually a well-maintained trailer and enclosed porch neatly situated at the end of a row of modest summer camps owned and managed by Mike's parents. The property was carved out of a high bank that rose up steeply from the lake's shore.

Mike and I didn't hang around camp much; instead, we explored the uncivilized expanse south of the lake, following the creeks and rivers, climbing Maple Mountain, going on overnights to remote Gage Lake (on some maps it's spelled "Cage"), a ten-mile hike into the interior. I was quite taken by the territory surrounding Star Lake, particularly where real wilderness stretched unbroken for dozens of miles to the Stillwater and Bog River Flow.

That winter as a sixteen-year-old must have been a long one. First I passed time looking at topographical maps—a half-dozen old maps from the turn of the century—and my favorite, a new map that I had purchased, of the Star Lake quadrangle. That particular dreary winter the maps must have seemed small, their details cramped. I guess I needed more space for my imagination to roam.

From the paper supply store in my hometown of Ogdensburg, I purchased a large sheet of drawing paper and commenced to cover it with a penciled grid of squares. I did the same with the Star Lake map, dividing up my treasured territory into blocks one-quarter the size of those I had drawn on the blank paper. Then came the labor of love (though some may think it closer to lunacy): for the next two months, painstakingly, grid by grid, I scrivened every brown contour line, every light blue squiggle of creek, every elevation benchmark, every green tuft that represented swamp land. Whatever was on the quadrangle, I redrew with colored pencils onto my new map.

Contour lines were the most arduous, not only because there were so many of them, but also because they had to match up precisely, line by line, with all those other brown lines that waited incomplete at each adjacent grid. I learned to keep my pencil sharp and to wait until after I had finished copying contours for a whole section of grid squares to draw rivers and brooks. Working with contours, I learned where running water came from and where it went, where it had to go. Drawing contours, I learned to read a slope, and then actually to visualize it, to conjure from my imagination the sensory props of color and texture, scent and depth.

I don't remember what else I did that winter. Perhaps that was when Mike and I camped out for the first time in below-zero weather, and woke at night to hear in anxious wonderment pine trees cracking like rifle shots as sap expanded in the cold. Perhaps that was the winter tobogganing became more hard work than fun. Perhaps it was the year I learned to ski, and could finally perform stem turns rather precariously on the tame slopes nearby. Or perhaps I just stayed inside, copying and exploring the Star Lake quadrangle.

I do know that somehow it was necessary for me to perform this most mundane of tasks. And I do know that I was surprised—as I'm sure my parents were—at my dogged persistence. It wasn't to be one of those half-done and discarded jobs, or yet another ordinary task like snow shoveling or washing the same dishes every night. Hour after hour, day after day, I worked on my map and finally completed it. By then I knew that little quadrangle, knew the location of every swamp, the height and shape of every hump and hill, the gradient of every ridge. That winter, in my high-octane imagination and with my big map before me, I hiked the length of every dotted line I drew, canoed the perimeter and diameter of every pond and lake.

The contour lines—each light brown line was an elevation of twenty feet, while each dark brown fifth line was one hundred feet—were carefully studied and drawn, their intervals transformed to gullies, precipices, and hills. By painstakingly drawing the cliff above Aldrich Pond, I scaled it, and by connecting the gentle lines of Maple Mountain I retraced the steps my friend and I had made in past summers to its unremarkable top. I explored them all. That winter I lived in summer, revisiting places I had been, delving into remote areas I knew I would probably never see. I was at home in terrain which I had for the most part never visited before.

Moving with eye and imagination where my colored pencil had moved before, I splashed along creeks, scrambled up ridges, avoided swamps, and investigated the off-limits forests surrounding Streeter Lake, land that was then privately held by the Schulers of potato chip fame. By carefully rendering its every topographic detail, I had trespassed on the Schuler property and violated the privacy of that pristine lake. It wasn't until spring that I rolled up my paper kingdom, my customized, personal piece of the North Country, stuffed it carefully in the back of my closet, then dug out and scoured last summer's grease-caked, campfire-blackened mess kit.

I have never since redrawn another topo map, never since had the least desire to, but I must tell you that I still love to read them.

Looking now at an Adirondack Mountain Club map of the Adirondack Northern Region, I check out Dry Timber Lake and its surrounding wetlands, jumping carefully from tuft to tuft. My imagination soars, I slip; my feet get wet.

MAITLAND, ONTARIO FROM WEST OF OGDENSBURG

The St. Lawrence is my home river. Living near it, I have taken it for granted; living away, I have missed its presence. Like those things that are both potent and good, the river speaks in simplest terms of things we understand with every atom of our bodies: power and serenity, ebb and flow, life and time.

Who could hold a harsh thought at this river's shores? Why, the waves, the gulls would snatch it away.

This is a picture of the St. Lawrence River five miles upstream from Ogdensburg. It is half an hour after another mind-numbing sunset, and directly across the river the largest hydrogen peroxide plant in North America lights up its stacks and towers. How can a plant that produces thirty percent of North America's hydrogen peroxide be beautiful? Blame it on the river. Just as the river magnifies the impact of the bleeding sun, so it carries ribbons of multi-colored lights from Maitland's Dupont plant streaming and shimmering over its surface.

The faint hum of the plant, of the workers' voices even, are captured, redefined into sonorous undertones, conveyed to us by the river. A scant mile distant from this industrial complex, on our pebbly shore, the trash barrel (a rusted old hog cauldron) flares up with a bonfire of driftwood and dried river weed.

Looking back from the end of the dock, I can see that its flames, too, are claimed and converted to long spears of light, orange streaks that wriggle and flop like goldfish on the back of this greedy and generous river. My two children dance around the fire, but for some reason the river has stolen their voices and footfalls; they perform their impromptu ritual in uncharacteristic silence, their firelit faces shadowy and garish.

In the growing stillness, I can barely hear the river lick the log cribs of the dock. I can see the muskrat coming in from her evening swim, the vees of her mild ripples weaving a soft but insistent counterpoint through the mirrored shafts of light. Now, on this ordinary , extravagant summer night, the stars, too, drop to the water one by one. Without a whisper, they land and ride each tiny wave.

DIRT ROADS AND GYPSY MOTHS

This is a vanity postcard. It's of me in a dusty station wagon alongside a North Country dirt road in the summertime. I've got a paper cup in my hand. Look at that smile.

We each deserve at least one job in our lifetime that gives us pure pleasure. I was fortunate enough to land such a job and hold it for three summers during my college years. I worked for the Plant Pest Control Division of the Agricultural Research Service of the United States Department of Agriculture, or, in acronymic shorthand, the USDA PPC of the ARS. But I never thought of the bureaucratic monikers, only of the job. I was trying to trap gypsy moths and hoping I wouldn't find any.

Three of us shared St. Lawrence County; I was given the center slice, from the St. Lawrence River south to Piercefield. Our traps consisted of paper cups; around their insides we applied with a snub-toothed wooden comb an even layer of a very sticky substance called tanglefoot. Halfway down the inside wall of the cup we then inserted a small wad of cotton, sticking it fast to the tanglefoot. Using an eyedropper, we squeezed a single drop of bright red sex scent from a tiny bottle into the cotton. We then covered the cup with a lid that had a hole in the center just big enough to accommodate passage by a lusting male gypsy moth.

All that was left to do was follow the maps given us by our supervisor and, by its fold-out handles, tack a moth trap on a tree in a hedgerow or at a verge of the woods at the sites indicated on the maps. The trap site map was a composite of old relief maps, some dating back to the 1940s. My map was measled with 350 red dots, each of them representing a trap site.

While many of the sites were accessible by paved roads, at least half were located on dirt or sand: back roads in farm country, abandoned roads, camp roads, and hunting club access roads. Not a few of the roads were on private property, and I was often required to gain permission and borrow gate keys to travel on restricted land.

The first summer I started by working fast. I made up 350 traps and had them all set out in two weeks. Then I spent each weekday revisiting two or three dozen traps, cleaning out dead bugs and flies (but no gypsy moths), and restocking the tanglefoot.

One day, after I had been on the job less than a month, my supervisor caught up to me and told me to slow down. Heeding his advice, I relaxed my pace and began to take notice of the countryside. I'm glad I did.

I became attuned to the particulars of North Country landscape. Above the woods and pastures, I watched great mounds of cumulus clouds build up on the horizon on hot July days until they broke into thunder showers in the late afternoons. There were the high cirrus and jet contrails that hardly moved, the sound of the jet barely discernible, its faint drone drowned out by life buzzing in the rusty meadows where I made my paths.

I marked the way rain sometimes strolled ceremoniously across still fields, its gauzy veils cloaking distant woodlots and pastures. I came to know the way wind would lift and drive those gray veils into sheets of cold rain or hail. I marveled at the swiftness with which those storms would cease, water drops gathering on barbed wire, clutching the hairs on rough blades of meadow grass, dropping large and cold from the shiny leaves of woodlot maples. The huge silence of still meadows, I listened for the last rumble of thunder.

I drove with the large map next to me, on the alert for telltale orange surveyor tape hanging from roadside tree branches that marked the path to a trap. I became a friend to barbed wire; I could leap it or pass between its strands untattered, and on carefree days, I would bounce off a top strand as if propelled from a springboard.

The roads I followed led everywhere—and nowhere. Sometimes roads became two ruts in the high grass that swished noisily beneath the car and often hid rocks. Occasionally the ruts dwindled to less than a tractor path, and I would find myself in a meadow in the middle of the North Country outback. I would stand in that meadow and allow myself to fill slowly with song: the wind in my ears, the cries of larks and warblers and swifts, the locust's piercing scream, the vibrant tremor of millions of insects and bees.

Once, after leading me four miles down a narrow tree-lined alley, bumpy, pot-holed and with a high center hump that scratched harshly along my car's oil pan, a long-neglected path abruptly ended in a pile of boulders.

With no turn-around evident or possible, I had to back out, twisting my torso out the window to scrutinize for a second time the unschooled terrain. During breaks to relieve my strained neck, I counted each tenth of a mile the odometer rolled back. This bumpy and interminable drive backwards lost the mileage both in and back, regaining for my poor car a slightly former youth but netting me zero mileage reimbursement and a frittered-away afternoon for my efforts. At least I hadn't been foolish enough to place a trap at road's end as the map had indicated.

Herds of deer, usually young and without antlers, gathered on hunting club roads. I would slow the car and creep up to them, stopping almost in their midst. There I would turn off the ignition, and we would spend long minutes staring at each other. Usually the deer would grow bored before I did and would nonchalantly wander off into the woods, nibbling their leafy lunch as they went. Coyotes, foxes, porcupines, and other ramblers of the woods and fields also shared the back roads with me, even if only for a brief moment, a streak of orange, a gray shadow slinking into the underbrush.

Less romantically, but, unfortunately more frequently, I became unavoidably acquainted with cows, both on the road and in the pasture. I discovered that the intractability of loose cattle increased in inverse proportion to the width of the road they wandered, the opportunities for their escape, and the heat of the day. Cows were unfazed by my car horn, and usually moved only slightly whether I nudged my car into their midst or ran at them yelling and waving a stick.

Closer to their homes, I found cows to be less passive. I ran from bulls and other angry bovines who may have lacked testicles but not nerve. Boisterous heifers sometimes butted me into retreat, and cows often surrounded me in restless groups, staring at me wide-eyed and suspiciously as if I were a runty alien or a sour salt lick.

There is something unnerving about staring down a cow who is in turn contemplating you, its nose dripping and bubbling, gnawing relentlessly on a cud, sharing with you swarms of flies, the fragrant summer air punctuated by the sounds of substantial elimination, a moist barrage that seems nothing less than arrogance and contempt.

For three summers I manufactured and hung my traps. For three summers I followed my traplines diligently, but leisurely, succumbing to nature's notions of calendar and clock. And for three summers I found nary a gypsy moth; my territory was officially free of infestation. Then my school days ended, the long arm of the draft beckoned, and I left behind my maps and cups and tanglefoot, a half-empty bottle of sex scent, and my life as a government trapper. Although trees have since grown and fallen, pastures turned to meadows, and meadows to maturing stands of poplar and pine, I still have the urge to brake when I pass an old trap site. Sometimes I still do, if only to sit on a grassy shoulder and watch butterflies flutter on loose pebbles in the road or listen to blackbirds rustling about and singing their *cock-a-rees* in the thickets of marshes.

Today, dirt roads are disappearing quickly as highway departments widen, straighten, and pave, complying with the relentless mandates of progress. Now paved is the Tooley Pond Road that in 1960 snaked 20 miles from Degrasse to Cranberry Lake, dirt from start to finish. Now paved is the Stone Church Road in the town of Oswegatchie, so close to civilization yet once magical and inviting, the limbs of its roadside maples meeting overhead to form a long, leafy tunnel. Now paved are countless other roads criss-crossing North Country farmland.

Each summer, road crews with dozers and dump trucks, asphalt machines and rollers, work overtime to transform more dusty, secluded lanes into broad, smooth swaths of pavement and cleared right-of-way that ensure minimal contact with the surrounding landscape—a green blur perhaps, a flash of gold—and promise those of us in a hurry a more civilized ride, a quicker passing-through.

ON TOP AT DAWN

Summits of High Peaks offer special rewards for those who would sacrifice sleep and some comforts to stand far above the night-filled valleys to glimpse the splendors of dawn: those first smudges of purple and pink, the bold red shaft upward cast that sometimes precedes, like the cloak of a Roman god, the grand entrance, step by regal step, of the sun.

Look at these uplifted magenta rocks soaring into the morning sky. Those who have climbed Cascade Mountain during the day would hardly recognize this image. One of the lowest of the Adirondacks' "high" peaks, Cascade is nonetheless notable for its bare summit and sweeping views. Only a short two-mile, 1900-foot ascent from the trailhead on Route 73 between Lake Placid and Keene, the summit of Cascade Mountain is conquered by busloads of sneakered daytrippers every halfway-decent day in summer. A herd of young chaperoned campers can struggle up the rocky trail, run around on top, lunch, and storm back down to a waiting bus in a morning or afternoon.

In the pre-dawn hours one fall morning, three of us climbed Cascade by flashlight. The slight breeze at the trailhead increased with each step as we ascended steeply through the white birches. It had turned into a gale by the time we reached the top. Leaning into the buffeting wind, we crouch-walked carefully across the expanse of summit and found shelter in a trench-like crevice between two great upturned slabs of rock.

There, out of the wind, we sipped cocoa and watched the stars disappear with the approach of daybreak. We checked our camera gear and hauled out our tripods. As the black night turned gradually into purples and pinks, we scattered across the summit, leaning into the wind or crawling, seeking the best vantage points for grabbing sunrise shots. The gale tore at my storm jacket and sang insistently in my ears. Even when unextended, even when held tightly with both hands, my tripod hummed in the wind and was useless for camera support. Conversation was impossible, though we three were separated by only a few feet. The wind, the rough rock, the growing light consumed us.

Individually and as a group, we were existing at that moment someplace far from the rest of humanity, removed from civilization.

I recall the scene from *2001: A Space Odyssey,* with the hominids and the bone flung skyward. On Cascade that morning we were the monkey-men attempting to capture the heart of existence by a gesture, ours a click of a fashioned eye, an impression upon light-sensitive memory, of an occasion at once ordinary and utterly unique.

Before we could see it rise, the sun first touched the tips of the Great Range and, to the north, the observatory atop Whiteface. Then on the eastern horizon we saw a thin, fiery arc, and sunlight was upon us. We watched—my hiking friend of thirty-five years, my son, and I—as the sun's rays melted slowly down the mountain sides, as night's shadows retreated into the deep valleys.

To the east, Lake Champlain appeared as a scattering of gold shields that spread as we watched into a glowing chain, describing the far rim of the North Country. Above the summit monolith, the gleam of a munchkin moon persisted, dime-sized, fragile, and remote.

The image now hangs behind and above me as I write. Turning to look at it, I can hear the wind tearing at the ancient rock, see the pastel sky obscuring the darker riddles of the universe, once more limiting senses to the songs and substance of earth.

See how tiny the moon is now: no more than a suggestion of dust, a lost balloon, the ghost of a star.

THE SCOTTY: A RIVER REFLECTION

"Zoom . . . she's off, Flash she's back! . . . that's the Sea Lyon! Watch her bank the turns at full speed . . . gracefully, easily turning in her own length . . . giving you the ride of your life! Then watch the man at the wheel and his passengers . . . how thoroughly they enjoy the sport. . . . Come, take a ride in a Sea Lyon." (Howard W Lyon, Inc. advertisement in The Rudder, *July* 1930)

My stepson the sailor has departed after a short visit. On the coffee table he has left behind a 1930 mint copy of *The Rudder* ("The Magazine for Yachtsmen"). In it is described the maiden trans-Atlantic voyage of the *Etak,* a twin-masted diesel yacht built in Germany. It is the same ship, under a different name, on which my stepson sailed some years ago. In a snapshot accompanying the text, the ship looks too small for the Atlantic, too vulnerable for the high seas.

Here in the North Country, my water of choice would never accommodate the *Etak.* I crave a quiet stream only deep enough to float a canoe, only wide enough to turn it around, or a small, tree-locked pond where the whine of outboards is replaced by a loon's high whinny or a beaver's sharp slap. But as I page through *The Rudder,* I am reminded that my love of solitude, shallows, and motorless water craft was not exactly inborn.

I grew up on the St. Lawrence River at Ogdensburg. As a preschooler, I used to watch from a window seat as red-hulled steamships spilled black smoke into the sky, their whistles sharp and sudden. Before the Seaway was completed in 1954, these stubby steamships ruled the river.

During my school days my family had no pleasure boat, but one of my best friends had two. The one Paul used the most was a Dunphy Perch, a small open runabout with a rounded hull fashioned from marine plywood that would ripple when the eighteen-horse Evinrude outboard was cranked up. In the Dunphy we would spend hours on the river, often at full throttle, cooling off in the summer, enjoying the bracing air of fall, shutting our mouths and squinting our eyes in late spring when thick clouds of shadflies would drift toward us.

Often we would travel up and down both shores, cruising fifteen or twenty miles, looking at the cottages (called "camps" on the American side) from crowded rows of tiny bungalows to once-stately Victorian homes, their gingerbread trim, great cobblestone fireplaces, and airy verandahs retreating into mossy oblivion among the cedars, birches, and sumacs that grew up like weeds around their decaying flanks.

On the Canadian side the old summer homes were even more

extravagant, and their collapse even more imminent. There we would explore abandoned island derelicts, and with rich fancies that only children and dreamers possess, imagine lives of the wealthy back in the heydays of our grandparents. On the mainland we would tie up at Prescott, or Brockville, or Cardinal, seek out a customs officer, then wander out into those tiny towns in search of the slightly exotic: fish and chips, strong-tasting cigarettes in hard packs, or firecrackers.

Before the Seaway, many locks were operated manually, and the lock tender at Cardinal was always willing to enlist our extra pairs of hands to raise and lower ships around the vicious Galop Rapids. Nearby, dominating the shoreline landscape at Johnstown, was the grain elevator, a white, scallop-sided monolith about a thousand feet long and fifteen stories tall.

One day on a whim we docked near the elevator, banged on the nearest door, and asked the first person we saw if we could look around. Perhaps surprised by our naive brashness, he agreed and gave us a thorough tour of the cavernous facility, including a creaky ride in an open-cage elevator to the roof, from where the river below twinkled in deceptive calm. From our height the wakes of powerboats gleamed like tiny silver slivers; even commercial vessels looked like toy boats. Across the river our hometown, surprisingly foliate and pristine, spread out along the shore, its treetops punctuated by tips of church spires, water towers, and smokestacks, familiar landmarks that from our novel perspective somehow resisted quick identification.

Light and fast, Paul's Dunphy was perfect for duck hunting (I'll not tell here of the morning I bagged a decoy), seagull chasing (they always flew safely away, as we knew they would), and pulling alongside and matching the speed of laden freighters, riding a wave crest within arm's reach of rusting hullplates, standing precariously in our little craft, which was nearly awash in the churning roil, and glimpsing into portholes.

Sometimes we were seen and sworn at, often in foreign tongues, and occasionally those sharp syllables were repeated with more authority by stern, megaphone-toting officers on a lofty bridge. The adventure was always worth it, though, as on a high wave we balanced shakily—riskily—between our mundane teenage existence and the romance of the sea. It was quite worth it, if only to surprise the denizens of those ships who might by chance glance out a porthole and see, rather than sky or foam, a young face, half- grinning, half-terrified, bobbing and reeling by.

Four decades later, it is not the sailing vessels or larger cruisers that attract me to *The Rudder*. I am drawn to ads for slim inboards, particularly the Sea Lyon brand. A full-page ad depicts a flapper waving to me while being towed on a surfboard as wide as a door behind a Sea Lyon more curvaceous than she; another illustration shows a sleek Sea Lyon with ten overdressed passengers spilling onto its lustrous decks. These men and women, mostly outfitted in commodious stem-to-stern bathing suits, are middle-aged, overweight, somehow out of place.

At the wheel, dressed in white shirt and tie, the owner/skipper could be a Kennedy, a Rockefeller, a Luce. The craft's brass-tipped bow rides slightly up, cleanly slicing the water into streaming whitecaps. As burdened as it is with hefty passengers, the inboard is obviously going, as Paul used to say, like a bat out of hell.

Paul was the custodian of his grandfather's Sea Lyon, a sleek, graceful twenty-four-foot craft named *The Scotty*. Of the same vintage and design as the boat in the ad, its decking and hull were of double mahogany, and many of its fittings were brass.

Amidships, between the fore and aft cockpits, hidden beneath curved hatches, was a monstrous 125-horsepower Chrysler marine engine that devoured a gallon of gasoline every three miles.

The Scotty wasn't the fastest boat on the river, nor was it the largest. Lightweight speedboats with fat frog-green Johnson outboards were quicker, and the multi-deck cruisers that sauntered by at a respectable distance from shore bore greater evidence of luxury and elegance. But *The Scotty* was classy in a different way. Over twenty-five years old, it was considered nearly an antique, and its cousins were more likely to be found farther upriver in the Thousand Islands.

Around Ogdensburg, however, *The Scotty* was a *rara avis*

and garnered both curiosity and respect. I can't say that we didn't like the attention, but that wasn't why I loved to go out in *The Scotty*. Like the Victorian camps, Paul's nautical charger represented another age, a past with which I was only tenuously connected. It was a past of sensory impressions: the smell of pre-war car interiors, the silky or velvety feel of Victorian furniture upholstery, the cries from night trains in Canada, the rich bass sound of the big speaker in the floor console radio.

My earlier childhood memories of an excursion to Dixon Island, downriver from Ogdensburg, evoke the scent of kerosene lamps, their gold light dancing with shadows among the rafters. I can hear aunts and grandmothers in a darkening kitchen cleaning up after dinner, the banter of men playing cards.

Bored, we children escaped outside into the huge night where stars overflowed the sky and the Milky Way sparkled like a magnificent soaring bridge. There, on a finger-shaped island doomed by the coming Seaway, we chased and hid from each other, the current of one of the largest rivers on earth streaming by us on all sides. At the river's edge, *The Scotty* tossed lightly in its boathouse moorings, waiting for us to grow older, for Paul to add that ignition key to his custodial collection.

I drove *The Scotty* only once. One summer afternoon, Paul was desperate to ski the high, crisp waves characteristic of *The Scotty's* wake. There, in the middle of the river, he gave me a crash course in boat operation, safety, and navigation. All too quickly, he slipped overboard, ski rope in hand, maneuvering the slalom ski tip out of the water.

I'm not sure who was more apprehensive. After a few false starts, I finally gave the boat enough throttle to pull Paul up and drag him wallowing through the water. Finally, it dawned on me that we needed more speed. I gave the craft full throttle, its bow slamming down like an angry fist, and Paul began to fly across the water's surface, criss-crossing the wake, soaring happily into the air.

I kept busy with the throttle and wheel, looking ahead for boats, buoys, and other obstacles, and occasionally behind, stealing glances at Paul, whose pleasure was mitigated by the necessity to provide me with hand signals I didn't understand and shouts I couldn't hear. For the delight of a few minutes of skiing he had placed our fates in my hands, hands which after five years of trying couldn't yet tie a slipknot.

Behind the boat Paul was waving, waving. Gradually, it sank in that his gestures were becoming more impatient than friendly. Aha! He wanted to come in. I can still hear my friend, bobbing in the middle of the shipping channel, watching me wrench *The Scotty* into a sweeping turn, its bow then pointing his way, bearing down on him, yelling at me to steer around *him—please,* not to come too *close—please.* I imagine him wondering if I heard, wondering if I could steer the craft at all, and all the time the boat coming closer and closer, looming larger above him.

Paul survived, but I was never asked to run the boat again. We both knew why, and the reasons were better left unsaid.

Little by little, *The Scotty* fell on hard times. In its sagging boathouse home, it was carefully lifted out of the water each fall by block and tackle attached to huge beams upstairs. Once, the tackle was wrapped around a large wooden barrel. Over the winter months, the barrel crushed slowly from *The Scotty's* dead weight and its contents—molasses—oozed out over the floor, between the cracks and down upon *The Scotty.*

When Paul and I went to put the boat in the water the following spring, we soon recognized what had happened. I distinctly remember volunteering to help clean up somehow, to help remove the thick, sticky goo from the decks, the seat covers, the fittings, the bilges. But my offer was never taken up. Perhaps those reasons, too, were better left unsaid.

When Ogdensburg's downtown boathouses were demolished during urban renewal, *The Scotty* moved upriver to Paul's family camp in Morristown. One fall, as it was being carried in a stake-rack truck to its winter quarters, the boat shifted and a stake punctured its mahogany hull. Mortally wounded, terribly disfigured, the ancient craft was sold upriver. Since then I have imagined *The Scotty* stripped of engine and accoutrements down to its skin and bones, and the restorer, finding sticky traces of long-fermented molasses deep in the innards, putting two and two together and concluding that the innocent *Scotty* must have been the nimble river transport of a rum-runner during Prohibition.

Of course. That explains the Sea Lyon ad in that prohibition-era issue of *The Rudder,* and why those stodgy middle-aged folks on board look like the ride is more for business than for pleasure.

The *Scotty* I like to remember, the one without molasses in its bilges or the hole in its side, still tools around in that partly sunny, partly foggy, magical place where all my favorite old vehicles now reside—the three-toned '56 Pontiacs that Paul and I each owned, the string of convertibles and sports cars.

In my mind, I am never driving that majestic river beast. I'm always riding shotgun in *The Scotty,* just along for the ride, enjoying every second.

North County Seasoning

Lynn Case Ekfelt

Printed in small letters next to March 21 on my desk calendar are the words "First Day of Spring," just as they are on the calendar of my friend in Nacogdoches, Texas. But no one, neither my friend nor I nor any other human being, actually lives the life prescribed by those flat, glossy pages. We measure our years not in evenly spaced three-month spans, but in much different segments—seasons of the mind and heart.

Particularly in the North Country—where nature has not been caged and domesticated as it has in more urban settings—weather and geography shape our lives, often more than we would like. It is more difficult to miss the signs of change walking through a tunnel of trees—one day hunter green, one day glowing crimson—than through a tunnel of steel and concrete, changing only through the gradual accumulation of grime and graffiti.

Hungry city dwellers, usually located within a leisurely stroll of several specialty markets, notice the cycle of seasons less than do those more who are dependent on the natural world to satisfy their cravings. Small wonder, then, that we in the North Country tend to break down the year into segments along lines defined by our stomachs.

MUD AND SYRUP

In northern New York, our year begins with *Mud Season.* Starting somewhere between March 15 and April 15 and extending into early May, mud season is the logical result of large amounts of melting snow soaking into two inches of thawed earth on top of ground still too frozen underneath to absorb the runoff. Add to that the layer of grit left on the walks and streets after a winter of sanding, and you have a group of unhappy homemakers and building custodians. The mudroom, common to many North Country houses, serves as a decompression chamber, preparing us for the rarefied atmosphere of the hearth after a venture into the mucky depths of the world outside.

But mud season brings welcome signs of renewal for those who know where to look. Willow catkins, much more like small, unobtrusive gray mice than "pussies," quietly appear to announce that change is taking place. Loud cracks and pops speak not of out-of-season hunters but of breaking ice on the rivers, sounds followed later by those of the rivers themselves, energized by melting snow, roaring their challenges to puny wooden docks and footbridges.

Binoculars move permanently to a chair by the window so my husband, Nils, and I can watch returning travelers as they join the faithful chickadees and cardinals at our feeder. Some of the newcomers will take up summer residence here; others, like the dark-eyed juncos, will only refresh themselves before heading farther north.

Best of all, early mud season brings maple syrup. Even a person who can't tell a purple finch from an osprey can't help but notice woodlots tied neatly together with miles of plastic tubing. With this vision comes the knowledge that, as Swinbourne wrote, "the hounds of spring are on winter's traces." The *Watertown Times* made dire predictions this spring about the low price syrup might bring and quoted economists who speculated that some farmers might not even bother to tap their trees. Far more telling was the comment of the farmer who said, "They may decide not to tap, but when the time comes, I bet they'll be in the sugar shed. It gets into your blood."

Syrup made after the middle of April is usually "buddy"—cloudy and unpalatable—so sugaring off really is the first promise of returning life. Maybe a sense that he is taking part in nature's slow awakening leads Doug, my archival assistant, to crawl out of bed ahead of the sun in order to empty buckets before heading in to work. Or maybe he just likes fresh syrup for his pancakes. Those fortunate enough to have a sugar bush on a slope can spare themselves Doug's chilly forays by relying on plastic hoses to carry the sap hygienically from tree to holding tank. But even they can't insulate themselves from the necessary slog into the woods through three feet of slushy snow to hammer spikes into tree trunks. Our Puritan forebears would surely point out that anything so good as maple syrup must be earned before it can be appreciated.

A steamy magnet in the midst of lingering cold, the sugar shack attracts the entire neighborhood to its convivial warmth. It takes a long time to boil down the requisite forty gallons of sap into one gallon of maple syrup, so there's plenty of time to solve the world's problems while tending the fire and lifting the paddle occasionally to see whether the syrup has begun to sheet. It's even possible to entice the kids away from Nintendo long enough to feast on eggs hard-boiled in sap.

But everyone knows those eggs are just a way to pass the time until the main event. Finally, the smell of the sweet steam rising from the boiling pan drives even us adults outside to stake out a patch of clean white snow. A quick drizzle of almost-syrup onto the cold snow hardens instantly into a tooth-challenging rope of jack wax, or wax-on-snow. Through cemented jaws, older kids pass on to their younger friends the time-honored strategy for increasing one's wax capacity—use a crisp dill pickle to cut the sweetness and you can pig out blissfully for hours.

Once sugaring is over, there begins a round of maple syrup

festivals and pancake breakfasts, sponsored by local service organizations, that serve to extend the sociability of the sugar shack to the entire town. Husbands who rarely lift a finger in their home kitchens flip sausages and pancakes in church basements, trading quips with their friends waiting in line to be fed. Wives dish up the food while their sons and daughters pour coffee and carry off the well-cleaned plates to be washed and refilled. It's much too muddy to begin plowing, so most everyone is happy to devote a couple of hours after church on Sunday to the pursuit of good food and companionship. For those few reluctant souls, there is the tongue-in-cheek justification that it's all for charity.

FLORA AND FISH

After mud season comes *Spring.* Not for us the long, lush spring of the poets. Spring in the North Country explodes onto the scene around the first or second week of May, rushing pell-mell to make up for its tardiness. One day trees are bare, the next buds are swelling, the next tiny green-fuzz leaves appear. Suddenly daffodils and tulips are everywhere, often poking through the last dirty rags of snow. Local birds begin drawing territorial lines, their dulcet tones daring anyone to set foot—or wing—across them.

Then, just as the idea of spring begins to penetrate our winter-dulled minds, it's summer. Daffodils that budded in snow begin to wither, blasted by the midday heat. In Canton, as my friend Jon often said, "May, not April, is the cruelest month."

The week of spring usually ends with the beginning of *Fishing Season.* The still-icy rivers and lakes are dotted with small craft, some high-tech models equipped with all the latest in electronic fish-finding gear, others more modest. I once watched two men, floating in an old bathtub, boat a fine muskie. Hospital emergency rooms become expert at fishhook-ectomies, removing hooks from the hands of neophytes like my visiting father who tried in vain to detach the lure from a flopping two-foot fish without pliers.

Bait shops, closed for the winter months, come alive, and hand-lettered WORMS 4 SALE signs appear, pounded at rakish angles into front yards or onto tree trunks. Men who have spent the winter daydreaming over "Rod and Reel" on PBS begin to sort through their tackle boxes, making sure their favorite Mr. Twisters, Little Cleos, and Meppses are sharp and ready for use.

My husband's fishing buddy Bob earnestly assures us, "Fishing makes good sense. It fills the freezer for free." The truth is that he, like most North Country fishermen, would continue to fish even it he had to pay a surcharge on every fish he caught. In fact, a few years ago a two-week long fishing derby was held on the St. Lawrence in which a bass was tagged and released. Anyone catching the tagged fish within the prescribed period was to win $1,000,000.00. Sure enough, a local man caught the fish early one morning. Rather than miss out on a day of fishing, he put the fish on his stringer, went back to casting, and turned in his winner when he quit for the night.

It reminded me of the slot machine players I saw on a trip to Lake Tahoe who didn't even bother to pick up their cascading jackpots. Of course, jackpots don't often come loose and float off, a nasty habit of loaded stringers.

Fishing is addictive. Nils is always sure that the very next cast is going to be the one that hooks the 40-inch Northern, even if the last five "very next" casts netted only seaweed. It's that hope that gets him and Bob up at 5 A.M. on the first day of bass season, that makes them sit with rivers of rainwater streaming down their necks while they assure each other that "fish bite better on cloudy days." In a world of instant gratification, fishing reminds us of the rewards of patience. And a fine reward it is to feel a big fish strike the lure and begin to run with the line.

There are almost as many breeds of fishermen as there are fish. Trout fishermen are the first out, taking pride in carefully matching their meticulously crafted flies to whatever insects happen to be in season on the Adirondack ponds they are casting.

Bullheaders are specialists, luring their prey with rolled up balls of bread that would cause a Northern to turn up its razor-lined duckbill.

Bass fishermen sneer at Northerns as inedible—too many bones.

Those who pursue the elusive muskie are the big game hunters of the river, scorning anything that fails to bend their industrial-strength rods.

And every "real sportsman" looks down on the humble panfish as providing insufficient challenge.

Challenge? Maybe not. But it's hard not to get excited when a school of hungry pumpkinseeds crowds around the boat, biting on bare hooks in a frenzy of self-sacrifice. Throw the line out, reel it back, stick the fish on the stringer, then throw the line out again. No matter how fast the rhythm, I find it hard not to resent the brief time the hook has to be out of the water. When you're used to a bite every hour or so, panfishing can be very gratifying. Besides, there's nothing sweeter than a mess of bluegills, panbroiled in butter and garlic powder.

Fishing, at least on North Country lakes and rivers, isn't much of a group activity. Solitary contemplation or quiet companionship with one or two friends are the pleasures of the fisherman. Once the fish are cleaned, the situation changes. The lure of a fresh fish dinner is irresistible, and fund-raisers know it.

Late May and June bring bullhead feeds—all the fish you can eat, to say nothing of coleslaw and potato salad and homemade desserts, and your admission donation goes to help the fire department or the rescue squad. No quiet contemplation at a bullhead feed—not with kids of all ages racing between the chairs and neighbors yelling greetings and news from table to table.

BLACKFLIES, CHEDDAR, AND ZUCCHINI

"Sure, we had summer last year. Let's see now: I think it was July 16th."

Well, O.K. that's a bit of an exaggeration, but the truth is, *Summer* here is all too short. With nighttime freezes possible year-round, northern New Yorkers learn to prize summer in a way Southerners and Californians don't. We reach out and grab the warm, sunny days with both hands and squeeze every moment of delight out of them. A rainy Saturday becomes a personal affront. It's an incomparable pleasure to relax outside, shoulders held normally instead of hunched against the cold. We burst out of our winter cocoons, reveling in the variety of colors that have replaced winter's white, brown, and dark spruce green.

Summer is too precious to waste inside, so we seek excuses to leave the house. I hurry home from work to get in an hour or so of weeding before dinner. The warmth invites friends passing on the street to linger for a chat; sometimes they'll even pull a few weeds while they talk. Our neighborhood is alive with leisurely strollers after dinner. They amble along, admiring their neighbors' gardens, then wind their way downtown for a green-mint-chip-on-a-sugar-cone.

We fix picnics and head to the woods, or the river, or the lake, or anywhere else as long as it's outside. Many of our friends even pack up and move to camp for a couple of months, happy to accept a longer commute in exchange for the pleasure of drifting off to sleep to a lullaby whispered by pines.

Every weekend there's a festival, fair, or field day of some sort offering outdoor socialization and good food. It's almost impossible to drive around the North Country on a summer Saturday without passing at least one firehouse veiled in the sweet-smelling smoke of barbecuing chicken. Treating visiting nieces and nephews to a day at the St. Lawrence County Fair reminds me of a lesson learned long ago by their father and me: best to eat our favorite sausage and pepper sandwiches and fried dough with cinnamon *after* going on the rides.

Even when we're not eating mass-produced outdoor food, we're having a few friends over for hamburgers or fish on the grill. Summer is the time when you can invite out-of-town guests and know a snowstorm won't close the highways. Relatives who refuse to visit any other time of the year clamor for an invitation to escape more sultry climes. Luckily, summer is easy: no one expects you to fuss. Complicated sauces are unnecessary when you have fresh air for seasoning.

If every silver lining has its cloud, summer's is *Blackfly Season.* Unlike mosquitoes, blackflies require running water to breed, so they love the snow-melt-swollen streams of May and June. Voracious, the all-but-invisible blackfly views any unprotected bit of skin—the part in your hair, the small opening in your sleeve above the buttoned cuff—as fair game.

My friend Nancy seems particularly attractive to black flies. Swathed in the same netting she uses to care for her bees, she sallies forth to weed her flowerbeds, preferring to be pot roast inside a moon suit rather than steak tartare without it.

Bloody but unbowed, northern New Yorkers used to spray on noxious-smelling bug goop with names like Old Woodsman or Deep Woods Off and venture out their doors anyway. Then one glorious day a beleaguered nature lover discovered that Skin-So-Soft—designed by Avon to attract, not repel—can serve equally well to discourage blackflies. Now, even beefy forest rangers encountered on back country trails are redolent of sweet flowers. We have taken back our summer!

June is Dairy Month across northern New York. Actually, in a region reputed to have more cows than people, it might be fair to say that *Dairy Season* lasts all year. In Canton, the Dairy Princess parade is sandwiched between rows of spectators three or four deep. (By contrast, the Memorial Day parade two weeks earlier is mainly attended by the marchers' families.) Kids jostle for the best position to catch the caramels flung from the Kraft float, parents for the best camera angle to photograph their daughter portraying an ice cream soda in the 4-H entry.

After the parade, it's on to the park for ice cream served by Her Royal Highness, the Dairy Princess. Earnestly, yet with a winsome smile, she presses leaflets with milk facts and recipes on all passersby.

As for other dairy products, just try to get a northern New Yorker to give up cheese. I'd sooner steal a bone from a Rotweiler. Our love affair with cheese began as a marriage of convenience: in the days before refrigerated trucks, the only way farmers could transport milk to downstate markets before it soured was to turn it into cheese. Every four corners was home to a family-owned cheese factory. Modern technology has removed the necessity for cheese making, but not the inclination.

Some of the best cheese in the country still comes from small factories in northern New York. I've heard more than once that Kraft's Philadelphia cream cheese is named for Philadelphia,

New York, not the City of Brotherly Love to the south.

A reasonable variety of cheese travels south from the North Country, but there is no doubt about which is the Queen. Like a glitzy starlet, Wisconsin cheddar continues to draw rave notices nationally, eclipsing New York cheddar, the more established actress with less glamour and more quality. Good cheddar bites you back, tingling on your tongue, and crumbles rebelliously if you try to slice it into dainty slivers—as uncompromising and unpretentious as the northern New Yorkers who love it.

Summer's end brings *Zucchini Season.* Maybe because we prize most what we have least, most of my friends are avid gardeners. January seed catalogs are irresistible, their bright colors viewed against a dead-white backdrop. We comb them eagerly for varieties promising early maturity. Reluctantly we pass the peach, grape, and sweet cherry pages, settling for the more cold-tolerant apples. Then, we plant tomatoes and zucchini—lots of them, because we know they'll probably survive to maturity.

And they do. Like the sorcerer's apprentice we find ourselves inundated by the results of our folly. Shopping with a co-worker shortly after I moved to Canton, I instinctively pushed down the lock as I closed the car door. My friend scoffed, "Hey, this is a safe town; you don't have to lock up just to run into the store." Then, she paused and added, "Well, maybe you'll want to during zucchini season or you'll come back and find your seat loaded with them." In desperation, we create zucchini bread, zucchini casseroles, stuffed zucchini, zucchini quiche, zucchini chocolate cake, and yes, even zucchini lemon meringue pie. And still they come.

The most poignant zucchini story I ever heard came from my friend Pete, himself a gardener. He told me that his son, out on the Little River for an afternoon of fishing, had watched a flotilla of baseball-bat zucchini float by. We shared a moment of silent contemplation, considering the anguish that gardener must have felt when he realized he couldn't even *drown* them!

Mid-August until first frost in early to mid-September is a short-lived paradise of fresh-from-the-garden corn, squash, and tomatoes. If only we could have tomatoes like these all year. But no, annually we cure ourselves of our taste for fresh tomatoes by surfeit, then begin hopelessly to crave them again when faced with winters' pallid offerings. If we're lucky, we may have the foresight to shout down our jaded taste buds in September and make provision for future scarcity.

I am always grateful I remembered to freeze some gazpacho for a hot day in July when my own tomatoes are still tantalizing green marbles.

Those who don't garden think of themselves as public servants, helping to relieve the bountiful burdens of friends and neighbors. Free of the need to deal with the ample harvest, they have even more time than the rest of us to appreciate the farmer's market. It's a sensual pleasure to wander from table to table in the park, comparing recipes with other browsers, pulling back husks to check the freshness of corn, sampling Becky Harblin's latest herb jam, picking up a bittersweet wreath to decorate the front door. On market days I long for a painter's skill so I might capture the vivid colors—the red of the apples, so different from that of the beets and the new potatoes—and the textures, ranging from the lumpiness of blackberries to the silkiness of sun-warmed tomatoes.

Whether we're gardeners or gleaners, this is the season for putting food by, for stocking a snug burrow in which to survive the long, cold time to come. Feverishly, Nils and I transform the last of the basil into frozen pesto. The fragrance of simmering chutney, made with green tomatoes picked the night of the first frost warning, fills our house, then lingers pleasantly for days. The price of a few canning jars and some tomato seeds brings juice for breakfast, spaghetti sauce for noontime dinner, and stewed tomatoes to put into ratatouille or soup for supper. Even those of us who can afford to stock our larders at the P&C take part in this annual ritual.

Environmental concerns drive some of us; worry over our family's health spurs others. But mostly, food just tastes better when we've grown it and prepared it ourselves. There is something soul-satisfying in seeing those rows of jars lining the shelves and knowing that we've taken a hand in our survival.

GLOWING LEAVES AND VENISON

A few trend-setting trees in the Adirondacks begin to try on fall finery about the middle of August. We try to ignore them, saying, "Oh, those trees—they're sick." But we feel a shiver of apprehension. Then in September, their lowland neighbors decide to join the fashion parade and we can lie to ourselves no longer. *Fall* has arrived.

Nils and I divide our weekends between lawn chores and leaf peeping. Always alert to a bargain, we paddle down placid streams whose reflections offer two-for-one specials on bank-side glories. We know such splendor can't last; our eyes would wear out from too much looking. By mid-October, the wind has completely disrobed the participants in fall's carnival and suddenly we can see much farther without the leaves to block our view. The neighbor's house beside us and the school behind emerge from behind their screen, reminding us that we are not so pleasantly remote from civilization as we had imagined.

Walking in the country on the last mild days in October, savoring the browns, rusts, and mustards that have replaced the riotous crazy quilt of early fall, we hear popping in the woods and know *Hunting Season* has begun. North Country women may join their husbands and fathers in the fishing boat, but only a few venture into the male preserve of hunting camp. Many a family we know holds an all-female Thanksgiving dinner because the men are in the woods, not wasting a day at home.

Suddenly, the supermarkets are filled with men stocking their camps, looking a bit sheepish as they eye unfamiliar labels. I once watched two men picking out a can of cocoa powder and wondered whether they knew the difference between cocoa and hot chocolate mix. Perhaps they did. If not, there will be another good story to tell around the fire next year.

"Did you get your deer yet?" becomes the refrain whenever two men meet. Stopping for a red light often brings you face to face with a buck draped limply across the trunk of the preceding car. One more North Country family will eat well this winter. If hunting were simply a matter of provisioning, the camps would empty out slowly as one after another of the inhabitants carted off his prize. But it isn't. Hunting camp is a place for male bonding, a place to escape the fetters of female civilization, to live on the edge. And if you die, shot because your partner was too eager for his deer, then you die doing what you love best. Sitting recently at the funeral of my friend's son, I raged at the waste and was grateful that Nils is content to bond with his friends in a fishing boat.

From Thanksgiving to New Year's, we hold the winter at bay with the *Holiday Season.* Houses mimic fall's colors with bright decorations. Suddenly there are two and three parties every weekend, and we feast on fellowship along with food. The lack of big-city variety in our local restaurants has turned my friends into accomplished ethnic cooks. Potluck parties allow each the luxury of fussing over a single masterpiece, so we feast on hummus, taramasalata, lemon lentils, moussaka, and Sachertorte. We're so busy there isn't time to notice the cold, and the colored lights make coming home from work in the dark more endurable. The snow is a welcome ally, offering a white Christmas, soothing guilt as it covers up the last unraked leaves.

COZY FIRE AND COMFORT FOOD

We awaken January 2nd to the realization that it's *Winter,* and it will be for a long time to come. We turn off the Christmas lights, though we often leave the wreath to brighten the door until March. And we settle in. A Southerner who's never slept in a house covered by a four-foot-deep blanket of snow can never really understand the meaning of Gruber's phrase, "Silent night." Only the occasional soft plop of snow falling off a branch breaks the hush in a countryside wearing a thick white muffler. Winter is a time for sitting by the fire, for chess, for sewing, for reading. We hate to break the silence; we feel as if we may be the only people left on earth.

Like the rest of the animals, we eat heartily to insulate us from the cold. Bean soup, beef stew, great pots of chili, things that simmer for hours on the stove, slowly improving their flavor as the day wears on—these are what we crave. Now we really appreciate the garden's bounty, preserved in the pantry. When I look out the window and can't recollect distinctly what the garden looked like, it's comforting to heat a container of frozen green beans and remember.

We venture out to work or to shovel, then hurry home to cradle a mug of hot buttered rum, Earl Grey tea, or mulled cider. We envy the squirrels their bushy tails; when *we* curl up to sleep, we have no built-in nose warmers. Life is pared down to the essential struggle to stay warm.

By February, I begin to fear my cabin fever may be terminal. I cheer when the groundhog sees his shadow on February 2; *only* six more weeks of winter. Heartened northern New Yorkers decide we're not going to let the weather rule our lives, and we plan winter festivals. Every North Country town has its own mid-February extravaganza with snow sculpture contests, sled dog races, ice skating, and lots of hearty food. Church basements are filled again, this time with people eating ham and scalloped potatoes or chicken and biscuits or turkey with all the trimmings followed by homemade pies. Sometimes we wander among the sculptures at high noon, bundled to the eyebrows against -10 degree temperatures; sometimes a thaw retitles every statue "Melting Ice Cream." But at least we're out of the house.

Nils and I invite friends over for soup and bread. We're not alone, and suddenly the long nights don't seem nearly so interminable.

We wax skis, sharpen skates, strap on snowshoes, and decide to take back the outdoors. When we do, we're rewarded with more signs of life. Chickadees answer Nils' call and hop from branch to branch beside us. We find where a red squirrel has feasted on pinecones, leaving a pile of rubbish for the next snowfall to hide. A tidier mouse has stitched a neat line of tracks into the snow from tree to tree. Even the deer, seeming to know they are safe for another year from the hunter's bullets, venture into inhabited areas. They seek handouts; we engage in a staring contest with a doe until I sneeze. We're part of nature; we're all in this together. Hearts warmed, we head home to our own cozy den.

Slowly, the winter passes. Spaghetti dinners and church socials keep us in touch with our humanity; bird feeders remind us that humanity itself is only part of something bigger. The sun rises a little higher every day, and even on cold days, icicles develop runny noses. The cardinals begin to sing. And one day, finally, I find I have to use the cast iron scraper beside the back door to clean the mud off my boots.

The Nature of the North Country

Chris Angus

I'm sitting on a simple stone bench, staring up through the branches of a towering white pine tree. These trees, so many of which went floating down northern rivers to provide masts for the ships of eighteenth-century commerce and war, evoke visions of a wilderness I can never know.

The white pine nearly disappeared before man moved on to do similar damage to the butternut, the chestnut, the hemlock, and countless others. The very wilderness itself disappeared, the wilderness of James Fenimore Cooper and Francis Parkman, of Champlain and Father Jogues, and, most of all, of the Mohawks and Algonquins—disappeared to the logger's ax, the pioneer's plow, and the hunter's muzzle-loader.

But while the disappearing wilderness has changed this part of the world forever, it has not completely altered its pioneer character. A short paddle up a quiet stream only minutes from town can give one a credible illusion of being in the wilderness. That sense of connection to the natural world remains strong in the North Country.

Isolation has always been central to the idea of the North Country. It was isolation that first set the region apart, gave it its identity, and gave rise to the independent pioneer spirit. That isolation continues today, albeit to a lesser degree. We still need to make special efforts to travel outside the area. Rail and air transport are nearly non-existent. Drivers must make do for the most part with winding two-lane highways. Until recently, there was little access to that ubiquitous twentieth-century creation, the shopping mall. We are isolated by travel time, by lack of services, by fewer medical and cultural resources, by the very homogeneity of the population.

Beneath these magnificent pine trees, my thoughts run to feelings of isolation, for I am sitting in a graveyard, one of many sprinkling the North Country. It holds the remains of men and women who lived closer to a time when real wilderness could still be seen and felt.

Beneath me lies Irving Bacheller, a celebrated author who lived in these parts in the 1860s when they were still a "howling wilderness." Bacheller had a farm in the Adirondack foothills, just a few miles south of Canton, called "Paradise Valley." Except for a roadside marker, there is little to see there today. Indeed, someone has struck a dirt road through the woods to a gravel pit. But I can still recall the old barn that my father pointed out to me when I was a boy in the 1950s, and that place with the romantic name became my own personal frontier as we headed into the mountains. For generations of sportsmen, loggers, river-drivers and college students, Sunday Rock—the glacial erratic now protected in a small roadside park outside South Colton—marked the boundary between civilization and the deep woods. For me, the boundary was always Paradise Valley.

In Bacheller's day, there was little need for such markers. He could hear the cry of the wolf and the panther from his doorstep. His family lived in a world of utter separation, barely removed from the days of the pioneers. Of his mother and the other women of the period, he wrote, "They were a wonderful race of women—each a spinner, a weaver, a nurse, a doctor, a wise and tender mother. . . . Their lives were lonely . . . thinking of the old friends and beloved scenes they had left forever, and yet they were not more than a hundred miles from them—a journey so long and difficult that they dared to think of it only in dreams."

Here, too, are the remains of Frederic Remington, best remembered for his images of the final days of the American West. But while documenting the end of one way of life, Remington lived another, that of the early Adirondack sportsman. Guided by men who were themselves legends, he canoed and hiked and fished the primitive Cranberry Lake wilderness and the Oswegatchie River.

Remington was a true son of the North Country. He spent time on each of its boundaries—in the Adirondack Mountains, and at his island retreat, Ingleneuk, in the Thousand Islands of the St. Lawrence River. And he was born in Canton, midway between the two—born, wrote Atwood Manley and Margaret Manley Mangum in their book, *Frederic Remington And The North Country,* to a time when ". . . civilization had barely touched the virgin forests of the Adirondacks and the silent power of the mighty St. Lawrence River. In the clusters of villages perched near a virtual wilderness region, he had spent his childhood, unconsciously nurtured and influenced by the forces of nature."

Others lie here beneath these pines. Their names are not so famous, yet they have resonated down through the decades and can still be found today in any local phone directory. Indeed, towns were so small and insular in the 1800s that cousin could marry cousin, a widow might re-marry to her late husband's brother, and children who grew up together as neighbors would one day have children of their own.

The North Country was isolated—the mountains to the south and the river to the north could certainly be barriers—yet it was also a meeting place, a place where geography and nature schemed to separate and bring together at the same time. Bacheller's description of the mental boundaries of the North Country of the 1860s was telling: "In the East was history, in the West mystery, in the North the British, in the South the Democratic party, while above them was a difficult heaven and beneath the wide-open and capacious hell."

But this very separateness also made the North Country recognizable as a region. And there was much to attract the post-pioneers—fertile farmland, ample timber, excellent fishing and hunting. The northern boundary—the St. Lawrence River—also served as natural highway, bringing settlers and supplies in and shipping timber out as enormous rafts of squared-off logs to the markets of Montreal.

And so they came, a trickle at a time. There were many who came from northern Vermont. "They were a hardy race of men," Bacheller wrote. "Their fathers had been the Green Mountain Boys—a daring lot of raiders, woodchoppers and fighting men."

Bacheller was the first to coin the phrase "North Country" to describe this region. It has always seemed a perfectly apt name to me, though not terribly original. There are North Countrys everywhere, in many states and countries. I have even toyed with the idea of determining how many North Countrys I might be able to find resting on top of each other. There are certainly some north of us in Canada, and I have friends in New York City who seem to believe the North Country begins in Poughkeepsie.

The nineteenth-century writer W.H.H. Murray is usually credited with doing more than anyone to entice people into the wilderness of upper New York State. Yet more than a century ago, he wrote prophetically that "The tendency of our times is to quit the fields, and crowd into the street. . . . The tide of our civilization sets towards the cities. The drift of the age is all urban."

These poor city dwellers live lives of quiet, desperate separation from nature, even though most would deny it. One theorist has speculated that people separated from nature become psychologically poorer for it. And that seems about right—obvious, even—when one looks at the panoply of human craziness that occurs in cities. One scholar of social ecology has gone so far as to say that knowledge, mental skills, inspiration, verbal expression, the exploratory urge, and the appreciation of beauty and harmony all owe something to man's proximity to nature.

So we are connected, whether we like it or not, to the world that created us. Yet that world is disappearing rapidly, and despite the best efforts of a few, will likely cease to exist completely within a generation, barring changes in human behavior and population control that seem unlikely to occur.

In a sense, we are an island in the North Country: we still have the chance to connect with the natural world, still have the chance to achieve psychological balance. But the pressures from outside chip away at its boundaries, and it may not last much longer as a haven.

Irving Bacheller died in the year of my birth, 1950, and it feels good to know that we were both alive at the same time, however briefly. He connects me with the past, with the disappearing wilderness. He connects me with the true soul of the North Country. I can feel it still.

But its strength grows dimmer.

Island Frequencies

Bill McKibben

It's 8:30 on a June evening, sun just set in the gap between the hills. The blackflies achieve a diminuendo, the frogs reach a crescendo, and I sit on the dock in my pond, fiddling with a transistor radio, waiting for night enough that the signal of WFAN, 660 on the AM dial, will propagate up from the borough of Queens, bringing me the night's installment of the New York Mets.

This North Country, this big space that stretches roughly from the St. Lawrence down to the Sacandaga, floats in no particular urban orbit; that's one of the things that distinguishes it. The best shorthand I can think of for explaining what I mean is to say, Which baseball team are you supposed to root for? Depending where in the region you are, the nearest major league franchises belong to the Red Sox, the Yankees, the Mets, the Phillies, the Pirates, perhaps the Tigers, maybe the Indians. What? The Expos? Of course-but that's the point.

The Expos are in a different country (exactly which other

country it is hard to say, for the moment); their announcer speaks a different language; the border keeps proximity from becoming identity. But there are other kinds of borders, too, just as effective. If you lived just the other side of Lake Champlain, you'd root for the Red Sox—the furthest Aroostook potato farmer tunes into Fenway, pulled by some sense of New Englandness that holds no sway the second you debark from the ferry on the west side of Lake Champlain. We live in New York State, but the swagger of the city teams seems infinitely distant, a steamy, salsa-inflected happiness as far away as rent control and performance art and the knish. There's something simpatico about the Rust Belt clubs hunkered down on the far corners of the Great Lakes—but they're in Ohio, in Michigan, in the *Midwest*. We live in an odd and undefined island—a tired place, its human magnificence mostly past, possessing little even in the way of energy for conjuring up garish booster visions. Our sister cities, truth be told, are not Burlington or Montreal, but Utica, Rome, Gloversville, and the rest of that decaying necklace of failed industry strung out along the old canal. And somehow, that is our glory.

There's no *need* to live in a geographical eddy, of course; not even here. CNN and TBS have replaced the Roman road as the vehicle of empire. You, too, can watch the Braves—America's team, which means nobody's team. Chinese peasants wear Dodgers T-shirts as they trudge behind water buffalo, so why shouldn't we? But if you want to, living here gives one the privilege of existing a little outside that imperial terrain. If you unplug the cable, rip out the satellite dish, a rare kind of quiet descends that is the bonus awarded the marginal.

There's no local TV to unite us all, to focus us in on the same murder; there's no dominant newspaper. Nor even any common city or town, any county seat; on a psychological relief map, Plattsburgh and Watertown and Glens Falls and Potsdam all bump up the same short distance. For certain folk, there's North Country Public Radio, the only voices that reach the whole region. But they're soft voices, happily.

I'm not certain why this chance for distance, for a kind of

silence, seems so precious to me. For more people, especially those with little choice in the matter, it likely feels boring, as if the world is passing them by. But I've known other places, felt chattered-at and sign-seduced until it all seemed toxic. Deep in the Adirondacks, where we live, it's possible to go weeks without anyone trying to sell you anything—no billboards along the road, no storefronts. Our zip code is backward enough that we can eat dinner without solicitation from someone representing the Good Life in its many incarnations. There is some small chance of hearing your own heart amid the din of the communications society, the information age, the blessed electronic communion that now stretches through every spot on earth but concentrates on those places with more money, more power.

We live in one of those small pockets the army didn't bother mopping up, up at the end of the bloodless war for our souls. I don't know a single person with a cellular phone.

And so what is there to do? What does the old world have to offer that the shinier, newer one can't match? Gossip and weather, and gossip about weather. A kind of repetition at odds with the novelty-urge of the larger culture. Snowstorm, snowstorm, snowstorm, fall leaves, fall leaves, snowstorm, snowstorm. Individual events stand out for a little while—a blizzard for a week in your mind, the Great Blowdown of '95 for a few years, the Ice Storm of '98 maybe forever—until the visible scars diminish. You are smaller than your surroundings, smaller than the feet of snow piling up inexorably in the lake-effect counties, smaller than the huge and untrailed woods of the Adirondack core, smaller than the economic forces turning farmland to scrub across the dairy belt. In a country—and now a world—where people loom very large, this place has a way of reducing them; you scream and yell and holler and make a commotion, and it dies out against the muffled approach of never- distant winter.

I make no romantic claim for this turning and returning cycle; it is, in many ways, dull. Thank God we are free of the New Agers, celebrating the simple. But there is a certain solidity about life here, freed from the unnerving growth and forced cheerfulness that dominates at www.suburb.com. As I say, it is possible to escape it easily, sucking down the dominant life through the coaxial cable. But this is a backwater, an *eddy, a* place, one of the few in this nation, where you can still choose, where you can find some shelter from the current.

All I want is to stick my toe out in the main channel now and again. We've got no TV, but we do have a radio. On clear nights—late nights, June to September—I root for the Mets because the city was once a part of my life, and because they have the good radio signal. In midsummer, it's usually the sixth or seventh inning before I can hear Shea Stadium over the static on the radio and the rubbery belching (always the same, though never quite) of the frogs.

Growing Up

Rumblings

Peter Owens

As I drive west on Route 11 toward Chateaugay, I can see the hot afternoon air frying on the horizon, rising up a wall of misty thunderheads like smoke. In less than an hour, we'll be paddling into this grouchy, hair-trigger sky in boats hardly bigger than bathtubs, heading to my island on the Lake St. Francis stretch of the St. Lawrence River, a breeding pool for ocean-like waves and white-knuckle squalls.

My wife, Mary, sees the same sky and thinks we can wait until morning, but in nearly thirty years, we've never driven the eight hours from our home on Cape Cod and let foul weather stop us. Silently, we review our emotional options: fear of capsizing, fear of drowning, fear of being struck by lightning. On a lesser scale, short of mayhem and death, there is fear of being swamped, food and clothes soaked; fear of being sucked miles down river; fear of needing to be rescued; fear of hypothermia; fear of exhaustion, injury, humiliation.

All that's missing is fear of heights, a special affliction I acquired from daredevil stunts in my youth on the West Canada Creek, a vigorous quasi-river that spills from the southern Adirondacks, carving spectacular limestone gorges over geologic eons until tamed by dams early this century. Both of these formidable North Country waterways frame my lifetime of fascination, attraction, and sometimes dread of water akin to the tug of moths to flame.

But always, the St. Lawrence and the island beckon first. The river has been a part of my life now for nearly fifty years, while the creek has drifted into distant but no less vivid memory that churns in my belly every time I climb a ladder or witness waterfalls. Both waterways evolved from a wild past to which they will inevitably return, despite our clumsy and sometimes hairbrained attempts to civilize them. We are just brief blips in that process, witnesses to temporary human self-indulgence dwarfed by flashes of nature's indifferent revenge.

On that sweltering summer afternoon in 1998, we arrive at the river and chat nervously with Bob and Callie Smith, who own a shoreline camp a half-mile downriver from our island. Bob, a retired physician from Massena, is an avid windsurfer who sometimes goes out in 30-knot winds, yet has a healthy respect for the river when it whips itself into a frenzy.

As we unload our supplies at their dock on this thickening afternoon, the wind picks up and the sky out of the west darkens. In fewer than fifteen minutes, a fierce thunderstorm rushes toward us, whipping the calm water into a froth of four- and five-foot waves. Luckily, we arrived late enough so that we weren't trapped halfway between the island and shore when the storm struck. We sit on their porch and admire the jagged lightning bolts, and after twenty minutes the first squall line passes, leaving brilliant skies but a strong residual wind—a prelude to nastier events building on the horizon.

Should we or shouldn't we launch my own 12-foot *Rob Roy* and my wife's 10-foot *Wee Lassie,* the boating equivalents of skinny-dipping? I've used outboards in the past, but winds from river storms tend to circle the island, making it difficult to protect large boats and requiring that they be pulled from the water, a hazard for those with bad backs. Finally, I stumbled upon Rushton canoes—originally built last century in Canton by the famous Henry Rushton. I had several hulls made for me by Bart Hauthaway, a legendary small-boat builder from Weston, Massachusetts, and I finished off his fiberglass hulls with pine gunnels, frames, and decking. These tiny boats originally designed for the St. Lawrence River became my vehicle of choice, and if not overloaded, are as seaworthy during river storms as any craft you can find—and far nimbler than the $300,000, thirty-five footers so common these days.

Still, nature can be very scary, and people who see you in a 10- or 12-foot canoe paddling into the teeth of a gale tend to think, perhaps justifiably, that you're nuts.

After considerable hemming and hawing, we decide to make a run for the camp, carrying only light loads and sealing our cockpits with spray skirts. My small English cocker spaniel, Zoe, jumps into my boat, pops her head out from my spray skirt, and we shove off.

As we paddle west toward a larger expanse of the western sky, we see another squall forming. It is a race against time, wind, waves, and current that I reckon we can win, but it is one of those risks I begin doubting as we pass the halfway point. Our fears rise as thunder rumbles in the distance, and the blazing blue sky again turns dark and ominous. Another of the virtues of such small boats is that they ride like corks between the troughs and peaks of St. Lawrence waves. It is a truism of risky navigation that if you move very slowly, you can stay quite dry, but we need to paddle hard to beat the storm, and as we pick up the pace, waves splash over our bows and spray our faces with bracing 65-degree water.

Three quarters of the way to the island, a huge channel cuts diagonally downriver from southwest to northeast, causing a tricky, chaotic chop and a hard tug away from the island. When we reach the channel, the current tries to push us back and the waves turn steep and churlish in the channel rip. As the black clouds climb the sky, the wind begins howling, and our progress against wind, waves, and current slows. We labor hard, taking deep, hurried strokes, trying to reach the lee of the island, whose tempering effects begin only three or four hundred feet farther west.

Though Zoe loves the water, she gets skittery and nervous when she senses the same in me. She begins whimpering and wiggling, deciding that swimming to shore might be a better option. So here I am, trying to calm the frantic dog, trying to paddle as furiously as possible with arms growing leaden, and Mary struggling a few yards back, jaws set with worry and disapproval, face gleaming with spray, hair soaked, and carrying a look that says, "Now, this was a really stupid idea." But she is too scared to shoot me a scolding scowl.

The key to both endurance and strength when paddling is to push hard with the top hand while holding the lower hand as a pivot. It doubles your power over the more intuitive reflex to pull more feebly through the water with the lower hand. So I start yelling, "push, push, push." Heeding my own advice, I feel my boat accelerate, and within a few minutes we break out of the channel and into the island lee. Shortly, we pull into the sheltered dock of a small northeast corner bay fully protected from the wind. It has always struck me as remarkable how thirty feet of thick woods can cut furious winds to a whisper. We pull the boats up on the bank, flip them over, and rush up to the island point where the camp looks west over the wide-open expanse of Lake St. Francis.

Only five minutes later, the next line squall strikes. We watch from the window inside the camp. Huge rollers rush at us, pounding the rocks on the island point, spray erupting fifteen feet up the bank. Rain erupts in waves, swatting the windows. But even the camp is vulnerable. It sits under a perched canopy of tall trees, teeth to the wind, a high point in a vast sweep of water on all sides inviting lightning to strike and causing us to twitch with every flash and thunderous crack. It is wild, desolate, primordial—the great willow perched over the point, waving her arms like some frantic angel flailing in the cusp of chaos.

*

Always when I am there, gazing out on the expanse bordered south by the Adirondacks and to the distant tree line of the north shore, I am struck that people hundreds and even thousands of years ago experienced identical trials and looked out and saw the very same sweep as we experience time and again from the island point. Those many years ago, the river was a warpath for Indian canoes and French, British, and American gunboats that waged continuous battles for continental dominance. Before that, native peoples relied on the river for sustenance and spiritual connection to what must have seemed a capriciously harsh but bountiful universe. Today, it is best known as a pathway to the Great Lakes for ocean freighters plying the St. Lawrence Seaway, but that deep channel is only a small fraction of the river's totality.

Along the way, there are huge expanses—the river lakes that can whip up killer storms—and deep, surging narrows where powerful currents can suck people and boats into endless treacheries. Along shore, people are largely safe from the wild beast, but if stranded on one of its hundreds of islands, ancient dangers lurk, waiting patiently for unwary fools who defy the river's furies.

My family's treks to the St. Lawrence have now spanned four generations. My own introduction to river life began when I was six. My grandfather, Harold, and father, Jack, would haul me out of Holland Patent Central School in early May and drive me north up Route 12 past Boonville and Lowville, skirting the mountains along flat farmlands edged by the stony relics of the Black River Canal. We cut across to Carthage and through portions of Camp Drum, where Army tanks rumbled amid arid landscapes of shattered trees, giving ominous cast to the abstract images of the Korean War playing out on the TV news at the time. We passed through the town of Gouverneur, remarkable to me for the outlandish fact that cars parked in the center of the road, then onward to Potsdam, alternately stately and drably depressed, heading toward a little island on the St. Lawrence River.

I recall with mystery passing as a young child through customs at Dundee, where the national boundary crossed through the hotel tavern and allowed a person to straddle the U.S. and Canada and thus unify one of the world's largest land masses.

My grandfather had bought his island in 1943, less than three months before the death of his youngest son, who along with the crew of his B-17 bomber flew into a thunderhead over Papua, New Guinea and was never heard from again. Lightning was no friend to his son, for sure, and the island a place he could never visit, an absence that must have crushed my grandfather over and over again.

Two years later, I was born and named after this airman lost to lightning. His body fragments recovered fifty-five years after his death, were buried anew in Arlington National Cemetery in 1998, his grave site divided between some of the world's fiercest jungles and seemingly endless, orderly rows of human mayhem.

A few miles past Dundee, we turned north for a mile to a little green boathouse with sagging roof where my grandfather kept an aging cabin cruiser splattered with barn swallow droppings, a boat he called "The Bluebill" in honor of the river's most durable ducks. Here we rendezvoused with a French fishing guide named Joe Hart, a wiry middle-aged paladin with chiseled chin, a silvery moustache, immense, callused hands, thick French-Canadian accent, and infectious laugh. He would escort us onto the river in storm or blazing sun or high winds, undaunted by the river's whims. He was employed by men who believed in big boats and hefty motors to beat the river—motors that often did not work, thus requiring Joe to be a master at rescue and parts procurement.

My grandfather had purchased Buchanan's Island from a Montreal physician and immediately dubbed it Duck Island. It was tucked in a broad bay near Cedar Point, a few miles west of Cazaville, where Upstate New Yorkers—friends and family—came to unwind, fish, and hunt. On my very first trip, I slipped on a dock and fell into the river; the May water was *cooold* and would begin my immersion into life in the border region on one of the world's great rivers. My grandfather dutifully recorded the event in his island log: "Peter baptized himself at Duck Island by falling into the river the first day. Went in all over and was one wet kid. No harm done otherwise, and he got his lesson quickly and good. Never shed a tear."

It was a baptism into a nautical life largely rooted in the rituals of men. Though women came to the island and enjoyed it as a vacation hideaway, what most immersed me in the river life was the male world of endless tinkering with boats, motors, outhouses, toilets, and gadgets in a perpetual struggle with nature. For a family of engineers and hunters, at a time when women were expected to cook and attend to domestic chores, the river seemed at first a test for all things masculine. It was a throwback to a primitive era and ancient rites, the most important being the fall duck kill.

The first visitors at Duck Island were a bawdy lot who took glee in writing naughty verse, drinking whiskey, and wagering on who could catch the biggest or the most fish on any outing. But duck hunting was the most solemn enterprise, and during a stretch from 1943 to 1954, Harold recorded Duck Island hunters killing 2,027 ducks, with most trips including four to six hunters, two or three to a boat. An adolescent, I went on a couple of those duck hunting trips, and though I never became a hunter in later life, I learned much about the river's harshness and the sanctity of the kill.

Preparation for the hunt began during the summer, when Joe Hart found prime locations for duck blinds. Some were on the island, but more often, they were placed near reed beds and marshes with favorable angles to the prevailing winds, where decoys could be set and ducks were likely to settle. Hunters drove cedar stakes into the riverbed with their names and the year—"Hart 59," for example. As the season approached, Joe and his brothers and cousins would cut cedars and build the blinds, skeletal frames camouflaged with cedar boughs where boats slid into place as if into a slender, roofless corset built of sticks and branches.

Building your own blind was no guarantee on the morning of the shoot that duck blind poachers wouldn't steal it. So Joe enlisted the bravest and burliest of his brothers and cousins to go out the night before the shoot to occupy the blinds. They warmed themselves with whiskey, slept in their boats, and sometimes had to fight off poachers who waved their shotguns and shouted threats, which the watchers reported later in shaking voices, faces pale from fear.

My first hunt was early in the season of 1957. I was twelve. My father woke me at 3 A.M., and along with his friend Bill Westcott, we headed out in the dark on opening day. The weather was warm and balmy, the river flat as we motored in the damp black of night, navigating by the glow of the wake and the distant dim shadows of shoreline trees. When we reached our blind, the men spoke quietly with Joe's cousins, sentries through the night, who pulled out and melted into the dark. Every sound was sharpened by the damp air and night stillness. Oars clacked loudly as we set the decoys in diamond formation, windward of a reed bed. Jack eased the duck boat into the narrow blind, where we peeked out through scraggly branches and cedar bows. He handed us our shotguns, and the men loaded the first shell, chambers slamming shut with a steely clang that echoed sharply over the still, black water.

We waited in the dark, from time to time hearing the distant whine of outboards as other hunters prepared. Even before the first dim light, guns started erupting up and down the river, building to a cacophony of explosions like the finale of July Fourth fireworks. Jack and Bill cursed up and down that all that shooting in the dark was pointless, illegal, and would just spook the ducks and prevent them from settling in among the decoys. They were right. Soon, stillness settled again.

Dawn broke slowly on the eastern horizon, wisps of deep blue, horizontal clouds streaking the gray sky, the slowly rising sun painting their edges with streaks of pastel pinks. We sat for hours with Bill whispering jokes, but no ducks were to be seen. I was bored and dozing when suddenly a small flock flew overhead at breakneck speed. Bill and Jack leapt up and fired, the explosions startling me from my slumber and setting my ears to ringing, a symphony that continues today. Two ducks fell in crumpled arcs, splashing into the reeds. My heart pounded with anticipation, but that was it—a sudden savage flurry, then deathly quiet as I stood, gun in hand, ready to fire.

Later that morning both men squawked incessantly with their

duck calls, and when all seemed hopelessly futile, a small flock circled our decoys and came in to land. As they approached, they tilted their chests toward us and set their wings wide to a flutter, breaking their speed, their webbed feet spreading, bodies fully exposed and wavering as they slowed. The men leapt up and fired, myself following, the birds flaring, several dropping, the high-velocity loads kicking my shoulder hard. And then silence.

"Atta boy, Pete," Bill said, swatting my back with his huge hand, offering credit even though I had no idea who hit what.

"Good shooting, Pete," said Jack, making me think they knew something I did not—including the possibility that I had missed. Soon all was quiet again, and in a few minutes, we eased out of the blind and collected the floating bodies.

I never proved much of a hunter, and may have shot only two or three ducks by myself over five days, though the men generously credited me with more. I was never good with the killing part, but to the hunters, killing ducks was the ultimate measure of manhood and the essence of an honorable communion with nature. They never shot a bird in the water unless it was already wounded, and viewed "the kill" as a necessary touchstone of the meaning of life, a confirmation that there is no bloodless harvest for those who eat meat.

My first hunt was one of the best opening season trips in years, with 173 birds killed. Harold noted in the log, "There was good shooting and much very bad shooting, and this old man did his share of both." He was eighty years old.

During summers, my mother and four sisters accompanied me on island trips. For them, the river was a place for swimming, water skiing, tending to Joe's pet mallards, and fishing expeditions that seemed to me mysteriously feminized. The girls had little relish for stabbing a wiggling minnow, wondered if the hooks hurt the fish's lips, and when Joe filleted live perch, they watched with fascinated horror as the bony racks of ribs twitched and flapped.

"Is it dead yet, Joe?" my sister Sally asked through thick-lensed glasses, gazing at their frantic eyes that seemed to strain for a final look at their fleshless ribs. Joe grinned inscrutably,

"Ees dead; don feel not-ting," and would stab the trembling wrack with his ice pick and flick the wiggling corpse into the water. Then he pulled the next flopping perch from the stringer and stabbed the pick through its tail, inserting his huge, gnarled forefinger through the gill and cutting parallel to the gill, blood oozing from the deep gash as Sally looked on, mouth agape, certain of its suffering.

I watched with equal fascination, torn between the brutal indifference expected of men and my sister's tortured compassion, but I always sided with Joe. "They don't feel a thing," I said smugly. "It's just nerves. Right, Joe?"

He nodded wisely. "Jes de nerves; don feel not-ting," he said, slashing off the side, yanking out the pick, flicking the perch over, and jamming the pick down hard through its cheek, causing Sally to twitch.

But the fish were not entirely defenseless. On one fishing expedition, I was reeling in a perch and leaned down to pull it into the boat from the leader, when a huge, dark shadow surged upward inches from my hand. A big fish slapped the side of the boat, splashing us all. "Jeez," Joe exclaimed, leaping to his feet, grasping a gaff and leaning over the edge. "Muskie," he grinned, bracing his hand on the gunnel and peering into the water. "Fifty-sixty pound, hey?"

Then he turned to me. "Jeez, Pete. He almos' took yer hand for dinner. He want dat perch, hey? Beeg damn fish. Jeez."

Fishing for muskie was considered men's work, evidenced on the island by numerous dried muskie jaws, smiling eerily with hundreds of needle-sharp teeth, their grinning heads nailed as trophies to assorted trees.

To rescue us both from the intense and insular bonding between girls and women that rendered us largely irrelevant, Joe often invited me to help him with his nightline. We drove by outboard into the deep channel, his boat slamming the hard waves, causing me to bounce harshly on the splintery wooden thwart. His hard, angular jaw was set high as he gazed the tree line for the angles marking the immersed line. Joe slowed and moved the boat at idle, tossing a grappling hook and dragging the bottom, seemingly in the middle of nowhere. With one or two tosses he caught a snag, then pulled up a taut line dangling with large hooks every foot or so. As he moved along the line, cleaning hooks draped with weeds, he would invariably brighten. "Got one," he grinned, and played the line over the gunnels until it began to shudder from the hard thrusts of a hooked sturgeon.

As he pulled the huge, thrashing gray fish into the boat, lethal hooks danced and jabbed the air. He then removed the hook with pliers, pierced the sturgeon's rubbery white lips to fasten a tie-line, and, in a few moments, tossed his huge catch over the side and knotted it to the oarlock. That was money in the bank for Joe; for me, it was a chance to reach down and rub the rough, sandpapery skin on its back or to tickle the soft, slippery feelers around its strangely human lips.

My grandfather's logs are filled with references to bad storms, gale force winds, ice on the river, and a never-ending litany of boat and motor repairs, construction projects, and improvised gadgets patched together to make island life resemble the life of creature comforts on shore. From the very first days after purchasing Duck Island in 1943, Harold began making wisecracks about bathrooms, pumps, stoves, lights, generators, and domestic doodads. But none proved more entertaining or prescient than his thoughts on the island outhouse which he described in verse dated September 23, 1943, excerpted below:

> "The Ballad of the Island John
> There it is my friend, and we point with pride,
> To our John where it stands at the river's side.
> Not always was it as you see it now,
> So pause my friend while I tell you how
> Through hardships suffered, it's come to be
> A palace of comfort and luxury."

He refers here to the original outhouse, resplendent with "splinters and bumps" that caused complaints from guests and led to the construction of a classic two-holer, finished on the outside with red shingles, and for some years, the island's primary bathroom.

> "And there came a day when a guest we brought.
> Ah! What a change has since been wrought.
> This guest's behind, which he called his moon,
> Was chafed and cut, when very soon
> After landing here, he sat upon
> The serrated seat of our Island John. . . ."

Construction began:

> "Both Joe and he hard labored and wrought,
> A smooth polished surface, with satiny sheen
> Appeared in the place where the slivers had been.
> Next Joe brought his wife with her brushes and paste,
> And she papered the John to suit everyone's taste.
> When you sit out there dreaming, just look at the wall,
> With its teapots and posies and pitchers and all. . . ."
>
> Harold Owens, Sept. 23,1943

A few years later Harold, Joe, and Jack replaced the outhouse with an attached bathroom with a wooden toilet seat perched at the top of an enormous drainpipe, eighteen inches in diameter, that dropped into a deep black hole reaching groundwater at fifteen feet with a resounding splash. While there wasn't much danger that an adult could fall down that huge, cavernous pipe, the toilet was a haunting sight to a child. It disappeared into a dark liquid abyss that seemed as close to the notion of darkest eternity as my young mind could imagine. What a way to drown, I shuddered ruefully, whenever I gazed upon this engineering spectacle.

It was all this tinkering and fixing, though, that often defined these people, setting in microcosm the struggle of industrial-age men using their minds to outwit nature and conquer her whims through ever-bigger boats and clever gadgets.

In 1950, Harold purchased an island from Rene Deschamps, a legendary fisherman who was getting too old to manage trips onto the river. About an acre and a half set between two deep channels a quarter mile off Cedar Point, Deschamps Island was wild and thickly wooded. Its two opposite points faced into the prevailing fair and foul weather winds, making it ideal for duck blinds, but neither Harold nor Jack ever developed Deschamps, and in 1982 my father was on the verge of selling it when I protested and asked him to let me buy it. He said okay and for one dollar handed it over, his own days on the river largely finished as a result of frequent camp break-ins, vandalism, and declining duck hunting.

I built a camp on Deschamps, and having seen the extraordinary efforts grown men had devoted year after year to fixing and repairing gadgets, I built an old-fashioned outhouse and pledged myself to a minimum of moving parts and mechanical contrivances. Hence, the Island John was reborn, an outhouse built of glued composite sheathing of breathtaking ugliness and a sanctuary to spiders and sometimes bats. Its only sop to modern engineering is a glorious blue, plastic, padded toilet seat.

As the late summer sun bakes the land in Upstate New York, afternoon thunderstorms stain the western sky all shades of black and brown. Sweltering heat rolls up the cool slopes of the northern Adirondacks and collides with rising greenhouse gases tumbling across the Midwest and western New York flatlands. They build into massive anvils flat-topped at 30,000 feet and climbing. My family and I watch with recurrent admiration on the island point as these squall lines rush toward us over miles of open water.

Boaters scatter for shore. Cold gusts swat the water, turning up skittery windrows that grow to frenzied waves, then the wall of wind hits and large droplets crash from the sky like soft bullets. In moments, a full gale and lashing rain erupt with ruthless furry, raked by lightning jags and instant, crackling explosions of thunder.

When the storms pass, hundreds of wind swallows curl through the island air, trapping great breeding swarms of moths and bugs. Raindrops gleam on wet leaves, the water settling sometimes to a perfect calm, the river suddenly mirror smooth. Often at these times, we launch our canoes and paddle along the island's shore, watching sandpipers skip along ancient logs and moss-green rocks, snapping up bugs with their yellow beaks. Huge basswoods and willows lean out over the water, forming canopies whose leaves and branches shelter prodigious bugs whose wings shimmer and glow in the late afternoon sun.

In an odd confluence of forces, nature and men have conspired to make the river strangely wilder in recent decades. PCBs and metallic toxins have reduced fishing in this area, retiring a hardy breed of commercial fishermen undeterred by winds and storms. Huge, expensive cocktail lounges masquerading as boats roar up and down the river on summer weekend afternoons. Most people have become fair-weather boaters who flee at the first sign of a fresh breeze.

Jet skiers buzz in aimless circles, chasing their wakes like dogs after their own tails. Joe giggles knowingly from his grave. Sleek, low-slung racing boats shriek across still waters, outpacing the Doppler roar of testosterone tumbling past like sonic booms above shimmering wakes. As night falls, wary blue herons land on the point and hover in frozen stillness before stabbing the water for baitfish. Night herons soar into island trees hanging over the water's edge, breaking the silence with their croaky squawks. At dawn, songbirds chatter and sing. Nervous loons work the edges of the channel, crying out in distress as the day emerges.

Because I live on Cape Cod, my drive to the river these days is along Route 11, a stark and wind-swept ribbon of upstate highway paralleling the border, criss-crossed by the Great Chazy River, and speckled by villages that have not changed discernibly in a quarter century. At the cemetery just east of Ellenburg, wind-swept poplars and cedars permanently bow to the winter's frozen gales.

I am always struck here by the Spartan landscape; I imagine how pinched life must be from November until March. I grew up enduring these upstate winters. Bleary-eyed from nearly eight hours of driving, my mind fixates on the bleak landscape, evoking memories and sensations rich with an odd mix of nostalgia and dread, as if those cold winds could grasp me and pull me back home into a world so cold that snow squeaks at your feet and turns the hairs in your nose into icicles.

This stark vista echoes like some elemental nest, a swirl of memories yanking me back to childhood in Prospect, an Adirondack foothill village creased by another formative North Country waterway, the West Canada Creek. I wandered its towering limestone cliffs and deep gorges through much of my youth, acquiring a lifelong fear of heights in a series of dares that began at the Rumbly Bridge, a three-mile bike ride downstream in the village of Trenton Falls. Each summer trek to the river rekindles those roots and stirs dormant dendrites in my brain that reach back into the murk of memory, reminding me that what I did back then is what I am, and that will never quite blend with the saltwater beaches in the place I now call home.

West Canada Creek (pronounced 'crick' by us locals) flows in a deep gorge not far behind my childhood home, a huge chunk gobbled out of the cliff side by the Prospect stone quarry my grandfather owned. Often I watched from tall, sandy cliffs above the pit as huge loaders dumped immense rocks as big as cars into the backs of dusty Euclid trucks with tires taller than men. The creek was diverted and used to wash the crushed stone passing through giant screens, the silty water drained into a settling pool before flowing down the narrow gorge toward Trenton Falls below. Every few weeks, drilling rigs moved onto the flat limestone ledges, where the workers drilled into solid rock with diamond bits, carving the holes wherein they would drop huge dynamite charges. The muffled blasts that followed shook the village with the rumble of industry.

The creek served many masters, once as a logging trail, later as a spigot emptying runoff from the Adirondack Mountains into pipes that eventually flowed into Utica's urban sinks.

After tumbling down countless falls between Prospect and Trenton Falls, the creek flattens into a section of shallow rapids spanned in the 1950s by the Rumbly Bridge, a rusty, steel truss straddling the creek like an iron spider with wobbly, arthritic knees.

If you "got any guts," my friend Bill Groben told me one morning looking upward at its top span, "you'll climb it and cross up there." He was eleven and I was ten, and thirty feet above the road, the rusting top steel girder looked distressingly narrow. "You'll need good sneaks," he said, in reference to his own non-skid PF Flyers. I envied those PF Flyers with every ounce of my being.

He immersed his forefinger into his mouth, extracted it quickly and held it to the air to gauge the strength of the wind. "No sweat," he said, spitting on his hands in preparation for climbing the sharply angled steel riser upon which the long girder was riveted along the one hundred-fifty-foot span, perched at least eighty feet above the rocky rapids below.

"I dare you," he said. I gazed up at that skinny ribbon of steel and felt my heart thunder in dread, knowing that I was as compelled by an official dare as if by gunpoint to walk that rusty steel tightrope over the Rumbly Bridge.

The mid-1950s was a time when country kids handled their boredom by embarking on daily missions that would land them in a shrink's office in today's world, woozy from psychoactive drugs. Bill was a city boy who spent most of the year in Utica, where daring and risk were a daily part of his life. I was a simple country boy, but tempting fate along that treacherous creek was an ongoing ritual that would prepare me for a lifetime of acquired cautions and latent phobias.

The Rumbly Bridge with its towering overhead steel spans is gone, replaced by a modern engineering contrivance of drably efficient reinforced concrete. Cars pass over now with a whisper rather than a rumble. Not much else is different: Prospect had a population of 300 then and does even now. Trenton Falls was little more than a crossroads then and now, but a century earlier, the two villages were stopping-off points for wealthy tourists who gawked at both Trenton and Prospect Falls with an admiration reserved for Niagara Falls today.

The magnificent limestone gorges and thundering falls still exist, diminished by dams but still magnificent. Today they are fenced off by the Niagara Mohawk Power Company with ominous "DANGER" and "NO TRESPASSING" signs that cut me off from some of the fondest adventures any child could ever experience. Revisiting that history is forbidden by new generations of fearful corporate managers, horrified that a litigious citizenry will blame them for nature's ruthlessness. Of *course* it's dangerous. That's how kids grew up then, roaming free with time to kill and challenges to meet.

On that summer day nearly a half century ago, I followed my friend Bill up the 18-inch steel riser angled so steeply we had to brace our "sneaks" on the rivets while holding firm to the edges of the girder as we climbed. At the top the wind blew in dizzying gusts, and we could see for miles. I would have preferred crawling across the span, but Bill stood and walked, and after I crawled half the distance at his heels in undignified horror, I finally stood—the very memory of which makes me dizzy as I write—and looked out on the magnificent limestone gorge that slices northeast and climbs 600 feet to headwaters deep in the Adirondack wilderness. The memory of that fear has slipped deep into my being to the extent that nine feet up a ladder to this day sends me into a horrified swoon of trembling dizziness, wobbly knees, and pouring sweat.

Bill stood and spread his arms and spat, sending a glorious goober on a lazy arc before it broke up into a gooey spray that splatted undetectably in the dark, glimmering rapids eighty feet below. My mouth was so dry from fright that I passed up this grand gesture, dropped to my knees, and hugged the girder as a car thundered across the bridge below. They didn't call it the Rumbly Bridge for nothing; I thought for a moment that we were history. In a very small way, we *were.* This event—an odd mix of foolish bravery and childish machismo—is frozen in time, place and circumstance, displaced in today's world by video games and organized soccer. Back, then the world seemed safer, parents less worried, less hovering, easier to fool.

It's a shame that the creek's greatest beauties are now fenced in and swallowed by the region's most powerful electric utility, because down in those gorges are wonderful hidden swimming holes and great cliffs for diving and teenage fun as filled with history and initiation as any place on earth. I, for one, played my first game of spin-the-bottle in the Trenton Falls Gorge, made all the more delicious by the fact that I was too young and mortified to appreciate the fun. It was my turn in a circle of young teenagers, and I remember the brittle clatter of the beer bottle spinning on the limestone. My gravest concern—having never kissed a girl—was what to do and how to do it. I think I was just as scared as I was that day on the Rumbly Bridge, and when the bottle clanked to a halt, it pointed to one of my sister's friends who volunteered her full, water-cooled lips with such rapidity that I nearly fell over as she quickly pulled away. There's a ghost of that mysterious moment wandering aimlessly in the gorge to this very day, wondering what went wrong.

To get to the Trenton Falls Gorge, you had to climb down a precipitous three hundred-foot cliff slick with muddy paths, but sprouting enough trees to allow enterprising climbers to lower beer coolers and picnic baskets with minimal risk. At the bottom of the cliff, the woods opened to vast walls of silvery limestone, carved by millennia of surging water into a series of flat plateaus, each with its own deep pools carved by towering water falls. Huge bypass pipes hung from the cliff sides, diverting the bulk of the water to power turbines and Utica's faucets, converting the gorge into a relatively tranquil spillway. It reduced what had been a ferocious torrent throughout the ages to a gentle stream of lovely, stepped swimming holes, tamed by Niagara Mohawk into an unspeakably beautiful gorge closed to the public.

We weren't supposed to go down there, of course, but we did. We weren't supposed to drink, but with a legal drinking age of eighteen, anyone fifteen could easily secure endless supplies of beer. Because it was an arduous climb and its few approaches splattered with "NO TRESPASSING" signs, the gorge was extraordinarily private. Instead of being initiated into teenage life by wandering in crowded public malls, we traveled to paradise, basked in the sun, and swam in the deep pools once carved by ancient waterfalls of immense power.

I should have learned my lesson about heights from the Rumbly Bridge, but the first requirement of male prowess in the gorge was to climb the cliffs and jump from forty, fifty, sometimes sixty feet into the dark water below. It was said that some of the pools had no bottom, or harbored deep caves and underwater whirlpools that could suck you into the limestone cliffs where you could drown and never be found.

I stood many times on the ledges looking down, my heart thudding with excitement and fear at the slow swirl and eddies of the brown-black water far below. Each pool and set of ledges included its own falls, and the steady hiss of cascading water added to the beguiling dread as I summoned my courage to leap. Below on the limestone flats, friends watched—guys ready to guffaw at a wimpy or tentative leap, girls I needed to impress with my capacity to soar. The manliest of us jumped feet first a few times in preparation for a grand swan dive finale.

It happened like this: not fond of heights, I climbed the sharp-edged limestone, feeling for hand and foot holds, pulling against the sun-baked rocks, the waterfall hissing loudly a few feet to my left. My knees began to tremble at twenty feet, heart raced at thirty, throat dried at forty , breath left me at fifty, where finally there was a broad ledge wide enough to stand. Far below, the water moved in what seemed slow motion, bubbles from the plunging water rising and swirling to the surface. The higher I climbed, the more muffled was the sound of water crashing into the pool below, a gentle, distant hiss.

Faces upturned from below. From here, voices echoed and curled off the rock faces. There was no way down except to jump.

"Go for it," someone yelled and sipped a beer. "How about a flip?" someone yelled. "A cannonball!"

These were not options. The force of hitting the water at this height was so powerful, it bruised your feet. A belly flop, it was said, could kill you. So you held your nose hard, or the water filled your head like a high-pressure hose. You tucked elbows hard against your ribs and jumped far out from the cliff to give yourself distance away from the wall and underwater ledges. You hit the water straight up and down.

You counted. One, two, three. Nah. Not ready. First some deep breaths. Below, the cheers turned to jeers. You curled your toes hard on the edge of the ledge for the best possible grip. Okay, ready. One, two, three, leap. And with all your strength, you jumped out into the air, grabbing first for your nose, the air whistling at your ears, your body tilted a bit strangely, forcing frantic kicks and arm swings to correct the angle of entry, the dark hard water rushing up, and then your feet hit hard and kabooom, an explosion of cold water crashing around your head, and the water tearing your hand from your nose, and blasting your sinuses into the back of your head.

You went down like a bullet, trying to stop before going so deep the mythic whirlpools would suck you away forever, and with eyes open you saw the dim, foggy flash of a thousand brilliant bubbles above, while below lay an eternity of darkness. You churned frantically now, your downward motion finally stopped. You felt the coldest water at your feet and surged upward in a desperate panic, and then burst to the surface, shoulder aching from having been wrenched, your head jammed with water and aching from the crinkly stuffiness of a thousand terrible head colds jammed into a single, throbbing forehead.

From the flats would come assorted cheers and jeers as you swam slowly along the warm surface water and slid up on a slimy underwater ledge to survey your wounds—reddening welts, emerging bruises, aching joints, jammed nasals. Time for a beer and some rest. Diving would take an extra measure of courage today and a good deal more skill.

When you dive, you need to close your hands into rigid fists and lock your elbows hard against your head so you can penetrate the surface before your head hits. If this fails, your arms and hands are ripped away, and your head hits the water as if landing on a board, leaving you woozy and in throbbing pain. My terrifying dive succeeded that day; my arms held.

As with the river storms along the St. Lawrence or my trek across the Rumbly Bridge, there was a strange and beguiling imperative in confronting my fears while preparing at the ledge. Some of this was social—a feeling that to step away or climb down would be a public humiliation. Some was more personal, internal, private as if being tested by nature to become part of her, to be an ingredient in the storm, the waterfall, the wind. It was a solitary confrontation ritualized so many times in so many places that I could not discern always what was foolish or even simply risky.

I suppose we allow ourselves these risks in part because someday they may be necessary passages, as unavoidable as death or profound injury. Some part of us requires that we prepare, sometimes in foolish ways egged on by dares and bravado, sometimes showing off and revisiting some vestigial reflex associated with ceremonial maleness and ancient rites. But at the core, I think, is a reflex to rehearse, to test, to push at the edges, in preparation for dire necessity. For a water person like myself, the threats of storms, capsizing, having to rescue or be rescued are really quite immediate possibilities; I ponder these adventures as controlled brushes with disaster, real versions of which may sometime dare me to hold my nose and leap.

Sometimes such disasters loom very close. A few years ago, when Quebec adopted very high cigarette taxes, huge boats roared by our island late at night with no running lights—smuggling cigarettes from the American shores into Quebec in a dangerous game of cat and mouse with Canadian and American police. On a near shore a drug smuggler was murdered, and a few years ago, a plane crashed near my island and two people drowned. I wasn't there that night, but could have been.

Only last year a heavy wind struck, and a boatman could not start his motor a half-mile west of the island. I motored out in the Smiths' small skiff, powered by a three-horsepower motor dwarfed by this man's 100-horsepower behemoth. I offered help in what must have seemed a ridiculous gesture in my tiny boat, but I would have towed him to shore. Instead I drove several miles to fetch his brother, who jump-started the stranded craft, and off they went, having beaten nature with modern engineering but perhaps not so decisively as they imagined. On several nights boats have landed in the dark on the island point—thieves or drug smugglers, perhaps—and when I called out, they quickly left me to my thudding heart.

The river has been the scene of recent violent disputes between native peoples and both Canadian and American governments—new twists on a very old and depressing struggle. It has been a pathway for running guns and dangerous drugs. It has been a playground for drunken jet skiers, overpowered water skiers, and besotted party boaters all careening obliviously in a chaos of pleasure. It is still well sprinkled by fishermen and duck hunters, rogues and poachers; in the winter, it is very nearly always a cold, dark burial ground for a few unfortunate snowmobilers who fail to see a dangerous channel beneath the thin layer of snow.

Perhaps the risk-taking is in preparation for one of these moments, vestigial to a stroll in the mall, but not to dangers on a great river or to soaring toward an enormous splash in the bottomless pool in a roaring creek.

Such places as these are thick with strange twists of fate etched with people's limitations. Old man Deschamps sold his island because he was getting too old to manage on the river, but this wasn't clear to him until one day he caught an enormous 200-pound sturgeon on his nightline off the north channel. The fish was too big to haul into the boat, so the old man towed it to shore to show it to other fishermen. It was the greatest catch of his life—an ancient fish yanked from the cold, primordial depths. After showing this great beast—worth hundreds of dollars—the old man let it go, and according to his son, never ventured onto the river again in his life.

Like the Adirondack Mountains and the West Canada Creek in its once wild state, the river is bigger and more powerful than the people who live on its shores and islands. It dwarfs people, buildings, boats, ships, and all things man-made. It is staggeringly powerful and astonishingly changeable, and while vulnerable to pollution and abuse, the river, like the mountains and creeks, is a reminder of how puny, fragile, and temporary people are in the larger scheme of nature. I figure I might have twenty more years worth of visits, and then sometime, plus or minus a few years, I will be gone from the river. Despite a lifetime on its waters, I'll be just a speck in its steady, unrelenting flow of time and current, just as my childhood already is along a ribbon of empty sky over the West Canada Creek.

These are places that are so much bigger than us, places for which we prepare, so that if they catch us on a wild spree, we will be lucky to be ready. They are places that shape us in profound ways, while in return, we hardly ever leave a dent.

Pontiac Memories

Ken Lawless

Thomas Mann's *The Magic Mountain* was a 1924 novel set in Davos, Switzerland, a place famous for its tuberculosis sanatoria. Mann chose Davos as the setting for his novel because it symbolized timelessness and decay.

There was a time when Saranac Lake was America's magic mountain, a hamlet where hope defied death in those years when tuberculosis was the most dreaded contagion in the land.

With the wonder drugs of World War II, science replaced geography in the war against consumption. But the name "Saranac" was so deeply associated with the disease that well into the late 1950s, older tourists were spotted driving quickly through the village wearing surgical masks.

There are true stories from Saranac Lake that resonate with the melancholy music of Thomas Mann—the tragic death of poet Adelaide Crapsey, for example, just before publication of the volume that would have made her reputation; or the transformation of Norman Bethune from social gadfly to folk hero. But

Thomas Bailey Aldrich, whose son died of TB, wrote of Saranac Lake to James Russell Lowell, who had paddled the lakes with Emerson many years before, saying, "When all is said there is a charm in the place. There is something in the air to heal the heart of sorrow."

The magic of Saranac Lake is not the magic of Davos. It is an American magic, an Adirondack magic, an orchestration of canny guides from mountain resorts, robber-barons from Great Camps, French-Canadian lumberjacks, artists, hermits, lovers of wilderness, haters of winter, world-class drunkards, and TB patients—the mainstay of the economy.

The patients brought more than money. They brought their families, their friends, their ideas. Tuberculosis struck all classes and conditions, but it raged worst in the crowded cities. The patients brought a sense of the metropolis to a tiny mountain hamlet, making it simultaneously rustic and cosmopolitan—a microcosm of American culture whose single temple for the popular arts was the Pontiac Theater.

The first time I went to the Pontiac Theater, I was a little kid during World War II. My teenage brother Jack, ordinarily too busy to bother with a brat like me, agreed to squire me to the Pontiac because of the paramount cultural significance of the event. "If you live to be a hundred, Kenny," he said, "you'll never see anything any funnier than this."

We walked down Lake Street and up Main to Berkeley Square, where the dancing lights of the marquee shone from halfway down the hill at the beginning of Broadway.

The lobby was redolent of popcorn, cigarette smoke, and just a hint of chocolate, a scent that existed nowhere else. It was an aroma I came to associate with the peculiar magic of the imagination, wherein one satisfies his sweet tooth in ritual preparation for the satisfaction of his appetite for fantasy.

On that occasion, when I was so small I could press my nose against the glass and look straight at the rows of candy boxes, I was supplied with Reese's peanut butter cups, a wild extravagance in honor of the significance of the occasion.

We sat way down in front in order to be away from the

grownups, free to hoot and jeer and roughhouse a little. There was a double feature plus trailers, a cartoon, the news, a Pete Smith special, and, best of all as far as I was concerned, an episode of a serial adventure called "The Perils of Nyoka the Jungle Girl."

But my brother was much too imposing a personage to babysit a pesky kid brother for ordinary fare. We were there for the talent contest. Or rather, for what had been billed as a talent contest; there was relatively little talent and absolutely no contest. The Pontiac was packed to its ornate gilded rafters with fanatics determined to award the laurels by acclamation.

The crowd went bananas when two teenagers emerged from the wings. They stood centerstage accepting the rowdy obeisance with solemn dignity. When the furor subsided to a mere tumult, Artie Levy and Joe Benarro sang "We'll Go Pfft! Pfft! Pfft! Right in Der Fuhrer's Face." No ambulance was summoned because no one actually split a gut, but there were people literally rolling in the aisles, clutching their ribs and gasping for breath in excess of mirth.

The Pontiac Theater had been built as a vaudeville palace when Saranac Lake was the nation's most important health spa for the treatment of tuberculosis, the modern white plague. Among the thousands whose lives were saved by the care they received on the slopes of Mt. Pisgah was William Morris, the greatest theatrical agent of his era. Morris used to invite his biggest stars to his camp on Lake Colby. Harry Lauder was a frequent summer guest who spent a good deal of time playing golf, but still managed to find time to play benefit performances at the Pontiac.

Morris inveigled many of his name acts to do Pontiac fundraisers. Eddie Cantor did a show, and so did "Red Hot Mama" Sophie Tucker. In 1927, Al Jolson did a three-hour solo. Much of the money raised was used to purchase equipment for the hospital, but many local charities also benefited. Among them was a children's day nursery where local kids got free milk from the Emma Morris Milk Fund, in the hope that it might keep them healthy enough to ward off the contagious disease to which they were exposed each day. Morris and another ex-patient, Sime Silverman, founder of *Variety*, were instrumental in the establishment of the Will Rogers Sanatorium for theatrical people.

By the time I was old enough to have a paper route so I could pay my own "two bits" admission, the Pontiac was primarily a movie house. It seemed fitting to me that so glamorous an institution should be managed by perennial mayor Tony Anderson. Great movies were made in those years—Olivier's *Hamlet*, for example, and the splendid screen version of Robert Penn Warren's *All the King's Men.* Jose Ferrer swashed, buckled, and waxed poetic as Rostand's noble-nosed *Cyrano de Bergerac,* and Brando emoted up a storm with moodily mumbled eloquence and a ratty tee-shirt in *A Streetcar Named Desire.*

I saw none of those films, though; young lout that I was, I could not have been bribed to sit through them. The cinematic art that beguiled me at the Pontiac was rather more, shall we say, elemental in its appeal. My favorite film at the time was *Skipalong Rosenbloom*, a hare-brained send-up of the sixty-six Hopalong Cassidy movies, each of which I had seen several times on successive Saturdays for many years. At the time I would have assumed it was illegal to have a Saturday matinee without black-clad Bill Boyd, his silver hair matching his silver horse Topper, so I was dazzled at the brazen effrontery of *Skipalong Rosenbloom* for daring to spoof the peerless Hoppy.

The gags seemed to me marvelously original. At one point, the narrator said, "And then night fell," upon which the screen went dark to a heavy thud. Not all of the jokes rose to that level of wit, but the quality of the acting struck me as Oscar-calibre. I remember being mildly indignant when that year's Academy Awards went to Humphrey Bogart and Karl Malden instead of Slapsy Maxey Rosenbloom and Max Baer, whose performances in *Skipalong Rosenbloom* had seemed to me to embody the acme and epitome of the actor's craft.

I consoled myself that both Maxes had held boxing titles and appeared in Abbott and Costello movies, accomplishments that, to the best of my knowledge, had eluded the likes of Bogart and Malden. Skipalong, the hero, was such a paragon that he fired square bullets from a six-shooter with a square barrel. Did Karl Malden have any jokes as hilarious as that in *A Streetcar Named Desire*? He did *not*!

The original title capitalized on the fame of Slapsy Maxey, who had been light-heavyweight champ during the early 1930s. Today's TV audience may have forgotten not only Slapsy Maxey but even Hopalong Cassidy, although *Skipalong Rosenbloom* still shows up on late-night television now and then under anew title, *The Square Shooter. Sic transit gloria mundi.*

Vaudeville was dead by the 1950s, but the Pontiac stage continued to present great live entertainment. It hosted one of the show biz legends of the era, Don McNeill, whose "Breakfast Club" reached millions of radio listeners from 1933 until 1968. The show usually originated from Chicago, but occasionally hit the road. The ears of the nation were tuned to the Pontiac for the hayseed comedy of Fran Allison's Aunt Fanny and the wisecracks of Sam Cowling. Johnny Desmond and Patsy Lee were the regular singers, with celebrity guests turning up.

Almost everyone in America loved Don McNeill, with the notable exception of archrival Arthur Godfrey, the most vituperative celebrity of the era. The animus was so potent that Godfrey fired his sidekick and bandleader Archie Bleyer for allowing his record company to cut a disc with McNeill, the man who had single-handedly made morning network radio a profitable medium. McNeill's exit line, once as famous as any in America, reverberated from the stage of the Pontiac: "Be good to yourself!"

The Pontiac found itself the center of a delicious little fracas in 1953 when it booked *The Moon Is Blue*, the first movie released without the Hays Office Production Code seal of approval.

Naughtiness and occasional nudity in silent movies had irked the ever-vigilant puritans enough for them to demand federal censorship, prompting Hollywood to pre-empt this with self-censorship in 1922 through the establishment of the Hays Office. This system survived into the era of talking pictures, when it was threatened by the enormous popularity of Mae West movies—so naughty, so bawdy, so much fun.

The Roman Catholic Church organized the Legion of Decency

in 1933, and by 1934 had installed Joseph Breen as official censor for the Motion Picture Producers and Distributors of America. The Breen Code was so priggish that married couples were always shown with twin beds. Words such as "sex," "hell," and "damn" were banned, but so were "guts," "louse," and both "nuts" and "nerts" because such vulgar slang was anathema to the genteel tone demanded by Hollywood censors.

In 1953, independent producer Otto Preminger decided to defy the system with a movie version of a risque romantic comedy from the Broadway stage, F. Hugh-Herbert's *The Moon Is Blue.*

Of course, it was ridiculously easy to be risque in 1953. The 1950s cannot be explained to the 1990s; you really had to be there. In 1953 Hugh Hefner founded *Playboy* magazine, but that was in Chicago—wicked, sophisticated Chicago. Boynton's Cigar Store did not carry *Playboy* in Saranac Lake. Even *National Geographic* was kept where children couldn't see it, lest we be corrupted by glimpses of tropical tribes whose ladies did not wear blouses. Not only Joseph Breen, but also Queen Victoria would have approved of the successful censorship of sex in 1953 Saranac Lake.

But I was a boy of fourteen, abysmally ignorant of and insanely curious about sex. I knew that stag films were nicknamed "blue movies," so I deduced that a film with a title like *The Moon Is Blue* would certainly explain all the exotic mysteries of that forbidden realm, elucidating and probably even demonstrating all the secret techniques of that taboo topic. Seeing *The Moon Is Blue* became my burning ambition: I would learn everything I needed to know from a seat in the balcony of the Pontiac.

But I was an altar boy.

I found myself clad in black cassock and white surplice, facing the entire congregation at St. Bernard's while Father Ward, after fulminating against the mayor for daring to bring this filth into our innocent mountain hamlet, administered the Legion of Decency oath. I could see my mother watching me from the family pew as everyone placed left hand on breast and raised right hand in air to swear the oath to boycott films banned by Breen's

Code. There I stood at the foot of the altar, the complete hypocrite, pretending to condemn what I yearned to see.

Unwilling to risk hellfire by swearing a false oath, I crossed my fingers and spoke gibberish: "I swear I will not doovah de wallawah de blah blah blah, amen."

After the oath was administered, the entire congregation, with me up front carrying a candle, marched out of St. Bernard's, down the steps, up Academy Street, across Berkeley Square, and down Broadway past the Pontiac. That was the kind of protest march we had in the fifties. It was like something from *The Little World of Don Camillo*, with Father Ward and Tony Anderson squared off like Fernandel versus the commie mayor in Italy.

A picture of our anti-smut parade appeared in the paper. There I can still be seen on yellowing newsprint, apparently as sanctimonious as Reverend Dimmesdale. But if my cassock could be torn open it would reveal a scarlet H, the emblem of my hypocrisy.

It was no cinch seeing *The Moon Is Blue.* If I had tried to buy a ticket, the woman in the ticket booth would have scolded me. "Why, Kenny Lawless, you ought to be ashamed of yourself. Run along home before I tell your mother. The very idea!"

There is an African proverb that says, "It takes the whole village to raise a child." That was the way it worked in Saranac Lake in 1953. All adults felt responsible for and superior to all children. Because this system protected us in valuable ways, many people are nostalgic for it, forgetting how stultifying, arbitrary, and oppressive it was. It tempted me into deceit and petty crime—an usher opened the door and several boys sneaked into the balcony from the fire escape. We settled into our seats bursting with gleeful anticipation of forbidden delights.

Few disappointments in life can approach what happened next. After committing both sin and crime, not to mention earning the wrath of my mother if she ever found out, I saw a dreary film with less sex than *The Bells of St. Mary's. The Moon Is Blue* has William Holden and David Niven after Maggie McNamara, but to what purpose is never even hinted at. If there had been any saucy lines in the Broadway version, they were all eliminated by that sly fox Preminger, who cleverly included the forbidden words "virgin" and "mistress" to force the Breen office to deny the seal of approval, thereby guaranteeing him enormous publicity for a tepid mainstream comedy. It was a brilliant marketing ploy, but it broke my boyish heart. If anything, I was more utterly mystified by sex after seeing *The Moon Is Blue* than I had been before. Having sneaked in, we couldn't even demand our money back.

The Pontiac made national news in 1954. Biblical epics were big at the box office, and Hollywood produced a lavish, star-studded adaptation of Thomas B. Costain's novel *The Silver Chalice*, the story of a young Greek who makes the cup used by Christ at the Last Supper. Stars included Virginia Mayo, Pier Angeli, Jack Palance, Natalie Wood, E.G. Marshall, Alexander Scourby, Joseph Wiseman, Walter Hampden, and, in his screen debut six years before galloping to fame on the Ponderosa, Lorne Greene.

It was also the film debut of the broodingly handsome method actor lured from serious roles on Broadway to star as the young Greek artisan, whose leather tunic would reveal dimpled knees that would pack theaters with love-struck women. But not even a bare-legged Paul Newman could salvage this turkey.

Producers may have sensed disaster, as the expensive production turned out foot after foot of boringly pious celluloid twaddle. They tried to salvage something by linking the film to a genuinely worthy cause in a grandiose publicity campaign: The community that raised the most money per capita in the first three days of the 1954 Christmas Seal drive would win the right to host the gala world premiere of *The Silver Chalice.* Some jerkwater whistlestop in one nondescript Carolina or the other tried to give Saranac Lake a run for its money, but those poor jaspers never had a prayer.

Art Linkletter announced on TV's "House Party" on December 3 that Saranac Lake had won. We had to read about it in the *Daily Enterprise*, of course, because in 1954 there was no television to speak of in the village. If one erected a huge, rotating antenna, it was possible to receive a signal from Carthage, but every show looked like Casper the Friendly Ghost in a blizzard, so virtually everyone still lived in the world of newspapers and radio.

The Hollywood contingent arrived by train on the morning of Thursday, December 16. Virginia Mayo was traveling with her mother, perhaps a necessary chaperone for a visit to a village famed for its Lotharios. Some of the stars are now pretty much forgotten—Pedro Gonzalez-Gonzalez, for example, and Ann Robinson, and Marion Carr—but on that winter morning forty years ago, Saranackers stood in the cold, craning their necks for a glimpse of those stars.

Others had yet to reach their real fame. Alan Hale Jr. finally hit the big time eleven years later as Skipper Jonas Grumby on *Gilligan's Island.* Heartthrob Tab Hunter was actually returning to this neck of the woods; he had studied figure skating with Gus Lussi in Lake Placid. Tab's acting career had begun with a two-word role in a 1950 Macdonald Carey movie with a delightful title. The two words were, "Hi, Fred." The title was *The Lawless*.

Local bigwigs rode the special Warner Brothers train along with the stars. Mayor Anderson got a peck on the cheek from Virginia Mayo. Roger Tubby, so recently banished from the big time (he had been President Truman's press secretary until the Eisenhower victory provided Democrats with lots of free time to publish smalltown newspapers), wrote a charming piece for the *Daily Enterprise* headlined "Stars Sing Their Way Into the Adirondacks." These stars spent Friday doing all manner of adorable and photogenic things. The fourteen-degree temperature must have been a bit of a shock after southern California, but the stars kept smiling through the noon parade and the ensuing ski party on Mount Pisgah.

A vintage Packard took Virginia Mayo and Art Linkletter to the Municipal Skating Rink, where they were crowned King and Queen of the Ice. The actual premiere of *The Silver Chalice* began at 6:30 p.m., with the stars appearing in the lobby at 8:30 before a stage show hosted by Linkletter and broadcast live over WNBZ, the nation listening a little later on the Mutual network. The New York *News* devoted the back page of its Sunday edition to photographs of the event.

Paul Newman did not attend the premiere. Instead, he took the astonishing step of placing an ad in a Hollywood trade paper apologizing for his blunder in accepting the role. The amazing ad is now *The Silver Chalice's* only claim to fame, its niche in Hollywood history.

A couple of years after Virginia Mayo trod the boards of the Pontiac, I got my chance. A community theater group containing stage-struck natives and old troupers from Will Rogers decided to do *Room Service*, a show that had been a huge Broadway hit when produced by George Abbott with stars like Sam Levene, Philip Loeb, and Teddy Hart. RKO had bought the rights for a 1938 Marx Brothers film.

I was typecast as the juvenile, a hapless hayseed, the role played by Frank Albertson in the movie. Barbara Wallace played the ingenue. Sol Drutz and Johnny Garwood played all three Marx Brothers. For me, the performances had a delirious, dreamlike quality. There I sat, my face covered with fake measles, doing takes while those two zanies ran amok, flinging food, shouting "Godspeed!" and getting as many laughs as the immortal Artie Levy and Joe Benarro had gotten for going pfft! pfft! pfft! right in der Fuhrer's face.

If I was a teenage bit player in an amateur theatrical in the boondocks, I was also an actor getting laughs on the same stage where Jolson had wowed them less than thirty years before. So many ghosts haunted that stage; being on it was magic realism for me. Every audience is an emblem of the community, but for me at that age, the audience was literally my world—my playmates, my classmates, my kin, and my kind.

As I looked out at that world, laughing at me doing the role I was born to play—the fool—I was afloat in another world. It was a realm that encompassed Nyoka's jungle and the Double R Bar Ranch; a realm where famous phrases were uttered—"You ain't seen nothin' yet!" "Be good to yourself!"; a realm where Virginia Mayo had smiled at us as she had smiled at Danny Kaye in *The Secret Life of Walter Mitty*; a realm where the most Mittyesque fantasies might come true, and did, and do.

Magic realists remind us not to be fooled by mere appearances. Much of the Saranac Lake of my boyhood has vanished like *les neiges d'antan.* Only in my memory can I climb the broad staircase in Sterns Hardware or ride the elevator in Leonard's Department Store, miss a layup in the armory, avert my eyes from the cuspidors in the Hotel St. Regis, flub an easy word in the spelling bee from the radio station in the Berkeley, or get my ears lowered in the arcade of the Hotel Saranac. But the Pontiac is still there in a way that the armory and the Alpine are not, because the Pontiac was never intended simply to be real in the first place. It was a temple of the imagination, a spirit realm where urchins gobbled popcorn while heroes defeated evil, where young couples smooched in the balcony while forty-foot faces kissed on a silver screen, where weary workers watched while the muse Thalia did pratfalls, where the highest art met the lowest buffoonery, where commerce sold dreams and Jujubes.

You can't destroy a place like that merely by burning it down. The ghosts that haunted the Pontiac, noble spirits and mischievous elves alike, are still there, magic citizens of America's magic mountain.

Try if for yourself: Go to Saranac Lake on a crisp winter evening and stand in the vacant lot on Broadway where the Pontiac stood for so many splendid years. Look up at the stars and listen. Keep listening. You will hear the America of my childhood.

Don't be cynical. Don't think, "Lawless is drunk again, on booze as usual or maybe on nostalgia." Have a little faith. Listen. The voices are not loud, but they are as real as death or taxes. If I can hear them, you can hear them, too. Listen.

Pffft! Pffft! Pffft! You ain't seen nothin' yet! Godspeed! Be good to yourself! Pffft! Pffft! Pffft. . . .

Water in a Paper Bag

Roger Mitchell

The commonest thing said of the Adirondacks is that it is many places. If you live your life, say, at the south end of Lake Placid on the old Plains of Abraham, you may never go to Newcomb. Newcomb is only about fifteen miles away as the crow goes, but as humans in these parts go, it might as well be Saskatchewan.

Growing up in the Adirondacks, as I did, is growing up in one or another isolated corner of them. I knew people who had lived their whole lives in the Adirondacks and never climbed a mountain, never wanted to. And I knew people who practically slept in their boots. Did these people live in the same place?

It's like the Midwest, where I now live. Depending on where you spend your nights, the Midwest is the streets of Chicago, the cornfields of Iowa and Kansas, the ten thousand lakes of Minnesota, the Indian mounds of southern Illinois, the sand hills of Nebraska, the Toledos, Akrons, Daytons of Ohio, the wooded ridges and bottoms of southern Indiana, the wheatfields of the Dakotas, just to list the obvious. It is more than any word can hold, and yet the word holds something.

The Adirondacks I knew centered in Saranac Lake, extended most often in the direction of Lake Placid, spilled occasionally down through Keene Valley (it was through this valley that the family moved in and out of our part of the Adirondacks), glanced in the direction of Tupper Lake. I knew the names of towns like Malone, Massena, Gouverneur, Chazy, and Canton; but except for one trip to Malone, I never went to any of them.

I did spend two summers to the north on Lake Meacham, and the family went skiing once at Mont Tremblant in Quebec. And if that isn't constriction enough, I lived in the Adirondacks a long time ago, from 1947 to 1955—eight and a half years total.

But these were my adolescent years. Years when everything happened, in no particular order. These were the years when something like stability or continuity underlay my life. It was before anyone I knew started the long, broken treks out of their houses and lives into retirement homes, hospitals, and finally, graves. For me, the Adirondacks was as much a time as a place. It was a time in my life, and a time, now somewhat benign and remote, in American history. It was, as these things go, rather brief.

As I am always a bit astonished to say to my friends, I have now lived in one house in Indiana three times as long as I lived in the Adirondacks. I left the Adirondacks over forty years ago. But still it is, or has become, the place I know as home. Or, since "home" is only an approximation, only a metaphor, the place I would like to keep as the place I started from.

I have never moved anywhere by choice, which means I've never lived anywhere by choice. If I wasn't following the trail of my father's jobs, I was looking for an education, a trail that took me from Massachusetts to Alabama to Colorado to England. Or I was following my own job trail, one that took me to Wisconsin and finally to Indiana. I *did* grow up in the Adirondacks, but it was on the fly in my family's forced march through life. I *did* grow up in the Adirondacks, but it would be just as easy for me to say that I live in Indiana. Easier, in fact: more natural. So, in saying I grew up in the Adirondacks, I'm staking some sort of claim—a claim I have a right to, it seems, but one that needs some insisting on to be real. I want to have come from somewhere, and I want it to matter. The odd thing is that though I had no control over where I lived in those years, I now do, and rather than let the Adirondacks go, be the object of a casual comment or two in some other life I might be leading, I now choose them. I choose those years and what I can remember of those experiences to be a point of reference, a tack against the hurricane-like winds that rip through our lives.

No doubt it is what has made me write two books and a handful of poems about the Adirondacks. What stands out are a number of bright facts and a few broad impressions. Part of what I see, I see with memory—good old wobbly memory. The rest I see through the filter of experience.

I remember the morning mother said it was 54 below. We all bundled up just to go out and see what it felt like. In five minutes we were back inside.

I remember reading a few years back about the great Thanksgiving storm of 1950 or '51. Whole mountainsides were blown down in an instant. What I remember is that one day we lost our electricity, and for four days we sat around the fireplace in blankets. My brother, sister and I all got pneumonia.

We were living then in the Mills Cottage, the old nurses' home on the grounds of Trudeau Sanatorium. It was joined to the new one by a glassed-in walkway that was always locked. Upstairs was a bathroom with two toilets, two bathtubs, and four sinks. Anne and I used to take baths at the same time (different stalls, mind you), but it was there we conceived the BTBC, the Bathtub Broadcasting Company.

We did imitations of the radio programs we listened to, complete with station announcements, advertisements, and news shows. Later, we got a huge cardboard box, drew a few dials and knobs on it, and sat in the living room inside it, performing our radio scripts for Mom, Dad and Garry.

We were living in the Mills Cottage because Dad had just taken a job with Trudeau Sanatorium. The switch from rural

North Carolina to rural New York, in mid January, was a shock.

We had a radio with one of those watery green spots in the middle of the dial, but there was no TV. I say somewhat proudly these days that I belong to the last generation not to grow up on TV. But we had "Yukon King" and "The Fat Man" (the program always started with the fat man getting on the scales and dropping a coin in the slot), and "The Jack Benny Show." When I was sick, I used to listen to "The Breakfast Club." "Good Morning, Breakfast Clubbers, a howdy do-ya," the song went.

The family was musical. My grandmother, Gamma as we called her, had once sung with the Philadelphia Orchestra before she became choir director for the Presbyterian Church in Glens Falls. Mother belonged to the Saranac Lake Oratorio Society, as I think it was called. Anne, my sister, who went on to a Ph.D. in Musicology, came close to a career in opera and still plays the piano with feeling and power. So, when I asked my mother if she would buy me a copy of "The Johnson Rag," she nearly choked. But she did it.

Remember "Cry Me a River?" Johnny Ray, who made no effort to hide the wire to his hearing aid. The first of the white "shouters." That's the time we're talking about. Popular music was about to round the bend and give us, full blast, rhythm and blues and rock and roll. Elvis was born the same year I was.

At Christmas time I went caroling with kids from the Presbyterian Church. Gene Bjorkman and I were precariously balanced on the knife edge of hormonal change, so we could sing any part from soprano to bass (and did). We liked to take small liberties, like singing the third verse while everyone else was singing the first. Getting about in a horse-drawn sleigh, too. Good cold early winter nights. I remember the night we all ran out to look at the northern lights. Huge waving sheets of light covered the northern sky.

I snuck out after dark once, onto the roof over the front porch, down the drain pipe, and over to David Klemperer's house where, having snuck out himself, he was waiting for me in the shadows by the back door. We went up in back of his house and sat by the pond and talked and looked at the stars. It was pretty exciting, though I've thought for a long time that my parents probably knew. Probably lay there in bed and listened to me tiptoe across the roof.

Mt. Pisgah had lights, and the warming shack had a jukebox with loudspeakers outside. We skied to top 40. Does anyone remember "Charley My Boy?" "You *thrill* me, you *chill* me, oh *Char*ley, my boy." It's a good song to ski to. I used to dance that rhythm down the slope, digging and jumping my steel edges into every beat of it. Frankie Laine singing "Mule Train." Patti Page, Theresa Brewer.

One night Doug LaBombard's father drove his car out on the ice on Lower Saranac Lake. It went through, and he drowned. Doug was the only skier who could beat me on the high school team. This was before Tommy Finnegan, though. Tommy was the best skier, and later skied for Middlebury. My father rented a piece of Bluff Island in Lower Saranac Lake from the state and we often went out there for picnics. I could never get it out of my mind that we might have been driving the boat over Doug LaBombard's father's car, maybe even Doug LaBombard's father.

I saw Art Devlin once in Lake Placid. He was America's best ski jumper and jumped for the United States Olympic team several times. The Devlins owned a grocery, I think, in Lake Placid. People used to say of Art that he could stand at the back of a flatbed truck and jump straight into it from a standing position.

Dannemora prison is not far away, and I remember a roadblock on the road to Lake Placid once after a prisoner escaped. Six or eight grim men in hunting gear with shotguns standing by the side of the road.

I did my first camping in North Carolina, so the challenge in the Adirondacks was to camp in the winter, as I did a few times with the local Boy Scout troop. We made biscuits in the snow by pouring a little water into the paper bag that held the flour. That always seemed a small miracle to me: water in a paper bag. We wrapped potatoes in leaves and put them among the coals. They came out burnt on one side, raw as rock on the other.

If I was bored, there was always climbing. We lived on Mt.

Pisgah. I couldn't begin to say how many times I climbed that little knob. Across the Saranac River was Mt. Baker. The oddest climb was up Mt. Ampersand. It had steps all the way to the top. When I climbed up Saint Regis, there was still a cabin at the bottom of the trail where the lookout lived. Most of the towers have now been torn down.

There was the time two friends and I climbed I can't remember what mountain sometime in February. I used to think it was Whiteface, but I'm pretty sure now it wasn't. We did it on skis with "skins," as they were called: seal skins tied to the bottoms of our skis. I still have them in a drawer at home. The mountain had an old ski trail on it. No lift, of course.

As it turned out, there was a blizzard at the top, and we had to rope ourselves together. One of my skis came off as we were traversing a steep, icy open slope. Luckily it caught on a thin snowdrift. The trail—when we reached it—was deep in powder snow, and of course, no one had gone down it in years. Skiing that unbroken trail with fresh powder nearly to our knees—just three of us, having spent most of the day climbing to get there—was hard to top. Keeps being hard to top.

I walked everywhere, didn't get a drivers' license 'til I was nineteen. I don't remember anybody at school having cars. It was early enough in the fifties, I suppose, that that kind of affluence hadn't quite arrived yet, at least to Saranac Lake. More likely, it was just the way most parents wanted it.

This was outside the culture somewhere. The movies brought it to us, but the big world was elsewhere. It was something to look at, not something to be in the midst of. New York City was the big town. We all knew about New York City. A few of us had been there. The rest of us wanted to go sometime. Well, most of the rest of us. There were those who knew enough about New York from a distance to know we didn't ever need to go there.

I was a Yankee hater from early on. The Yankees seemed to win the pennant every year, mostly by buying the best player away from my team, the Philadelphia Athletics, who, of course, always finished last.

More than anything, the Adirondacks I knew was a place

where it took longer for the culture to arrive. In those days, culture was TV, the latest cars, movies, and top 40 music. We had those things, or a version of them, but there was a small-town, backwoods habit of mind that told us that if you really wanted that sort of thing (and why would you?), you had to get out.

The big world of Mao's victory in China or the federal prosecution of union leaders for suspected Communist leanings, the McCarthy hearings and the House Un-American Activities Committee, the war in Korea, all these things were "out there" somewhere, but they were too far out to make very much noise either in the Adirondacks or in the adolescent ear. Though I do remember paying close attention to the peace talks in Panmunjom as my eighteenth birthday got closer. I did not want to die on some frozen slope in Korea, Or anywhere else, for that matter.

You can't underestimate the power of snow. When not just the leaves, but the ground disappears for months, you pay closer attention to the life around you. The exaggerations of the seasons put you right in their midst.

The Pontiac Theatre burned down maybe ten years ago. It's now a parking lot. But, like everyone else, I went to the matinee almost every Saturday. First the "previews," then the RKO Pathe News, always narrated by Ed Herlihy, the cartoon, and finally the feature. I'm forgetting the "serial," always some barely acted, underfunded, black-and-white cliffhanger about bad guys who never smiled and good guys who did.

The story would go on for weeks, and fearless Fred, who was apt to be our very own age, would get closer and closer to uncovering the ring of urban cattle rustlers (bad, awful men who stole cattle in trucks), but each week they would just elude his grasp and he would have to take a short trip "over the cliff" at the very end. I remember the week our hero actually went over a cliff in the back of a sealed truck with his hands tied behind him and a gag in his mouth. The movie showed him inside, and then it showed the truck actually, really going over the cliff, hitting bottom and bursting into flames. How could Fred get out of that one? We had to wait a whole week to find out. And, as it happened, between the time when we last saw him tied up in the back of the truck and the moment when the truck left the ground, Fred managed to untie his hands(!), pry open the back door and jump out. We were mighty relieved.

The feature was usually a Roy Rogers/Dale Evans classic, maybe Gene Autry. Cowboy musicals. The Riders of the Purple Sage sang their way through all of them, and room was always found in the script for Gabby Hayes and his broad caricature of the simple-minded but good-hearted sidekick. For variety we had Abbott and Costello and the Bowery Boys. Not very different, I imagine, from small towns (and big ones) all over the country.

This was the era of *Parents' Magazine.* Mother always had to check *Parents* to see if it was all right for us to go to a particular movie. If it wasn't, we didn't go. And somehow didn't miss it. This is the way life was, we thought. There were rules and stages and phases, and guiding and monitoring them all were Mom and Dad, the ones in charge, the ones who knew best. We complained now and then, of course, but not very seriously.

Something has happened to the Adirondacks in my telling about them. It seems to have slipped. The things coming to mind most easily are, in fact, those things that made the Adirondacks like every other place in the country, just another bit of small town America. What I seem to be stumbling into is that growing up in the Adirondacks had nothing terribly unique or striking about it, except for extremities of snow and cold and a mountain setting.

For one thing, adolescence is adolescence, a well down which we all tumble for a few years while we grope around in the darkness of our uncertainties and hormonal imbalances. For another thing, we also live in classes, social classes, and it is difficult, if not impossible, to deny this truth or minimize its impact.

Middle class culture with its ideals of striving and success, its belief in progress—which is to say, its belief in the possibility of the human control of life and of the natural world, produces a definite kind of human being and a definite kind of culture. There are a number of good things about that. My father, for instance, was a doctor. Early in his working life he decided that he wanted to devote his life not to the daily aches and pains of people, but to the project of stamping out tuberculosis. He gave up general practice and went to work in tuberculosis sanitoria, first in North Carolina, then at Trudeau. Trudeau folded in 1955 because they had found a wonder drug to cure it; no longer was it necessary to move into the mountains or out onto a desert to "take the cure." In other words, the medical profession had succeeded in bringing TB under control. It was a real achievement, and one about which my father felt some pride.

My parents built a house out on Trudeau Road no more than four years before it was announced that Trudeau would close. What was their reaction to that closing? I don't remember any response other than a kind of excitement that boiled up slowly as it became apparent that Dad was going to find work in Denver. In June of 1955 we moved there, and my father went to work for a chest diseases research laboratory. The struggle against tuberculosis became a struggle against other respiratory illnesses, and life went on.

What happened to the Adirondacks? It stayed where it was, of course, or, in terms of our life, it turned into an interlude—a particularly nice one—that we often remember with real fondness. What became gradually apparent, however, was that in some real and fundamental way we had never really lived there; we had lived on the *surfaces* of the Adirondacks. The surfaces of the Adirondacks are, of course, gorgeous and compelling. But we lived on the surface, I'm now convinced, because we were exemplary members of the middle class. Life was about personal aspiration and personal space. Life was organized around tasks like getting good grades or curing tuberculosis, or it was organized around markets, markets for movies, markets for music, job markets.

People "buy" into commercial culture because that seems to be the instinctive way (probably the only way) we measure material life. We don't live in *places* (like the Adirondacks), except insofar as they can be made to seem a part of the larger and implicitly more important "places" organized most around, or as, markets, the most important of which are almost never local but national. Those people who have local pride—real local pride— or local knowledge, seem rarely to be members of the middle class.

So, yes, you could live next door to someone in the Adirondacks who never climbed a mountain and never showed an interest in it because he or she very likely lived "elsewhere." Their home might be in Onchiota, but they lived their lives among the fantasies created for us by those who want to sell us things.

I wanted at one point to be a baseball player. It had nothing to do with any skill I had. I was a lousy baseball player. It was, rather, a fantasy of personal success, a perfectly straightforward middle-class fantasy of rising by your efforts to a pinnacle marked by spotlights and cheering. Boys like me had this dream all over America. It was American in some way to have this dream. We might as well have lived on the moon. We were measuring ourselves by yardsticks the culture gave us which had nothing to do with the Adirondacks and everything to do with those most transportable and fluid of things, money and fame. With one possible exception.

I was the bespectacled geek son of a prominent doctor, who in adolescence deeply wanted not to be any of those things: bespectacled, a geek, or anybody's son. I wanted to be a "regular guy," although as you can see, I wouldn't have minded being a World Series hero as well. I may be fooling myself, but some tiny piece of this longing now seems like it was really a longing for something else: a different way of life, a different set of standards or presumptions about life. At the very least, as a baseball player, I would have gotten to spit. On national TV, too. I could have stepped out of the class to which I belonged and into something that felt closer to the ground.

Twenty or so years after leaving the Adirondacks, after having lived in Denver, Boston, Boulder, Huntsville (Alabama), England, Madison (Wisconsin), Milwaukee, Poland, and living at the time in Oxford, England, I finally brought myself to recognize and admit that I had lived somewhere (on the lower slopes of Mount Pisgah outside Saranac Lake), but had never known very much about it. It had not been important or necessary to know anything about it. As a kid in school, it was far more important to know if Shirley Shore liked you or what the lyrics to the latest Patti Page song were. As your parents' son, it was far more important to get the grades that would get you into medical school and get you, most likely, out of town.

It was to repair my ignorance, an ignorance that I think is "natural" to my class, that I turned to the only aids available to me—namely libraries—and started trying to learn some of what I did not know.

Out of this effort came two books, *Adirondack,* a book of poems, and *Clear Pond,* the reconstruction of the life of the original settler at the Clear Pond south of Elk Lake. I have often been asked why I put all that energy into reconstructing the life of someone who was both unrelated to me and from a part of the Adirondacks I don't ever remember visiting when I lived there. My mother said, "Roger, why didn't you do all this genealogical work on your own family?"

I gave her some sort of answer like, "I was interested in a kind of Everyman figure." Which was true. But I was beginning to take an interest in the early and primitive days of the Adirondacks, when most of it was still covered by original forest. I wanted to know more about the actual place: it's history, geology, archaeology, whatever might tell me more about the place I had come from, more anyway than was routinely available around the dinner table or in the "Good Old Days" column in the local paper.

If you were looking around the Adirondacks today for a part of it that still has some feel of that original forest, I don't think you'd do better than the stretch of land between Long Lake and North Hudson, just south of the High Peaks. First of all, this part of the Adirondacks has no immediate glamour, nothing like Lake George or Lake Placid to draw tourists into it in any large number, no industry or none larger than the logging that goes on here and there all through the Adirondacks. There is, however, a hole as big as a mountain up near Lake Henderson where some kind of mining has been going on in recent years.

The little village of Newcomb lies right in the middle of this area, and nothing about Newcomb suggests that people want anything more than to live right there. It is not a "summer town" like Keene Valley or Star Lake. It is not geared up for skiers like Wilmington and North Creek. People live there, and the woods and hills surround them. When you drive along the road from North Hudson to Newcomb, you are driving through the woods. You are *in* the woods and driving through them.

Blue Ridge is a small place. I'm not sure they have a word small enough to describe it. "Hamlet" seems too big a word. It can't be a "crossing" since no road crosses there. But there it is, Blue Ridge, a place on the way to Newcomb. And to be honest, even Newcomb, which is far bigger than Blue Ridge, has trouble sticking together. It sprawls out—all 80 or so houses of it—for four miles along the road.

It is the woods you are in in Newcomb and Blue Ridge. The mountains are certainly there to the north, but they're off in the distance. Rather, it is the woods and the silences of the woods that greet you. You meet an occasional car or logging truck as the road twists and winds its way across the landscape, but then the silences come back.

Off to the east, the Northway blasts through the solid rock of the mountain, shears the face off the side of a hill, rises up over a river or a town like an airport runway. It's a road that tries to get by the Adirondacks—or into them—with a minimum of fuss and local contamination. It's for people in a hurry, people for whom this and every other place are a kind of clay to be arranged and rearranged according to their preconceived hopes.

Something about this remote corner of the world seemed authentic to me. When I started writing about the Adirondacks more than twenty years ago, I was looking for the place I could say I came from. I was trying to make it more mine than it really was. And what I think I did was to go to a part of the Adirondacks I knew nothing about and to a life and lives that lay outside the ideals and obsessions of my class, because there it might be possible to find an authentic piece of the life of the Adirondacks. Something that stuck there, as I had not.

*

I spent years wandering around the Town of North Hudson, twenty-five and thirty years after having left the Adirondacks, looking for hints and glints of a person (his name was Israel Johnson) whom no one could much recall. It was a challenge—a complicated puzzle to solve—and that was fun. It also got me out from behind my desk and, since I am mostly a poet, out of the labored hallways of my brain where I could both be a writer and talk to a wide assortment of interesting people. Knocking on the door of a perfect stranger in a small hamlet in the woods and asking a string of odd questions is much more exciting than most people can imagine. The little instantaneous drama of convincing someone on his doorstep that you aren't completely crazy and getting them to open up a bit, beats a night at the movies. But, here I am again describing what I did in terms of a task, a personal achievement. It's hard to shake those middle-class habits.

What I've come to feel only recently, now years after the publication of *Clear Pond*, is that part of what I was doing in writing that book was trying, finally, to find or invent a way for myself into what I could only sense was the real Adirondacks, both the place and the culture of that place. And, as I've been saying, I had to come at it from that other world, the world of middle-class mobility and aspiration, the mentality that says the world is our oyster to crack open. The mentality that always assumes there must be something more to do, something better to be made out of what's there, a better place to be than the ordinary alleys and rivers we walk or drive by every day.

I think we are all complicated people and inhabit a number of subject positions at once, but the middle-class piece of my mentality, my upbringing, my professional aspirations, kept and keeps me floating somewhere just above the ground, not quite attached to it. The writing of *Clear Pond* was an attempt to attach, to find, if only symbolically, a real culture to belong to, not the free-floating middle-class culture, which is, of course, America's culture.

Crazy? Maybe. The worst of it is that this entire psychodrama is apt to be just another way to "use" the Adirondacks. It exhibits the very vice I've been talking about, floating above the ground, belonging, in truth, to the freeways and the movies and the ads and all else that makes it easier for people to package us and sell us things. Paradoxically, but also of necessity, *Clear Pond* is a book full of long drives. From Indiana to New York, from New York to Indiana. Albany to North Hudson (on the Northway, too), North Hudson to Elk Lake. And of course, though that was not my intention, it helps to avoid the place—Bloomington, Indiana—where I have now lived most of my life.

I could be a hermit, maybe. For a while, anyway. It's nice to think, at any rate, that it might just be possible to live somewhere and some way that owes its vitality to the ground on which it happens and not to what can be done *to* or *with* that ground.

Saranac Lake had only one black family. I forget their name, but the daughter was in school. It didn't seem like any big deal, but of course, it had to be. Not for us so much, not for Saranac Lake. But as a statement of what it meant to be black in America, I can see now what it meant. We all see now. It was a very white place, Saranac Lake; but in some strange way, no one knew it. No one said anything, anyway.

Saranac Lake was an almost perfect place for the fifties to happen. It was small and quite contentedly behind the times. You might have belonged to a family with social aspirations, some sort of larger dream or hope. A family that would want its sons and maybe its daughters to go to college.

Then there were those who hoped for sons and daughters who would do well, but not so well that they would move away or think things their parents hadn't thought before them. Such parents took the risk of losing their children by sending them to college.

Finally, there were the kids whose families had been there forever, some with fathers who hunted to put meat on the table, people who spoke with the local accent.

I have to remember that Saranac Lake straddles the Saranac River. Lake Flower is a wide place in the river made by the dam. The river swoops down through the bottom of town in a kind of deep cut, and it's easy to miss it. Right at the bottom of the cut is the Dew Drop Inn, a place that invited story-making back then. In school, we talked about what we were sure went on down there at the bottom of the building, no more than a rat's ankle above the river, where it smelled of dead fish and rotgut whiskey. We had no idea what rotgut whiskey was, but it sounded good rolling off the tongue.

We had hermits, too: shaggy, unkempt creatures who would come into town occasionally for bullets and a sack of flour. They always walked, of course. Some lived not too far from town in places you could find if you wanted to. Others were as wary as otters; you could never find where they lived.

There were people, too, who lived somewhere between the isolation of the hermit and the regular life of the town. They were found at the edge of town in homes that were little more than shacks, with a crazed dog or two tied up nearby and every form of moveable object lying around the yard: tools, car parts, used lumber, anything that might at sometime in the future be of some conceivable use or was too heavy to take to the dump. These were people right out of fairy tale: warty and twisted, one-eyed, smelly. On one side of town Handel's "Messiah;" on the other, the mother of Rumpelstiltskin.

What does it add up to? Things don't really add up, at least by themselves. Life happens—sixty miles an hour—and before you know it, you're somewhere else. Though I had had a taste of the Adirondacks when I was very young (my father's home town was Glens Falls), I was really shot into them at the age of eleven in mid-winter and then shot out of them eight and a half years later.

I didn't come back for twenty-five years. When I did, I went looking for the Mills Cottage. It was not there. It had been completely and surgically removed. And that, of course, is true about the past—the whole past—I knew there. I can drive through Saranac Lake today and see many familiar places. Altman's was, until quite recently, still Altman's. Tommy Finnegan now runs the store his father ran.

The St. Regis hotel, with its grimy, tiled floor in the lobby and fat old leather lounges, is gone. So is the Alpine, across the street. When the Pontiac Theatre burned, so did all the stores uphill from it. The big change, though, is that all those people whose faces and gestures and accents I wound up remembering forever are gone, at least from my memory. It is someone else's place, the place not just of other people than those I knew, but of another people, a different culture, a different way of life.

For me, growing up in the Adirondacks meant, partly, growing up in America right after World War II. For all its isolation, Saranac Lake was in that world, even emblematic of the socially conservative side of it. The people who lived in that village of "7000 friendly people," which is what the sign at the edge of town used to say, wanted the small town virtues and values that were endlessly portrayed on the screen by Fred McMurray and Doris Day and Rock Hudson (he was pretending, too). It would probably be fair to say that we had those virtues and values with all of their strengths and every one of their limitations. If you had parachuted onto Main Street in 1951, you would have found a community of people much like other communities around the country, a community both away from the center of the culture and one trying to be in it as well.

Life for an adolescent was simply a matter largely of coping with the prescribed dramas of that period of one's life, all of which centered around high school: dating, sports, school, and what was then only beginning to emerge: youth culture. I was no "rebel without a cause," but I had incoherent and inexplicable struggles with my parents. Some sort of old order was breaking up in the country, and I think many parents felt it coming, even if they couldn't be sure what it was. It was much of what made the time so repressive.

There really was an effort made after the war, with its inexplicable and pervasive violence, to return to some sort of older model of society, one that was familiar, one that was pretty much stripped of the labor radicalism of the thirties and the sudden advances of women during the war. My sense now is that Saranac Lake and the Adirondacks in general were sought out by people who had some sense (not to say fear) of what was to come—and a longing to steer clear of it.

But then there were the Adirondacks—not just the physical place, but the long-standing culture of farmers, miners and lumbermen, people who had deep roots in the place. It was there. You could see it and feel it: people who lived there because this was truly where they came from and where they would stay. People whose contact with the land was deeper than aesthetics, who saw the views, yes, but knew where the good fishing holes and best blueberrying were. People who could read the snow on the mountains in early October, who could change a tire at twenty below, who volunteered at the local high school or knit muffs for the elderly on winter evenings.

This is a culture I knew but, to be honest, wasn't really part of. My angle of vision was skewed by having come upon the Adirondacks "accidentally." But I had the great fortune of knowing some of these people in school and in Boy Scouts. It was in the Adirondacks that I first had the basic experiences of this culture, most of which I couldn't have described at the time. I was a migrant, really, in a culture that would increasingly give itself to migration. After all, what percentage of the American population is it now that lives where it grew up? But I was young enough and unfocused enough to sense a deeper and more settled level of the culture, a culture *of* the Adirondacks, that I have admired and envied and tried numerous times to imagine or to put myself in the midst of.

The writing I've done about the Adirondacks is, in some way, about trying to put myself *in* the Adirondacks in ways I never was and, to be honest, never will be.

I had the experience recently of sleeping in the house my parents built on Trudeau Road. I gave a poetry reading at Paul Smith's, and the nice lady who had bought the house from my parents, and still lived there, graciously let me spend two nights in it. I dream and even daydream about that house and have for years, but to sleep in your parents' bedroom at an age greater than theirs when they lived there is an experience I don't know where to begin describing.

I recognized every room. Very little had been done to change the house: a deck added here, some bushes and trees there. The house looked very much the way it had on that day in June 1955 when we left. The furnishings were similar, the refrigerator was in the same place, and so on. But it was different, completely different. It was where a kind of life had been lived for a few years by people who are now so changed from those they were that the place had, for me, the quality of a museum.

To walk into the museum of your own life is a terrifying thing. To see what you were, to know that it is gone. I lay down on one of the two beds (my parents had slept in twin beds, too) and felt I had violated something, had become the parent of my parents.

Thirty-seven years had gone by, and my father was to be dead in less than a year. I could hear that death coming. I could feel it in the air. I slept in its sheets for two nights and dreamt of what had been. When I left, I kept saying thank you, over and over—to my hostess, of course, but to people who weren't there, too, to something I almost touched.

Across the valley of the Saranac River, Whiteface Mountain was nearly bare. It was October, the leaves were down, and the first snows would soon whiten its peak.

The Old Pump House

William Gadway

The old men in town told us that it used to be the site of a pump house, a place where water was drawn from the river to wash the crushed stone of dirt and roots. The building had long since gone, but the large cement slab that had supported it remained, jutting out into the small river cove, a testament of days past. It served as the perfect podium from which we kids could fish, swim, and skip rocks all summer long.

The river wound through our small village of Morrisonville, New York before arriving at the pump house. We kids would sometimes ride our inner tubes from the bridge in town down to the slab, then stop to swim in the shallow pool it overlooked. My father had taken me there when I was too young to leave our street, let alone go fishing by myself. By the time I was ten, I was eager to become a pump house regular.

The old pump had met its demise when the crushed stone plant was relocated to a more promising area for producing stone. Consequently, a better place for procuring water was also found further downstream and closer to the new site. A small lunar landscape was all that was left of the old plant's location.

Back when the pump house was first constructed, a small man-made weir had been built slightly downstream to enhance the water's depth, and when the slab was overcrowded, the weir served as an alternate site for casting. The hay field at our backs, with its bait shop of crickets, beetles, and grasshoppers, helped supplement the worms and bread dough we invariably ran out of. It also supplied a soft place for an afternoon nap.

Our hand-me-down equipment consisted of old, rusty reels and rods with broken eyelets, the latter adorned with various pieces of duct tape. These would occasionally dislodge and be propelled out into the cove. Hopelessly tangled knots were left intact, until such time as our allowances caught up with our expenses. A sprig to hold our fish was all that was necessary to round out the gear of our youth.

We never really caught anything more than a few perch, rock bass, or punkinseeds, but it was far better than suffering the embarrassment of going home empty-handed. On the weir, where the current was swifter, we would land an occasional trout—cause for much celebration, besides bragging rights for the lucky angler. Getting snagged on deadheads and losing our bait on the first cast was a regular event, along with straining to hook tree limbs and old tires.

About once every two weeks, a careless cast would demand our early departure to remove the small hook embedded in someone's scalp or ear. It was a good twenty-minute walk home that often took twice as long, due to our tendency to lollygag at the various frog ponds and marshes that were strewn along the way. It proved difficult to keep a straight face while gazing upon the forlorn face of a playmate wearing a three-pronged hook on his head, and even harder when a gaudy lure was involved. I guess the insults we threw at one another were worse than the pain of the whole ordeal.

The views on the trek back home kept our minds off the offending fish hooks. We would pass what was left of the old plant—mountains of left-over stone interspersed with twisted pieces of conduit and wire. There were old roads containing vast mud puddles we had to walk through, and then another delay to get a cold drink of spring water in a local farmer's field. If the season was right, we would then pause for a snack of wild strawberries or raspberries to give us energy for the rest of our journey.

In those days there were no houses to look at and no unnatural sounds to be heard, except for the distant pounding of the crushed stone plant. Across the river, the woods shrouded the sight of the village and the county fairgrounds. The only human voices we ever heard were our own.

As I grew older, much of the crushed stone from the pump house went into the building of the huge cement runway at Plattsburgh Air Force Base and was mixed with tar for its roads. Understandably, our small town was much busier suddenly, for Plattsburgh was six miles away and trucks traversed our streets constantly on their journey.

As time wore on, the town kept expanding more and more, inching toward the larger town of Plattsburgh. Most people preferred living in the small communities, so new housing developments kept surfacing.

The opposite shore of our sanctuary fell victim to just such a project. It was cleared of any trees that were blocking the river vista, and now children, clotheslines, and yapping dogs have taken their place. Ducks and geese no longer seek refuge in the coves, and the blue herons find a more sublime place to fish.

Recently, Plattsburgh Air Force Base closed, but the town is still sprawled around one of its other central features: the mall. I still like to fish, but the place's aura of desolation and solitude has long since vanished, visible only in the memories of a few lucky adults who, when they were ten years old, found a way to make the old pump house useful once more.

North Country Girls

Elizabeth Inness-Brown

Have you ever spent a season in the North Country?
Have you ever spent a season way up north?
Have you ever been loved through a cold winter's night?
Have you ever loved a North Country girl? *

The year I spent back in the North Country, it was the yellows that caught my eye. The last leaves of fall. The school bus roaring past my door. A yellow hearse in a barnyard along Route 68. The Schwan's truck delivering frozen goods across the way. Pencils on the sidewalk, dropped by kids walking home.

In the dead-white of winter, I borrowed a camera from Hal. Hal is a North Country person; you probably know him. Tall, wispy beard, glasses, funny. He lent me his 35mm without a question. I took it without asking any back. The first roll I lost altogether—all my yellows gone because I didn't know how to load the film. The second roll came out all right, but not how I imagined. Nothing could capture those yellows, so necessary against the snow.

I showed Hal the pictures. "I like the word yellow," I said. "I would have to say it's one of my favorite words."

"What other words do you like?" he said. "Rubber," I said. "I like the sound of it."

I'd been far away, and for a long time. I was 30; I'd been 22 when I left. Even so, when I came back that year, everywhere I went people knew who I was. I had no problem cashing checks, getting bank loans, renting a house. People might not know *which* of my father's daughters I was, but they knew I was a North Country girl. You probably know me too, even now.

I had come home in the summer of '84 after living in Mississippi for five years, after being gone from the North Country—except for vacations—since 1976. Not much had changed. The cracked sidewalks, the old neon signs, the dust in the summertime, and the sand in the winter. The landscape that seemed to go on around people, ignoring them. In the summer, wild growth. Even where the land was cultivated, it seemed out of control. And where someone tried to control it—by planting a little bed of marigolds and zinnias, say—nothing but a puny showing of garish flowers on tiny plants, the dirt hard between them. Anywhere else, they'd have thrived. Gardens seemed to get away from people, like dogs did—day lilies to the ditches, blue flags to the fields.

And in winter, snow. Not the pretty blanket people hoped for and imagined, but bricks of snow, walls of snow, mountains of snow, building up slow and steady over the winter. Snow in some places heaped so high it took 'til June to melt. For all the long haul of winter after December, the roads were white, tamped down, layered with sand, the streets just not visible 'til the thaw. Then, in the spring, the snow at the curbs going black and the sand making silty deltas at the ends of driveways. I remember playing in them when I was a kid, navigating twig-boats down them as if they were little Mississippis.

*

It was a long, dark winter, the winter of 1984. During the day, people scurried from car to building. The streets were empty but for moving cars, their drivers muffled inside them. At night, no place felt warm and lit. Back in the fall, I had helped my friend Jean stack wood in her dirt cellar; all winter we burned it to keep warm, the flames yellow between us and the darkness. Even so, the black seeped in.

But when the sap began to run, the countryside seemed to let out a shiver and Jean put on her tall rubber boots and collected the buckets. She built a hot fire in her sugar shack and boiled the sap down from its thin, crystal clarity to a dark amber. That was the year her income was $850. Her mother had just died; she was living rent-free on a farm her father had bought as an investment. That spring, the sun glittered on the snow, and the sap pinged in buckets, and the snow ran in rivulets down the roads. At night, everything froze, stopped, halted; in the morning, it ran.

Jean and I had passed through adolescence in the sixties. We had traveled with the same crowd. It was a crowd that seemed too fast for me, that seemed to speak a different code from the one my friend Vickie and I used to speak, with flashlights between our bedroom windows. It was a crowd I had to run to catch up with. So I learned to flirt and tease and kiss, and by 1969, I was fifteen and had an eighteen-year-old boyfriend who was more innocent than I was. When his parents weren't home, we lay on the family room floor with our heads between two speakers, listening to Iron Butterfly and giving each other hickeys, carefully placed so our friends could see them when we wanted (pulling the necks of our t-shirts down) but we could hide them from our parents.

My boyfriend's older brother went to Woodstock; my big adventure was going to the drive-in movie with one of my new friends, who used all her worldly charms to get us a ride there, in for free, a car to watch from, and home again without our parents being any the wiser.

This was Jean. Jean, whose dad owned the local department store. Jean, one of the most popular girls in town. My friend. At fifteen, she was making buying trips to NYC and helping turn her dad into a millionaire. I envied her New York clothes, her blond hair, her body, her tough and knowing manner. I thought she had it made. I didn't know what she was hiding.

When I came back to the North Country in 1984, I found her living on a farm and selling off her New York clothes for money to buy groceries and used clothes for pennies at garage sales: wool jackets and denim pants and rubber boots for mucking out the barn. She had shucked herself of that earlier Jean like it was a cocoon, had emerged from it clean and complete, dun-colored but alive.

We were thirty, a time for confessions. All through that icy, dark winter she told me about the alcoholism and abuse that had shaped her childhood, leaving her both vulnerable and tough. The nights the cops came, the nights she spent in the emergency room. Since then, she'd gone through her quota of "romantic" relationships; a failed pregnancy had taken one of her ovaries; her mother had died. Yet that winter, she looked toward the future with her direct and clear gaze, writing vet school applications and trying to forgive her father and her mother for the past that wouldn't let her go.

I liked the life she had carved out for herself; I liked the farm. So, that summer I moved out there, and learned the difference between soil and dirt. Dirt, Jean told me, was what filled the cracks in the floor; dirt was what tracked itself in on your shoes. Dirt was dead and useless and in the wrong place. Soil, on the other hand, was what you got under your nails when you pulled weeds. Soil was what gave us the asparagus we cut with a sharp knife, the iris we put in a vase on the table. Soil was alive, full of potential. Even in the North Country, things could grow—if only you treated your soil right. It was a good lesson, a lesson I needed to learn.

Jean was a true North Country girl, or so my friend Carla would have said. Back when I first knew her, in college, Carla had written a song called "North Country Girl." I remember sitting in the coffee house she had started in the unused basement of one of the buildings, listening to her sing and watching her play, her steel-stringed guitar whining and twanging under an old aluminum maple-tree tap:

> *Now each North Country gal has many special secrets*
> *You may try to find them all through the night*
> *You may stay a long time wondering,*
> *searching for the reasons*
> *That her wisdom makes her your Northern light.*

A lot of my college friends held the North Country in something like contempt. They came from wherever they came from-Long Island, Connecticut, Massachusetts—and to them what we had seemed shoddy and pathetic. But others it got hold of and wouldn't let go. Carla was one of these. She came from Pennsylvania Dutch country, where she had grown up watching the Amish shape their lives around the land. She knew the difference between "shoddy" and "necessary," and she liked, I think, the idea of shaping her life around necessity.

So, when I came back in 1984, Carla was still there—making do, getting by. She had a North Country husband now, and two North Country kids, a boy who played hockey and a girl who liked to fish. Carla herself hunted deer in the fall, and was a pretty good shot. Put up jams and jellies and preserves out of her own garden. Had made a living painting houses for awhile, but now had a frame shop in the basement of the house, a house she and her husband had built together.

Pretty often I found myself sitting there in the shop's smell of hot glue while she mitered corners and cut mats and hammered nails. Her hair was short now, all business, and blonder than I remembered, like a yellow-white flame above her sharpshooter's quick eyes. She listened to my talk and diagnosed my loneliness and fixed me up now and again with someone she thought I'd like. She liked to play matchmaker, that was for sure. Maybe because it seemed easier to fix up someone else's love life than it was to fix her own.

Her husband Rick could be genial, when he wanted to be. He was good-looking and good with his hands, and smart—had a degree from a good school. But he was walking anger, looking for a place to put itself: walking bitterness, looking for something to sour. Who knew why? Maybe it was because he hadn't lived up to life's own expectations, or maybe it was because life hadn't lived up to his. He had everything he wanted, but maybe it had come too easy, or maybe he wasn't sure that it was what he wanted after all. Maybe part of it was that he worked for his father, so that nothing he ever had he'd really gotten on his own.

Carla never talked about it; she didn't need to. She wasn't writing songs anymore. And when he walked into the house, it was like a light went out in her. No matter what she did, it wasn't right, or right enough for him anyway. He yelled at her as if she were a child, and yelled at the kids as if they were animals—disobedient dogs. I don't think he even knew I was there, listening. Or cared if he did.

But Carla could not be kept down. All that winter she was hatching a scheme: to reunite our favorite college band at the reunion in May. Because it just happened I had once had a thing for the drummer, who was still single, she figured to kill two birds with one stone. And sure enough, after a few letters back and forth, I started seeing Dan, driving the five hours every other weekend or so. Carla was as pleased as a mother would be.

April came and preparations accelerated. The band would need instruments, amplifiers: Carla borrowed them. A place to play: Carla convinced a local bar-owner to set up a little stage. A place to stay: since I was living with Jean on the farm that summer, Jean got swept into the plans too, and the old farmhouse got itself swept and scrubbed and organized. It was that college coffee house all over again—music and people and plans, and Carla putting them all together.

Reunion Saturday at Connie's Bar and Grill. The place was jammed. Carla was in heaven, sitting in on a couple of songs. Rick stood by, drunk and glaring because she hadn't told him she was going to sing. But Carla hardly noticed him.

Then it was over. I have a picture somewhere, of me and Jean and Carla standing in Carla's driveway, waving goodbye to the last of our guests as they drove off.

The fall of '85, I went back to Mississippi. I knew from the moment I got there, from the moment I saw that orange clay dirt and those lodge-pole pines and felt that hot wet air on my face, that I couldn't stay. I needed to be up north, where I belonged.

Not long after, I left for good. Got married, moved to Vermont.

Jean's life moved on, too, though she stayed in the North Country. Vet school didn't work out, so she got her teaching license and a job. Bought her own place, over a hundred acres. Married a man who said he wanted to farm, but later changed his mind. Blamed her when things didn't go right. Left her when someone else came along, waking up one morning and taking with him things that both were and were not his.

Meanwhile, one day something someone said made Rick's anger boil up into a shove, and Carla got in the way of it. Her head hit a friend's garage door. Rick didn't mean to do it, he said, but Carla said that was too bad, and took the kids and left.

We stayed friends, Jean and I, Carla and I, Carla and Jean. One April, ten years after, the three of us had dinner together at Carla's house. With the bitter pride of survivors, they sat in the yellow light of Carla's kitchen and talked of their brand-new divorces, raking over the bad moments like farmers hoping to find one last potato in the soil. It made me think about the women who hadn't survived—Jean's mother, alcoholic and dead of cancer; my birth mother, who had shot herself years and years ago; all those women who suffered silently and alone in the dark houses as winter dug its chilly fingers into spring.

And I remembered one time that summer ten years before, when a bunch of us sat in my friend Hal's cabin, hidden back in the woods near Morley. Hal had a black walnut on the property, and other valuable trees; he didn't have electricity, but he had a phone. Jean was there, too; maybe even Carla was. Hal started teasing me about "yellow" and "rubber." He joked about how we should christen Jean's farm "The Yellow Rubber Ranch." Then the phone rang, and Hal answered it. "Yellow?" he said, to the person on the other end. I nearly passed out from laughter.

This was in the cabin at the bottom of a hill where, years before, for no knowable reason, Hal's last girlfriend had doused herself with gasoline and struck a match. In my mind's eye, the flames were yellow and all-consuming. A regular conflagration of the soul. A last laugh against the darkness.

That's the North Country for you, I thought.

Up north, they say that abuse of wives and children reaches its height during hunting season. It's as if the men—powerless the rest of the year long—get the taste of that killing power in their mouths and want more. Maybe that's to be expected in a place like this, a place where the land and the weather and the economy leave a man feeling vulnerable more often than not. Maybe, for a man, such a place permits only two kinds of survival: the fighting kind of Jean's father and Carla's husband, or Hal's hiding kind, living in the woods, alone. For women, also, there are two choices: all or nothing. Those who learn how to work it find the soil rich; for the rest, nothing grows.

Carla's writing songs again, after a long dry spell. And Jean's garden thrives, orderly and green. And all winter, yellow flames keep the night at bay.

> *There's a wood stove aburnin' in her house through the night*
> *and some hot stew to keep your inners warm*
> *You cry oh me, you cry oh lordy my*
> *And you'll see something flashing in her eyes*
> *Don't make yourself too comfortable next to her*
> *She will always be a North Country girl.*

*From "North Country Girl," a copyrighted song. The composer's name has been changed to protect her identity, as have the names of most other people mentioned.

An African in the Adirondacks
Growing up in the Fifties

Alice Paden Green

The moment is permanently etched in my memory: November 9, 1994, 10:50 A.M.

There I was, Alice Paden, reared in the Adirondacks of New York State, standing in the doorway of an old slave castle on Goree Island in Senegal, Africa. The November air was warm and moist. In the slight breeze, I could almost hear the agonizing sounds of my ancestors as they were hauled to the slave ships that would take them to America, never to return.

I slipped quietly away from my companion for a moment alone to commune with the spirit of my people, who had been taken from these shores so long ago. It was important to connect with them and think about the long personal journey that had brought me here and, in some respects, allowed them to return through me.

My thoughts quickly turned to Annie and William Paden, my parents, whose spiritual presence I felt. I wondered whether they had ever thought about this place, or if it was forbidden in their minds as it had always been in mine. I wondered what it must have been like for them to venture north from the South, where even in the mid-twentieth century they still felt enslaved, to search for a better life in Witherbee, New York, nestled far away in the Adirondack Mountains.

It was in Witherbee that I, one of few black children in the remote rural community, learned about race in America. Our isolation from other black children made us feel like aliens—inferior breeds, forever the "other people" who were ostracized from town folk in work and play.

At the same time, we found white neighbors on our street and church who have remained our friends to this day. Although we longed for the black communities we read of in *Ebony,* our isolation from the violence of Jim Crow America—the lynchings, the cross burnings—made us feel safe and protected. It was the Adirondacks that separated us from the world, and there, basking in the natural beauty of mountains, hills, and forests, I felt a security and serenity that I carry with me to this day.

Witherbee, New York: landscape of my childhood, landscape of tranquility, of rage, and despair. Although my journey to Africa seemed inevitable in 1994, nothing in my childhood in the fifties paved the way.

My parents seldom spoke to their children about the lives they led before they ended up in Witherbee. It was only after their deaths in 1970 that we—myself and my two sisters and three younger brothers—learned more details of their lives from our much older half-sister and from several other relatives and friends who had known them. There is so much we don't know and probably never will. But then, we do know that there was little time for talk of the past; they had enough on their hands coping with the many problems life presented them.

If only I could have known how important their life experiences, feelings, and beliefs would become to me, I would have listened more carefully to the little they shared, and begged for much more. But, it is much too late; they are gone.

In the late twenties my father, William Paden, then a young man, left South Carolina and went north to work in the iron ore mines and blast furnaces in Lyon Mountain and Standish, New York. Mr. Allen Walton, an elderly African American who lived, until recently, in Port Henry, New York, recalled meeting him there in 1929. He characterized my father as a loner who did his work, but was fond of traveling to New Jersey on occasion to visit a girlfriend.

After two years in Standish, the Depression hit, and evidently my father left the Adirondacks for Jersey City, New Jersey. His stay must have been brief, because my older half sister, Sadie, remembers meeting him when she was eight years old in Greenville, South Carolina. She and my mother, on the run from an abusive husband, had just moved there from Spartanburg, and had rented a room in the same boarding house in which my father was a guest.

Soon after their meeting, my father began to court my mother. Shortly thereafter, in 1939, Annie and Bill married and started their own family.

Frustrated by poor employment opportunities and fearful of the oppression of the Jim Crow South, my father decided to return to the Adirondacks where he believed he could make a better life for his family. His older brother, Herman, who lived in Port Henry, New York, had urged him to settle there.

Dad, a thin, dark, sad-eyed man of medium height, arrived in early 1948 and was lucky enough to get a job working in the iron ore mines with the Republic Steel Corporation in Witherbee, New York. But even in the North, life would bring him financial uncertainty and danger. Shortly after he started working there, the company cut back on hiring, because of stiff competition from Minnesota, where iron ore could be extracted more easily and at less expense. My father always lived under the specter of a possible layoff and never knew job security, despite the union.

Even worse, of course, were the risks inherent in the job. Cave-ins were a frequent occurrence. In fact, a few days before my mother and siblings and I arrived from South Carolina to join our father, a black man named Mr. Gambrel was crushed to death in a cave-in, leaving his wife to raise their several young children on her own.

The fact that our arrival in Witherbee coincided with this man's funeral must have troubled my mother greatly, but whatever fears she had, she kept to herself. I really don't know how she coped with the anxiety. Wherever you were in our small town you could hear the alarms that sounded from the mine when there had been a cave-in or, more benignly, whenever it was time for lunch. When you heard the sound you would check the clock, and if it was noon, you would sigh with relief and go on with your day. But if it was any other time, you would gather in front of the mine's "change house," or locker room, to find out what had happened, and to whom. That was how many a woman would discover her husband had been killed, or badly maimed.

Although we never openly discussed these dangers, I know that I internalized the worries looming over our family—over every miner's family—because to this day, I am often frightened by the sound of a fire alarm.

I was only seven when my mother packed up all her children and everything we owned to join our father in the North. In Philadelphia, we were joined by my half-sister Sadie, twenty-five, who had decided to accompany us north. My memory of the trip is sketchy. I have only a faded recollection of arriving in what seemed to be the middle of the night and experiencing the cold, brisk air, typical of August Adirondack nights.

Only the sound of my father's gentle but firm voice greeting us on the platform at the station in Port Henry was familiar .His co-worker from the mine, a Mr. Matthews, was waiting with his car. We all piled in—sleepy or asleep—to be driven to our new home, a rented company house on what was known as Spanish Settlement in Witherbee.

My family would live in Witherbee for the next twenty-two years, surviving as best we could in a small white community that seemed cut off from the rest of the world. No one understood who we were, we didn't even know ourselves.

Language differences proved to be an immediate barrier. People laughed at our speech. I remember my mother describing how difficult her first visit to the grocery store was, how she was met with noncomprehension when she tried to order "ice potatoes" and "light bread." No one understood what she wanted and it took what seemed forever to translate her request for "Irish, or white, potatoes and a loaf of bread."

In the South, she was so accustomed to sweet potatoes and biscuits or cornbread that she thought she had to specify what she wanted. And, she tried, in the only language she knew.

There would be other practical, domestic difficulties. Mother found—as we would later—that in white, rural communities, the consumer needs of blacks go unmet. Items such as cosmetics, stockings, and hair products were unsuited to our complexion and hair texture; even "flesh-colored" band aids were made for white skin. Certain favored foods were also hard to come by. As a result, we grew our own collards and turnip greens.

My mother tried to help us overcome our feeling of isolation by seeking out the other black families living in the area. Only one other family, the Twilleys—a married couple and their young son—lived on our street. Much to her surprise, she learned that another black family of four lived only a couple of miles away, but they seemed unfriendly, wanting to remain to themselves. She later discovered a family of four, the Daltons, and another of five, the Bullocks, in Grover Hills several miles to the south.

Her search uncovered approximately ten other black families six miles away in Port Henry. Our father had introduced us to Mr. Matthews, the fellow mine-worker who had picked us up at the train station our first night. He introduced us to the Garrisons, the Gambrels, the Waltons, the Gateses, and the Hagoods.

My uncle Herman Paden and his new family of three lived in Port Henry, with several others that I never got to know. Strangely, they all lived on Elizabeth Street in close proximity to each other. The male head of each family worked in the mines. Most were related, and a number had emigrated from Greenville.

The small African American community in Port Henry tried to identify itself as such by starting a small church. Enlisting the services of Reverend Matthews from Albany, they were able to hold worship at least once each month in a small, shotgun-style wooden building located on Elizabeth Street.

If I remember correctly, the little church survived for several years. It was a place where my family could really be ourselves, and we went as regularly as possible. Because of the church's connections to Albany, black choirs would come through from time to time. We loved the music, loved how expressive it was. The black church was really the only thing we had in our lives that was reminiscent of our years in the South, and this was tremendously important to my mother. I was baptized in this church, along with all the other children in my family.

Unfortunately, the six-mile journey to this welcoming black church was difficult for us, because we had no car. Sometimes we got rides from Nathaniel Hagood, a widower with four children who soon after our arrival began courting my half-sister Sadie. She eventually married him, which worked out well for them, but the rest of our family was still stuck in Witherbee, where we were close to my father's job. Even if transportation hadn't been an obstacle for us, we would have still had to have made other arrangements, because the minister could only get away from Albany to the church in Port Henry about once a month. We would have to make do with the churches closer to home.

Religion was important to my mother. She, who had been brought up in a Methodist church co-founded by her grandmother in Taccoa, Georgia, was determined to raise us in the same manner. The problem for us was that Witherbee was a decidedly Catholic town. There was only one Protestant church, the Mineville Presbyterian, and soon we were all members—all except my father, that is, as organized religion was not a part of his life.

The church served as a much-needed source of friends and supporters. My mother was active in the "Ladies' Club," and all the kids attended Sunday School every week. We sang in the church choir, participated in the youth club, assisted at church suppers, and attended church picnics.

Our membership in the Protestant church also had its cost. We soon learned that being Protestant in a Catholic town would make us feel like outsiders in yet another way. Great reverence was paid to the priest, who had significant influence on the social life of the community. Among other things, he decided which films were inappropriate for showing at the Port Henry movie theater, and he selected the Friday luncheon menu at the school cafeteria. Later, some of our Catholic friends would taunt us with charges of heathenism because we were non-Catholic. Soon the pervasive influence of Catholicism caused us to feel that there was something else, besides race, that was wrong with us.

Nonetheless, we were overjoyed to feel a real part of a church family. Members drove us cheerfully and willingly to and from church, and when we were desperate for money and food—especially during the occasional union strikes that closed the mines—the church and its members always came to our rescue. One of the nicest gestures of all came when I graduated from high school and needed money to attend college. Five church families pooled their resources to help finance my first year.

From the time we arrived, the Mineville Presbyterian Church was a place of solace and support. We would soon need the support more than my parents could have ever anticipated.

After we had barely settled into our new environment, my father became the second black victim of a mining accident when his legs were badly crushed by an iron ore trolley car. For nearly a year, he was in the hospital. I don't know how my mother managed—caring for the six of us, finding rides to the hospital to be with her husband, and somehow keeping us financially afloat. I remember that the union would bring food and clothing during the holidays, but mostly, we had to depend on welfare.

Luckily, the company physician, old Doc Cummings, used his legendary skills to wire Dad's legs back together. After months of hospitalization and physical therapy, he could walk again. His injury prevented his return to mining, so he was given a job caring for the change house at the mine, perhaps the lowest-paying position in the company.

This meant that our childhood years in Witherbee would be heavily burdened not only by race and religion, but poverty as well. Of the three, race proved to be the greatest burden to bear.

I still regret that I did not have more conversations with my father. On weekdays, he focused only on carrying out what he viewed as his responsibility as a man and father—work and disciplining of the children when necessary. Weekends were devoted to beer drinking—a favorite sport in the Adirondacks—but we were glad that he did most of his drinking at home rather than in the bars favored by most. Alcohol made him lucid, animated, and easy to talk to. We found him to be brilliantly witty and insightful. But his loneliness and anger, particularly when it came to the frequent racial jokes and condescending attitude he encountered at work, made him bitter.

Almost by default, my mother, a stout woman with fair, brown skin and an engaging smile, became the family stalwart. Content with her role as wife and mother, she committed herself to the care of my father and, most importantly, the protection of her children from the pain she knew they would experience in a white community. When we started school, she took us there and enlisted our teachers in her campaign to protect us. When we were called "nigger" she fought our battles, and, when we cried, she cried with us. In her effort to make us "fit in," she tried to ensure that we had what was needed to participate fully in the life of the school. If a school pageant called for costumes, she struggled to make them. As fads in clothes changed, she would take on a housecleaning job to purchase what she could. In later years, I convinced her that I needed a typewriter, which we could ill afford. But, she bought it on the installment plan, paying one dollar a week from a cleaning job.

After a while, several of our classmates, now accustomed to our presence, became friendly. But others—including the adults we met—remained cold or else tactlessly curious about our physical differences. They would often stare, and they frequently bombarded us with questions about our skin color and hair texture. "Do you get tan? Do you sunburn? Does your hair grow? Why is it greasy?" Although these questions often represented innocent curiosity, they set us apart and caused us to feel different and inferior.

Hair was especially problematic for the female members of the family, as it has been historically for Black Americans since enslavement. "Good hair,"—that is, "naturally straight hair"—

was more valued, since it is a characteristic more closely related to the dominant culture's white standard of beauty. Unfortunately, my sisters and I had kinky hair that Mother straightened with a hot comb, teaching us how to maintain "the big secret" about our natural hair from whites. Not even our closest friends knew. In preparation for the bi-monthly ordeal of washing and straightening our hair, which could take three hours for each of us, we went so far as to lock the doors of our home to ensure that no white person entered unannounced during that time.

Mother also trained us in the art of keeping our hair moisture-free after straightening to prevent a reversion to the natural state which she feared would cause us embarrassment. We were taught to always be prepared in the event of rain by carrying protective gear, such as a scarf. Plastic scarves were at a premium. Sweating was to be avoided at all costs, and swimming was allowed only if we could manage to keep our hair dry. The latter proved to be a great source of anxiety as well as a real handicap when it came to enjoying water sports. Each summer, we attended our school's summer recreation program, which included afternoon swimming at Lincoln Pond. Although we wanted very much to learn to swim and play in the water with our classmates, we knew it would be forbidden. Therefore, in order to hide our secret, we would find some excuse for not participating. Occasionally we would walk into the pond to wet our swimsuits and then pretend that we had been swimming. Sometimes we were forced into the water for swimming lessons, but we resolutely refused to put our heads in the water. As a result of all of this, my sisters and I never quite learned to swim.

In retrospect, many of our efforts at deception about our hair seem silly, but at the time they were necessary protective devices. It was the fifties in Upstate New York, and none of us—includeing our parents—knew who we were and whom we were allowed to be. Although we made an attempt to assimilate, we soon realized that it was not possible for us as it had been for all the white immigrant groups that made up the town's population.

We were certain of one thing: we looked different than the rest of the people in town, and they saw that difference as a mark of inferiority, which we were in danger of internalizing. Mother did what came instinctively to her, protecting us from those who had the power to irreparably damage our delicate psyches.

Mother continued to monitor our treatment in the schools, including the quality of the instruction we were receiving. She was usually the first parent to arrive on Parents' Night, hungry for a progress report on her children. When we were all enrolled, the duty became heavy, for there were six of us in as many classes, all separated by one year.

There were my sisters Geraldine and Joan and our younger brothers: William, known as "Duke," Ralph, and the baby, Clyde.

Of course, there were so many things Mother couldn't keep watch over or protect us from. We each had to learn to deal with school life, in our own way. Generally, we each managed to adjust to being the lone black kid in our class, but often, particularly in elementary school, our teachers seemed especially insensitive to the situations and circumstances that were most difficult for us.

For instance, at the beginning of each school year, the teacher would ask each student to verbally identify the country of his or her ancestry. Being an iron ore town, Witherbee had been a magnet for immigrants looking for work in the mines since the turn of the century, and my classmates took pride in their European roots. While they would proudly proclaim—one after the other—their relationship to Poland, Russia, Spain, Canada, France, and Italy, I could hear my heart pounding and feel my body shaking with fear.

What could I say? I really didn't know where I was from. But if I mentioned Africa, everyone would laugh. That was the land of darkness, jungles, animals, and black savages. What if someone made some wise crack about Tarzan?

Often I would try to slide down into my seat, hoping to be passed over or forgotten. But, when my turn came, I could feel all those anxious eyes fixed on me and I would utter in a barely audible sound, "Africa." Sometimes they'd all laugh, but even when they didn't, I still felt humiliated and cheated—cheated, because I didn't come from one of those nice European countries.

There were, in spite of the racial barriers, several teachers who recognized and respected my intelligence and appeared sensitive to the difficulties that I was experiencing as a black youth in a white community. Their reach went far beyond the school and into my family and community life. Among them, James Sotis, a tall, athletic man with intense yet smiling eyes had, perhaps, the most positive and lasting impact on me and my brothers—particularly Ralph, who benefited greatly from his guidance both in school and on the basketball court. Just as he had promised, James Sotis attended my college graduation ceremony. To this day, he remains a loyal and close friend.

Those few kind people notwithstanding, neither my textbooks nor teachers addressed the issue of race throughout my schooling. Only an occasional reference—usually in the context of slavery—was made to blacks, or Negroes, as we were known in the fifties. At times, however, an obligatory brief acknowledgment was given to the two Negroes thought to have made the most significant contribution to America: Lena Horne and Jackie Robinson. Since I depended upon whites for my validation as a person, those brief positive references, flawed as they were, caused me to sit tall and beam with pride.

Nevertheless, the lingering message to my classmates and me was that the talents of those two Negroes represented the only significant contributions African Americans had made to this country. It was much later before I understood why only a singer and an athlete could be thought to be palatable at the time.

Racism continued to figure prominently in our lives. Although expressed more often in subtle rather than overt fashion, my classmates communicated their beliefs about our innate inferiority in a variety of fashions—from their occasional use of a mocking southern twang in our presence, to their obvious reluctance to physically touch us and their quickness to wipe their hands when they did, to their "slips of the tongue" and compulsory apologies for using the word "nigger."

My sisters and brothers and I would discuss these behaviors when we got home from school and sat together, safe around the dinner table. Although such treatment served to unify us as a family, each member reacted differently and developed his or her own strategies for coping. I was more inclined to internalize my anger and protest in silence by withdrawing socially, yet I stubbornly refused to engage in behaviors thought to validate negatively held stereotypes of blacks. So disturbing did I find the widely held belief that blacks were inherently inferior intellectually, that I embarked upon a self-proclaimed mission to prove it fallacious to everyone, including myself. Already considered gifted by some, I sought to offer myself as evidence that this stereotype was utterly wrong.

To fulfill my mission, I enrolled in a full range of extracurricular activities, maintained a perfect attendance record throughout my school career, and carried out a program of discipline and study. Yet, although I graduated as salutatorian of my class, I proved little to myself in the end. Having learned from a Eurocentric perspective that ignored and devalued the intellectual achievements of blacks, and having lived in a community that included no significant role models for me, it would take years for me to gain a degree of confidence in my own intellectual ability.

If it was difficult to feel comfortable at school, navigating through the social world outside of school was almost impossible. Many of the classmates who befriended us at school did not extend their friendship beyond the school yard. Rarely, if ever, was an invitation extended for birthday parties, sleep-overs, or other occasions.

As we reached adolescence, the social distance widened. Interracial dating was out of the question, which was particularly difficult for the girls in my family. Had we grown up in a community with more black families, my sister and I would have had an easier time finding boyfriends who would treat us with appreciation and respect. My sisters were tall and thin and very attractive and outgoing, and they could have had their pick of boys in the South. I was shorter, chunkier, shyer—more of a bookworm than they were, and not exactly a magnet for boys, which made my experience in Witherbee all the more trying.

Not only did we have no one in our neighborhood to date, but my sisters and I were often forced to fight off surreptitious sexual advances brought on by those who believed the stereotype that black females were sexually loose. Thus, gender added another dimension to the problems I faced growing up in the Adirondacks.

As high school teenagers, my sisters and I had to look elsewhere for available black males. In my junior year, intense anxiety built up over the impending junior prom. Luckily, we discovered the Plattsburgh Air Force Base, with its cadre of young black men from across the country who were equally anxious to meet black women. We found ourselves in the enviable position of having our pick of dates for the event. Under the glare of the entire town, my sisters and I, decked out in our gowns, entered the high school gym escorted by three black men in uniform.

Needless to say, we were the talk of the town. Although we won the battle, we felt that we lost the war. Racism would never allow us to experience what we wanted most: "normal" social relationships with our peers, both boys and girls.

There was, however, one advantage to being female in those years: no one ever tried to beat me up. The racist acts inflicted on my brothers were much more overt. On a number of occasions, Duke and Ralph were physically attacked, sometimes by mobs.

Although our position in the town was shaky, our immediate neighborhood was hospitable. On Spanish Settlement, we lived in one of the mining company's four-family housing units that were constructed during the early part of the century from bricks made of gray iron ore tailings. One of the families in our unit was the Sharrows. They had six children, two of whom had already joined the Air Force. We became fast friends with the remaining four—twin girls, Margaret and Myrtle, and their two older brothers, Alton, or "Haircut," and Roger, better known as "Tinker."

What was especially nice about our friendship with them was that we had something to offer in return: the warmth of our family. This made us value what we had as a family and made us feel more like anyone's equal. Mr. Sharrow and his wife were not physically demonstrative with each other or with their children. Mr. Sharrow was a quiet, reserved, and reclusive man while my father, in contrast, was high-spirited and witty, quick to put people at ease and make them laugh. The Sharrow kids spent most of their weekends at our house, where they felt freer to express themselves than they did at home.

Mrytle and Margaret Sharrow were probably my best friends, but we would learn as we got older that our interracial friendships would present obstacles we couldn't easily surmount.

Although life in Witherbee was often difficult, the town's location gave me a serenity and a feeling of security that helped me survive. Nestled in the beautiful mountains, rolling hills, and those ugly gray piles of iron ore tailings, I felt shut off and protected from an outside world that all of us in Witherbee—black or white—perceived as harsh. I spent a lot of time by myself and enjoyed the feelings of peaceful contemplation that isolation sometimes brings.

Late summer would find me wandering alone in the hills and bushes near my home to pick blackberries. It was a productive exercise that provided my mother with berries for cooking, and me with solitude—and the opportunity to let my mind wander and imagine what the outside world was like.

Few of the town's people ever left, and even fewer came into Witherbee from the outside. The only black people who came to town were the seasonal workers we sometimes invited into our home—in the summer, the domestic workers who worked for vacationers in places like Westport, and during the fall, the apple pickers who worked in Crown Point or near Elizabethtown. Except for the few occasions when a black choir or basketball team would come to the area to perform in places like Port Henry or Ticonderoga, we had little contact with other blacks.

All I knew about the world, I learned from reading magazines. I spent hours poring over photographs of beautiful, pampered white starlets and dashing, handsome actors who fell in love, divorced, and attended lavish parties. Occasionally, an old copy of *Ebony* or *Jet* magazine would come my way, and they provided me with some images of black people. Although the people pictured in *Ebony* looked more like us, they also seemed a lot like the people in the movie magazines. But *Jet* was a little different. Sometimes it carried pictures and stories that frightened me. By far, the most frightening and disturbing was one done in 1955 about Emmett Till, a fourteen-year-old black boy from Chicago who was beaten to death by white men while visiting Mississippi.

"What kind of world is it out there," I wondered, "that would allow such a horrible thing to happen to someone who looked like my brothers?" Although my family and I were deeply disturbed, the rest of the town seemed completely oblivious to the nightmare that had taken place in Mississippi, yet entered our world as a reminder of what white Americans could do to blacks with impunity. We were grateful to be hidden from the lynchmen of the South by the Adirondacks.

Early television contributed to my limited and distorted view of life on the outside. We first viewed it surreptitiously, through the windows of the few homes in our neighborhood with sets in the early fifties. This new medium brought some of the black personalities from the pages of *Ebony* and *Jet* to life for us; any scheduled television appearance of a black person became a must for the entire family. At the appointed time, we would gather together, at first at a neighbor's house and in later years at our own, to share the moment. We cared little about who the performers were, as long as they were black. Yet the experience left undisturbed my view of a limiting world out there, defined for blacks by white America.

Left to my thoughts, I pictured America as a huge, segregated land controlled by whites who were innately superior to all others. Those blacks who were thought deserving were allowed to engage in certain defined activities. To me, this meant that much of America was off-limits to most blacks. Care must therefore be given to what you said and did in the presence of whites.

As the Civil Rights Movement began to unfold in the South, I noticed that my schoolmates and other Adirondacks neighbors looked upon racial segregation and discrimination as uniquely southern problems. For the most part, they denied or ignored the institutionalized racism and discrimination that existed right under their own noses in almost every segment of their lives.

Perhaps the most vicious form of racism my family members experienced in Witherbee was employment discrimination. The tourist business—where all my white acquaintances got summer jobs—was the worst employer of all.

As teenagers, we eagerly sought employment opportunities to earn needed income for the family. Our parents were engaged in a difficult struggle to provide for our basic needs; strikes and dwindling demand for the iron ore caused layoffs and contributed to a worsening economic climate throughout the area. Conditions were so depressed that we were forced to accept welfare assistance. Housecleaning was the only after-school work I could get.

The summer I turned fifteen, I embarked upon a serious job search, determined to become a chambermaid in one of the tourist motels. I was confident because a number of my classmates had worked at motels in Lake George, Schroon Lake, and Westport the year before. A few had found jobs at Frontiertown or worked as waitresses and made what seemed a fortune in tips. Even then, however, I intuitively sensed that waitressing jobs were reserved for whites.

After a difficult search, my neighborhood friend Myrtle Sharrow and I landed jobs as chambermaids at Clautice's Restaurant and Motel, located in Paradox, New York. We were hired by the owner and manager, Mrs. Clautice. During the winter months, she and her husband and two daughters lived in Florida. Each year they came north to manage their tourist business. They also arranged for their loyal black chef and his kitchen assistant wife to come from Florida as well and to work in the restaurant.

The motel property included a large white two-story main building that housed the restaurant, a reservations office, and the private living quarters of the Clautice family. Behind the main house sat a dreary-looking barn-like structure, with the second floor divided into several rooms by thin partitions. Each of the rooms included a bed. A common toilet and washbasin were located at the far end of the second floor. Guest cottages were on a hill across the street from the main house.

Myrtle and I arrived the evening before we were to begin work. She and I had been close friends for most of our lives, and were happy over the prospect of living and working together for the summer. Mrs. Clautice greeted us and explained our work assignments and the lodging arrangements. Much to our dismay, she informed us that we could not live together. The reason? Myrtle was white and I was black. Myrtle would stay in the family's private living quarters and I would have to stay in the back building. We protested, but she was adamant.

When I was taken to my living quarters, I discovered that I would be housed in the barn-like structure with the chef and his wife and another black kitchen aide. The other employees—the waitresses and bartenders, all white—were housed in either the Clautices' living quarters in the big white house or in one of the guest cottages across the street.

Adding insult to injury, I was instructed never to be seen on the lawn in front of the main building.

Demeaned and confused about how to fight back, I went to my room. Since my assigned housemates worked during the evening hours, I was alone. Frightened and angry, I decided to go to bed with the light on and think about what to do. Soon, sharp squeaky sounds caught my attention. Scanning the room in fright, I caught sight of scores of tiny creatures lined up on the ceiling beams. Occasionally, one or several of them would fly across the room, spreading their large wings. Panic-stricken, I cried out for help; "Bats!" I shouted, but there was no response.

To me, bats were blood sucking creatures that lived in deep dark caves, flew around graveyards, and became entangled in your hair. After what seemed an eternity, my housemates came in after a long night of work. I jumped out from under the bedding and ran to report the presence of the evil bats. They responded with a brief and tired giggle, quickly dismissed me, and went to bed, leaving me alone to deal with my fear and anger.

Exhausted after a sleepless and fearful night and outraged at the segregated work force and the inferior living arrangements for the workers of color, I pondered the situation throughout the following day. Earning money was vital, and if the other blacks were willing to endure the conditions for the money, why shouldn't I be? Still, I knew I couldn't remain silent. I had to confront Mrs. Clautice about the conditions, and I chose to do so in the presence of everyone.

I unleashed my rage with great force. Trembling with anger and uncertainty, I loudly and commandingly denounced her and her racist practices and proclaimed that I was a human being who wanted to be treated like one.

My frenzied outpouring prompted her to interject just two words: "You're fired." Somehow, I managed a weak smile and proclaimed, "Too late, I already quit."

Myrtle, a loyal friend as always, left with me at once. I arrived home with no job, and no prospect of finding another. My mother seemed disappointed, but I hoped that she understood how much I had been hurt. I went back to the hills to find solace and pick blueberries and blackberries. With no money, I was unable to afford new school clothes, but returned to school with a new sense of self and pride that came from the rejection of enslavement. The experience with the bats caused me to develop a life-long phobia, but the decision to stand up for what I believed was right has served me well.

My brothers encountered even more vicious and brutal racism and discrimination in the resort business. Duke remains extremely angry and bitter over the harsh treatment and discrimination he suffered at the old Sagamore Hotel, where he was forced to work long hours in the worst positions for little pay. Only recently have Duke and Ralph been able to share the pain they endured while working in the resort hotels and recreation camps of the Adirondacks during the late fifties and early sixties.

Segregation, Emmett Till, Montgomery, Little Rock, and sit-ins resonated through my mind as I prepared to graduate as salutatorian of my class. I could almost feel the turmoil and social upheaval in store for the world outside in the sixties. While it is true that everyone who knew me expected that I would attend college, I was fearful and extremely reluctant to leave Witherbee. There was also a matter of money: I had none. Nevertheless, I left with a promise to myself that I would manage somehow and return with a college degree to the relative safety of the Adirondack mountains and the hills I had come to love so much. It was also my intention to stay near my family and provide the support they needed.

Before I had enrolled at the State Teachers' College in Albany, my youngest brother, Clyde, was killed in a car crash. His death was devastating to us all, but Mother would never really recover from the loss. His death made me even more hesitant about school, but friends and fellow church members encouraged me. Financial as well as moral support from the latter convinced me to proceed with my original plan.

Rejecting the enticement of the larger world and my new college friends, I headed home with a teaching certificate in hand. I was determined to find a teaching job in my hometown. I quickly applied for an opening at Mineville High School, my alma mater. Much to my dismay, every attempt to apply was blocked—without explanation. After accepting the fact that racial discrimination was destroying my dream of returning to Witherbee, I left with an anger that ignited a spirit of rebellion within me.

My anger intensified as I learned more about the history of black oppression in this country. Fortunately, that anger has been channeled and used in constructive ways throughout my adult life. It has also been a force that has pushed me to discover who I am, where I came from, and the impact life in the Adirondacks had on my development as a person with a strong sense of justice and compassion.

My parents and brother Clyde are buried in the Adirondacks. Their spirit, and a new sense of personal peace, draw me back frequently. With the help and inspiration of my husband, Charles, I purchased and rehabilitated our family home, which was in great disrepair.

Each year my brothers and sisters, their families, and our lifelong friends, the Sharrows, convene in Witherbee. We sit around a campfire and reminisce about days gone by. There is a lot of laughter about the good times and the bad. Now middle-aged, we are still struggling to confirm our identity.

I've been especially lucky to have continued my education, worked in urban communities, and traveled. Each of these achievements has helped me understand who I am. I have also been lucky to have found a few loyal friends along the way, like the Sharrows. I feel much freer now, and I have long since stopped straightening my hair. But to be truly liberated, I knew that I had to go to Africa, the land I feared for so long.

No words can ever adequately describe the euphoria I experienced as the black-piloted Air Afrique plane landed on Senegalese soil. I had arrived by way of Witherbee, New York, a long and often painful journey.

As I stood on Goree Island, I remembered those mornings in the school in Witherbee when I was ashamed to whisper what I now proudly proclaim: I am African!

Groceries

Tam Lin Neville

I don't know why, but the story I want to tell about growing up in the Adirondacks begins with Tony Galiano, who owned and ran a grocery store on Third Avenue in New York City. Manhattan was the other place I grew up in, going to P.S. 40 during the school year, and after school, alternately loving and hating my friends and siblings in and out of the crowded apartment we lived in.

Tony worked around the corner from our building, on Third Avenue, under the elevated train when it was still going, and then next to the relatively quiet roar of cars after the tracks were torn down. He loved the business of selling food to people, and his store had the atmosphere of a kitchen you could walk into at any time without hesitation. When I came in to buy candy, I felt he was both conspirator and parent, someone who took delight in my purchase of a large round mint wrapped in silver foil, but someone who would also stop me from buying five.

"One is enough for today," he'd say.

Tony was always home, unlike my father, a newspaper man who worked long hours every day, sometimes even going in on Sunday. In his absence, my mother raised five children, plus myriad cats and dogs, almost single-handedly. She always said if crisis came upon her, she would go to Tony first.

I begin in this roundabout way because of the particular inclusive atmosphere of his store. It wasn't Gristede's, which only Gramercy Park people could afford. But the vegetables and chicken were fresher at Tony's, and the people with maids and doormen would go to his store also, along with everyone else—those who lived in dark one-room apartments under the El, the Puerto Ricans whose numbers grew as you got closer to 14th Street.

Of course, in New York, the lines are not always clear. The bag lady collecting cans may be an heiress; the kid smashing bottles against a lamppost might grow up to be a famous basketball player.

There was a Puerto Rican boy I went to school with, named Junior, who used to do delinquent things in school like lighting fires in waste baskets—things which thrilled and terrified the "good" kids, filling us with envy and curiosity. I would be romanticizing the situation if I said that Junior was a friend, someone who might come home to play after school. He was not. Neither was he a threat; rather, another facet in the world of the fantastic I grew up in. (On any given day, you might see a woman walking with an iguana on her shoulder or a man coming down the street in a skirt.)

New York's troubles in the fifties weren't what they are now. Drugs, and their attendant crimes and fears, hadn't split the city so dramatically between the "haves" and the "have-nots," and for us growing up there, the world was an unpredictable, heady, yeasty mixture of things.

Then, overnight, everything would change. Each July we were herded into the old Chevy to begin the eight-hour trip to Keene Valley, a small town in the middle of the Adirondack Mountains. In the early days we set off at night, when there were fewer of us and three children could sleep side by side in the back of a station wagon.

When we arrived groggy in the morning, the valley was full of air and flowers and early northern sun, cool and aloof. We stepped out of the car into the big meadow of long grass, black-eyed Susans, daisies, and Indian paint brushes, with bluets and wild strawberries down in closer to the ground. In the middle of the field stood the brooding three-story summer house that had come down to us through my grandfather. The windows were shuttered and the porch was strewn and drifted with leaves.

After the euphoria of arrival wore off, it was time to open the house, sweep out mouse and chipmunk droppings, squabble over who would get what room, and grudgingly unpack our things. Then, finally, it was time to go to town for our first ice cream cone of the season. My father, whose job didn't allow him much time with us, loved this ceremony. Of course, I did, too. But as I got older and my peripheral vision widened, I began to feel the strangeness of the virtually unchanging, well-kept town of Keene Valley, its one street, tidy and clean, so radically different from those I was growing up in.

The townspeople who greeted us were often more wary than welcoming, guarded and dour as though they wished winter would go on forever or, at least, that they might find some way to by-pass this season's influx of people who came here to "summer."

Our family came, for two months out of every year, to play, not work. We swam, fished, and went up mountains. My siblings and I spent most of our time at the Keene Valley Country Club. A five-minute walk through the woods and over the bridge brought us to the club grounds set opposite the Post Office, local bar, and grocery store, between the town's main street and the river.

"The Club," as we called it, had been started by a wealthy summer person, a woman who wanted to keep her husband healthily occupied and away from alcohol. It had a swimming pool with a slide, a diving board, and high dive. There were six clay tennis courts, two bathhouses, a clubhouse with kitchen, a pool room, a piano, and a gathering room. Tea was served in the summer every Tuesday, Thursday, and Saturday at four in the afternoon. Adults sat inside in the big round room, its east side a long curve of windows overlooking the Ausable River. Children were to stay on the porch. We would come, barely dressed and still wet and blue from the pool, to drink juice and see if we could somehow steal more than the two-cookie limit.

One of the magical things about having so much to do is that this allowed us, sometimes, to do nothing. Our house is surrounded by a deep porch. As an adult, I've kept my childhood habit of spending long hours in the afternoon reading, and sometimes just gazing out, from one of its old Saranac chairs. But my old dreaminess is almost gone. The wariness of the townspeople, which lies subdued—hidden just under the surface—is no longer an invisible presence I can ignore. I know that while I am sitting and dreaming on the porch, by the river, or in my study in the attic, others are working overtime during this season.

But as a child, I didn't see this. I wondered what the muted atmosphere was that lay over the streets of the town. Once, we came to the valley during hunting season. Outside the local bar, in the gray November rain, two dead deer hung upside down by their ankles. I felt we were intruding on another world, one that was forbidding and austere. I wanted to go home and come back again when it was summer and we could swim and pick blueberries.

What could be wrong in this place, where every summer we built dams and swam naked in the river, slept outside, ran in the rain, climbed trees and mountains? Even rainy days had their own store of resources, things we hadn't thought of in weeks. Sometimes we built a fire, or made brownies or penuche. Once we caught a chipmunk in a suitcase. In the laundry room there was a hand wringer. At lunchtime we'd put sandwich bread through the rollers, turning it back into dough, then roll it up with jelly.

We fought about who got to use the old swing that hung over the attic stairs. The full attic, terrifying by night, was full of possibilities by day. We made a clubhouse in one of the rooms and painted the walls with ghoulish faces. From a fairly unchanging group of cousins and other summer kids, we made lists of who was in—and who was out—of our clan that season.

The swing is still there; when my daughter uses it, the rub and creak of the ropes on the wooden railing sound exactly as they did when I was a child. When I hear it, time collapses for a moment: I'm ten, and there are no intervening years.

When we got bored at home, we'd walk or beg a ride down the road to the Country Club. In the clubhouse, I'd play chopsticks on the piano with my cousin or lose myself in a game of pool, chalking the cue with one of those intriguing blue cubes, slipping it between my fingers, leaning over the table, feeling the thrill of focus. I'd beat my brother in eight ball and get beaten the next game around.

Through all these escapades, I felt I had the run of the valley, as though it were an Edenic playground set down on the earth for my pleasure. My siblings and I entered it every summer with an almost cruel innocence. Like most children, we were quick to recognize and secretly endorse class differences. We scrutinized any child we saw, on the lookout for proof that ours was the better, more enviable position. We noted details of dress, food, and dwelling, keenly observing them and storing them away: He rides a second-hand bike; she doesn't have the "cool" kind of sneakers; he's got peanut butter on bunny bread for a sandwich. Observations like these reinforced our primitive sense of hierarchy.

On rainy days, we sometimes played with the children of the owner of the local dry goods store, a man my father became friends with because both were passionate fishermen. His kids were ideal playmates—inventive, down to earth, ready for anything. They liked to come to our rambling old house, which had plenty of room to run around in. Those days passed quickly and saved us from the oppressive, brooding skies that sometimes hung over the valley for weeks at a time. Still, I knew that they would always be "townies" and not friends, unlike the kids we played with at the Country Club where we spent most of our time. And I'm sure that I let this awareness slip somewhere in the course of the day, in the form of one of those savagely snobbish remarks children are capable of: "How come your mother works at the gas station? Where'd you get those sneakers? No, I don't want to play with your doll. She doesn't have real hair."

Now as an adult, I see things less clearly. This summer, my husband and I and a visiting friend went canoeing on Saranac Lake. Since we do this rarely, what would have been a simple operation became a three-hour production. It took us that long to locate and assemble the right equipment: paddles buried under leaves in the shed, life jackets "somewhere" (last seen three years ago), sunblock, hats, rope to tie the canoe down to the top of the car. It took so long that we began making up a stream of obscene names for the boy scout knots we couldn't remember how to tie. When we started down the driveway and the canoe swung drunkenly over the windshield, we collapsed laughing, inebriated with Adirondack air and our own ineptness.

Finally, when we were on the lake, surrounded by waterlilies and stillness, I said to my husband, "What luxury to have half a day to *waste* on getting ready to play."

We also spent a lot of time hiking in the mountains around Keene Valley. The blueberries on the ridges were especially lush this year, hanging in almost grape-like clusters. Their clouded blue was all the more astonishing for its unobtrusiveness, set against the gray rock and green of the stunted mountain bushes. On this particular day, my husband and I were with newly married friends; as we picked and ate our way over these stretches, we commented on the bear scat at intervals in the path, deep purple with digested berries, the seeds already well on their way back into the ground. Everything seemed to breath an air of northern ripeness and fertility.

We returned from the day's long climb to drink beer and eat on our porch: steak, salad, corn, and blueberry cobbler for dessert. Leaning back, I found myself caught in all the contradictions of my pleasure-loving soul, happy yet embarrassed, trying and not succeeding to feel more guilty than I do.

When I went into the valley grocery the next day for more provisions, these duplicities hung in a cloud over my cart. I love to shop in this small store, but there are times when I want to disappear or at least shrink to the size of a fly on the wall: when the wealthy dowager plows down my aisle to greet a friend in a booming voice, oblivious to everything around her, as though the store were her living room; when a tan summer kid runs into the store, reaches into the freezer for a popsicle and, without glancing up at the long line, slaps a quarter down on the counter, eager to get back to his friends.

And there is the pasta salad, salmon, and feta cheese (all imported for the summer population) in my own shopping cart—groceries I wish were invisible, things I would like to say I don't need, but I do.

Mohawk Women Remember: Growing Up Akwesasne

Interviews by Randall T. G. Hill

During the winter of 1994, I had the pleasure of teaching a course on the St. Regis Mohawk Reserve. The forty-mile drive on winter evenings took me from the snow-covered rolling hills of Canton, New York, where I taught speech and theatre at St. Lawrence University, to a northern point on the St. Lawrence Seaway valley. This place between countries and between cultures somehow more quietly embraces the snow and the people.

The Reserve, split by the St. Lawrence River and surrounded by Ontario, Quebec, and New York was experiencing strained relations between the people of Akwesasne— "Land Where the Partridge Drums"—and her international neighbors. The source of the strained relations include the gambling casinos and the emergence of cigarette smuggling.

During my discussions with the people there, both in the classroom and outside of it, we talked about Mohawk lifeways, performance and ritual, and intersections between my tribal tradition (Lumbee) and their beliefs. Over time, it became clear to me that the antagonisms between the people of Akwesasne and her neighbors were neither new nor a primary preoccupation of the people. Similar conditions existed on many reserves and between most tribes and their neighbors. The lack of understanding between Native and Euro-American people with respect to each other's lifeways and their mutual distrust of each other have historically caused the indigenous people to give visitors who ask questions a cool or hesitant reception.

Fortunately, my own Native heritage and my weekly trips to the Reserve as a performance studies instructor provided a way for us to gather and tell stories and learn about one another. One of the first assignments in the course was to tell a personal story. Narrating an autobiographical moment in one's life is a gentle way into a performance class and a delightful way to make discoveries about the people you will be working with for fourteen weeks. I asked my class to tell their stories about growing up and living in Akwesasne. Two of the women in my class, Rebecca Papineau and Carol White, talked about their memories of growing up Mohawk, of times before gambling casinos and cigarette smuggling. Rebecca and Carol remember events from their childhoods and both situate their story in and around their homes. Rebecca tells us what the winters on the Reserve were like while Carol recalls that summers were especially memorable.

These women do not romanticize their early lives by reflecting on the past; indeed they tell of times before central heating, running water, and television. They do not recall their earlier lives as somehow simpler, more traditional; no nostalgic longing here. Instead, they recognize and articulate in marvelous ways the complexity of family and friendly relationships, they suggest the importance of understanding how their own lives have changed as a result of the stories they tell, they celebrate a familiarity with a certain landscape and a belonging to that landscape.

Their women's personal narratives represent gender differences in Native culture, whether written or collected by an ethnographer in the "as-told-to" tradition. While Native men's personal narratives usually center on historic events and moments of crisis in individual lives, most of the day-to-day activities and family and personal relationships are given cursory treatment or are completely omitted. Native women's personal narratives are generally more concerned with the private and intimate aspects of their lives and cultures. Women offer insights into their role in the structuring and preserving of traditional lifeways—particularly women speaking from within matrilineal cultures such as the Mohawk tribe. Rebecca and Carol offer us personal and intimate visions of life from the perspective of contemporary Mohawk women. We begin with Rebecca's story about the winters on the Reserve when she was a young girl.

REBECCA PAPINEAU, MOHAWK
ST. REGIS / AKWESASNE RESERVE

It's January 25,1994, and I've just gotten back from work. I walk in the house and turn up the heat, then I look outside and it's so cold and dreary and the temperature hasn't risen above zero in about a week. And I sit down with the mail and the day's paper and can't help but think back when I was growing up in my parent's home on St. Regis Road. And I think back about when my parents were still living. I am the youngest of eight children. There were quite a few of us. We do get together quite often because we all live here. We get together just to visit or on special occasions, on birthdays. We always remember each other's birthdays. We talk about different things. We have stories about my parents, a favorite aunt, a not-so-favorite aunt. My favorite-and-only-brother stories. Delivering the paper and Christmas stories and the favorite stories of ours from the winter spent in my parents' house.

Our house first belonged to our grandparents and there was no insulation at all in the walls or the ceiling. And when the wind blew, it seemed like it blew right through the walls and came through the windows. We would always say it's so windy upstairs you could fly a kite. The winters, I remember, we spent so much time around a big, black, round stove that was in our dining room. Well, we were so little that it seemed like it was high and big and round. And there were so many of us and we all sat around the stove with our feet up around it. Everybody in chairs all bundled up. We always had our feet on the stove because it was so cold. We probably couldn't stray two or three feet from the stove. I still remember the burning leather from our shoes if we left them on the stove too long. And in those days, women or girls just didn't wear pants or jeans. Even at home or even on our reserve they just didn't do that. We had long dresses and then we'd have long socks and not much of our legs would show anyway, but it was pretty cold in the winters. And we'd be standing around that stove, we just couldn't get close enough to the stove. And we always had burn marks all over our legs. It was so cold in the house that you could even see your breath as you talked and breathed.

One other thing I remember was that my mother was such a great cook. She never looked in cookbooks or read cookbooks. She just knew how to make all of these foods. Anything we were hungry for she would get up, and she made her own bread. That's what I remember from when we were young; we hardly ever had store bought bread. She made her own bread. She made her own donuts. Everything was homemade. And I miss that the most.

Our entertainment was whatever we could do right around that stove. We listened to the radio. We had no TV. We never did. We got the *Post Standard* every day and I remember fighting when the paper would come, everybody fought over the comic section and we knew what was happening in every one of those comics. Brenda Starr was our favorite. At night, with the long nights, we played monopoly and everybody played, my father and my mother. And I still remember there were so many of us that we filled the whole table. Of course, the table was right there next to the stove. We filled the whole table and it was just so much fun because we did so much together.

My father's token was the shoe. I don't remember what mine was, but that's what his was. We played cards. Every game possible. Solitaire. War. You name it. We used to play for matchsticks or whatever, not money. We didn't have any of that.

Getting water was really difficult. We didn't have any running water and for drinking water we had to go about a quarter of a mile. We knew the wells, all of the wells in the neighborhood, and my sister and I were about the same age, two years apart. We used to go together, carrying this pail down the road about a quarter of a mile. And in the winter, we would have to put it on a sleigh and pull the sleigh down the road. And it was fine if there was a pump on the well, but sometimes it was broke or we'd have to go to another well. And sometimes there wasn't a pump on it. It was just a long pole, it looked like a gaff hook. Just a long pole with a little hook on the end. And you put the pail handle on there and you'd lower it into the well. And a lot of times as soon as that bucket hit, it's quite deep sometimes, ten feet, and we were reaching trying to get this pole, both of us hanging on to it, to get it down to get some water, and we would lose the pail. Oftentimes that happened. And we'd get home and my parents would be really mad because we'd have to scramble then and somebody else would have to go get it. Find another pail. If we managed to get the water we'd be coming home and, of course, bringing it out of the well, we would lose half the water and spill the rest of it on us and get home all wet with half a pail or less of water. I remember that so well. And that was our drinking water.

And then we had to have other water, soft water, for washing and cleaning. During the winters, it was really hard. We had these men in the neighborhood who would deliver water by horse and buggy. And they'd have these big huge barrels and they would bring water in them. We'd have to have a barrel in our kitchen and they would bring these barrels and put the water right in our barrel in the kitchen. But you couldn't always get the water. It was hard for them to get it. They'd have to chop through the ice in the river and it was pretty difficult, depending on how much snow there was. And we'd call, or we'd have to walk down to tell them that we needed water. And it was sometimes a week, sometimes two weeks or longer before we got it. In the meantime, we were chopping icicles off the roof and bringing in snow and you name it, if there was a way, we were able to get water. But that was a big problem.

Washday, if we had the water, was usually on Saturdays with the old wringer washer. It was an all day affair. And then in winter, my mother always believed that we had to hang these clothes on the line outside. No matter how cold it was. We were freezing and freezing our fingers trying to hang these clothes on the line. But we did it. And then they'd be hard as boards trying to get them off the line. But she always said it made them white and smell good, so we did it.

Bedtime, because it was a coal stove that we couldn't have it going all night, when everybody went to bed, the fire went out and that was it. So, everybody piled on the blankets, coats, and whatever and it would be really cold. And with the weight of the blankets sometimes we could hardly breathe. There would be no fire or anything. My father would get up about five o'clock in the morning and start the fire. And we wouldn't get up until it finally started getting a little warmer and bearable so we'd finally get up and our day would start over again. You'd think that as cold as it was at home that we'd really love school, going into a warm school, but we didn't. But looking back on it and telling the stories, especially with our family, there was just so much togetherness and love among all of us that we look back on it and smile that we could see the humor in it. And our kids don't believe it. And that's all I have today.

Rebecca's story reflects the importance of family and of the difficulties of daily living on the Reserve during the winters. Her memories give us vivid images, glimpses of what the world was then, of the cold that surrounded and crept into everything: everything except the relations between friends and family. She begins the story with the current day, takes us into the past, then she references her own family's storytelling as she brings us back to the present. Similarly, Carol White takes us into her past, but her memories are scented with wild strawberries and touched by the summer sun.

CAROL WHITE, MOHAWK
ST. REGIS / AKWESASNE RESERVE

Well we'd sit around and start to tell stories at home so when I was trying to think of something to tell, I thought; what was it really like compared to today? And usually what kind of sparks my memory is the summers. How nice they were and warm. You didn't go from just hot to cold and warm to cold. It was a really nice time. And if the sun was out, there were just so many things you could do. What was really great about it was there was no TV. You got your chores done in the morning, you were free to go out and do what you wanted. But you also had to be back in time, for mealtimes, especially. And if it started getting dark, you'd better be around the house.

So we went out, ventured outside and it was so nice, you know. What could we do today? I'm with my sister Claudia, sitting around, and all of a sudden we could smell strawberries. Wild strawberries are out. We could do that. Let's go pick strawberries. She said all right. We ran back to the house and got our little cups and we went out and, of course, we didn't go very far and we started finding strawberries.

So we went and I said gee this grass is getting kind of long, it's going to be hanging pretty soon. I said it's going to be a little harder to find strawberries. She said well it won't take us long, look it. Just all over. Look at these strawberries. And we kept picking and we'd eat some. Then we'd pick some more. And we'd eat some more. And without realizing it we kind of wandered a little farther than we thought.

It wasn't until we came to this rock that we realized how far we'd gone. It was always the rock in the middle of the field. And even when the grass grew high, you could always see the rock. So we said we've come quite a ways. But we could still see the house too. So we said, let's get up on this rock. Okay. We'll wait here for a while and then we'll decide which way we want to go back. Do we want to go back through this field to the road, and then go back by the road, or do we just want to go toward the pasture and then come back around the other way?

We stand there thinking and then all of a sudden, well let's go this way and we'll hit the road first and we'll come back around the road, it'll be easier. Okay. We're talking about feet, not miles either way. But for us it was quite a ways. And no, we're not more than seven or eight or something like that. So that's quite a bit of walking, it was quite a way. So, we decided to go one way.

We started to get off the rock and all of a sudden the grass moved and we looked. And all of a sudden, we just grabbed each other like this and started screaming to the tops of our lungs. And we're saying, "Mom, mom, help!" And the more we jumped around and hung onto each other, we were pulling on each other's dresses and everything trying to stay on the top of this rock. Because the more excited we got, the more we were teetering all the time. We held each other close and all the while we're screaming, "Help, help, help!"

Finally my mother comes. We could see her at the end of the lawn before it gets to the field. And she's yelling. "What are you doing out there? Get back here right now." "We can't. We can't. Help. Somebody help us." She is just not even thinking about our fear. Maybe she's trying to hide her fear, but she's just saying you get back here right now. Never mind; help, help. Get back here. And we can't. Because every time we jumped, the grass would move in a different place. And then it would move in a different place. And soon it was like they were all around us. And we're going, "Snakes, snakes." And then she realizes we're not just fooling around.

So, we stand out there. And we thought, oh my god, my god, when are they going to come? When are they going to come? We must have been standing here for hours. Actually probably minutes. But all of a sudden, my brother Joel comes running. And he's got this pitchfork. And he's running out there. And I don't know, we don't know how many there were, or what they looked like. To this day when we tell the story, we just knew they were snakes. So I said, I don't know, it seemed like they were coming up from everywhere. And Claudia goes, they were, they were. And I go but how did we get off the rock. She says, I don't know but Joel got there and they were all gone. We jumped off the rock and he's saying hurry up, get home. And he's right behind us. And he's only two years older than we are. But he's yelling at us all the way back to the house. And we were just so afraid to even go near the edge of that field again.

But we got back to the house and we were trying to tell our mother. "But they were all over. We couldn't get off the rock. They were there. And every time we jumped, some more came out." And she kept saying, "no there couldn't have been that many." "Yes there was." And she wasn't believing us. "Well you shouldn't have been that far away from the house. You were just going a little ways. And what were you doing way out there?" Well we didn't realize it. I said you should see the berries out there. I said we didn't realize we went that far. "Where's your berries?" "Our berries. We didn't get our berries."

So we sat there and she was just totally disgusted with us and saying you know, you could find something better

> to do than scare the whole household. So we went and we tried to find something else do and, of course, it was probably near another meal time.
>
> But we just have so much fun with this story when we all get together. And they go, well what kind of snake was it? I don't know what kind of snake it was. I don't know what kind of snakes there were in those days. I've been deathly afraid of snakes ever since. But it seems like every time we tell the story, you know, we probably started off with a few, ten or twenty, and then it came to be a hundred, and I think we're talking about thousands of snakes now. But it's just like nobody experienced that except us. And we know how many snakes were there. And don't tell us they were baby ones either because they were big.

Carol's story is obviously a family favorite—and like most good stories, it gets richer with every telling. Like Rebecca, she situates this telling in the context of her immediate environment during an especially memorable season. Both of these women remember and re-tell stories that have been told many times, to many people, and that are particularly celebrated among their families. And too, both of these stories depend on the peoples' relationship with the land. The oral tradition is alive and well.

These two stories work metaphorically to describe my own emerging relationship with the people at Akwesasne—from a chilly climate to a warm and hospitable one. This is a place of much joy and hopefulness. In talking to Carol and Rebecca, I have replaced some of my own ignorance of people who have inhabited this part of the world for thousands of years with a burgeoning understanding of what happens when Mohawk women remember.

A Letter to My Father in Late Winter

Jim Gould

I awake at 5 A.M. to sugar maples cracking like rifle shots. During the night, a stiff breeze must have tossed away any blanket of clouds; the stars prove it.

I let the dog out, remembering to put gloves on first. The night before last, my moist hand stuck to the frozen doorknob. Outside the kitchen window, the thermometer reads eighteen below zero.

The all-night man on our local radio station tells me—I must be the only listener this early Sunday morning—there's a storm warning in effect for the northern Adirondacks. Temperatures will rise, probably into the low teens, and another foot of snow is coming.

I remember your stories, Dad, when you were a young boy on your aunt's and uncle's farm up in northern Ontario. Tough winters there, too: plowing snow with the horses, stoking the stoves every hour, keeping the chicken coop warm enough so they would lay, and praying, during each evening's Bible readings, that the money and food would hold out until spring. When the wind blew, you said you could see your breath in that small wood-frame house. When you went down the road to school—a one-roomer where one year you were the whole sixth grade—every child brought a helping of coal or hardwood for that day's heat.

I feed our wood stove with some maple and beech that has seasoned all year. It acts as if it's been soaked in kerosene, immediately blossoming into yellow, red, and blue flames. I look at another piece of stove wood; I think I recognize it.

Since this wood splitting business isn't a very efficient affair, I know I've probably touched this piece several times: cutting sixteen-inch sections from a log, throwing them in the back of my truck, then unloading in the backyard near where I split and stack, and then finally, months later, hauling them into the house for burning. Some pieces I do recognize, especially if they have a knot or twist that took some sweat to split around. I am not sure I recall this one, but it's a beauty. The grain is straight and golden and red, a bit like a salmon fillet. The draft roars like a jet engine when the stove door is open, and it sucks this piece in whole.

You said that up in Canada on that rock farm—that's what your uncle called it when he was tired of dulling plow points in the rocky soil of the Canadian Shield—you never went hungry. There was a big vegetable garden, of course, and a root cellar, and chickens and pigs for eggs and meat. They even had a little stream where you fished for trout—just little ones, you said, careful not to exaggerate—and Aunt Effie would clean up enough to fill a skillet.

When you told me these stories, even the one about your skinny boy's body shivering under the covers all night, you had a warm, tender look on your face. A smile, even.

I know you wouldn't be smiling here with me now—even though the woodlot near the house is layered with champagne powder, even though the sky is glowing blue-black and the sun will fill up this clearing as soon as it clears that hill. When I turn the key in my old truck, it turns over in the sluggish, caramel-like oil, but does not catch. I try it again and again, feeling the lifeblood of the battery turn the starter and light the cold plugs. But the plugs aren't firing.

This has happened before; that's why I keep an extra set of new plugs under the seat. They'll fire up hot and clean, creating a fire in each cylinder that even these freezing temperatures cannot quell.

My fingers burn to the touch of bare metal. I must start each new plug without a glove on to avoid cross-threading. I try not to get cross myself. When you worked at a stubborn chore like this, you would go into a slow burn sometimes. I've learned to ignore that tightness in my jaw, in my chest. Ignore it, relax it, and go through the motions.

The plugs go in methodically, one by one, as if I'm watching a slow-motion replay. There are eight plugs in my light, four-wheel-drive truck. Two on a cylinder. Ingenious design. It maximizes the burn, the combustion in each chamber. A set of four goes on the intake side, another set on the exhaust side. The first set goes in easily, but I'm starting to lose feeling in my hands, even though I'm warming them after I ratchet in each plug.

I cannot hurry. But I do, or maybe it is some snow that causes the ratchet to slip, bang into the hard plastic distributor cap, and crack it. This half-hour project is now extended another twenty-four hours, when I can hitch a ride tomorrow to the auto parts store in town for a new cap.

You had an older cousin on the farm, and you helped him with chores. One day while milking the farm's only milk cow, after taking too many kicks from the cranky animal, your cousin took his milking stool and smacked that cow flat in the forehead, full-force. The cow dropped to the floor and soon stopped breathing, making for one of the saddest days you could recall on the farm. Your cousin didn't mean it, you said. His temper just got the best of him.

I'm trying hard not the let my temper get the best of me. After I shovel out a path to the woodshed, I hear the dog crying the way she does when she wants to go for a walk. I take her and a pair of snowshoes and tramp through the backyard toward Jenkins Mountain.

The first mountain I ever climbed was here in the Adirondacks. It was Cascade Mountain, only about thirty miles from here. After years of working and living in different places in the Northeast, I took a job up here on a friend's recommendation. I was guided up to the top of Cascade, following a stream and then a rockslide, and then bushwhacking through heavy cripplebrush to a bare rock dome of the summit. It was so clear that day we could see Lake Champlain and Vermont fifty and more miles to the east, and endless wooded mountains and hills in every other direction.

I didn't know then, right there, cutting up chunks of hard cheese and bread and oranges for lunch, that I had found a new home. My bones must have known, though, because I settled in quickly, like a coyote, scavenging up new skills and adapting new ways to flourish in these woods.

After you left your aunt's and uncle's farm, you returned to gritty Buffalo. You and your mother, brothers, and sisters got through the Depression without a father by taking in laundry, candling eggs, and working the grain elevators down in the First Ward, Buffalo's Irish ghetto. Yet after nearly forty years of working two jobs every day, of humping it in steel mills and on the docks and in the rail yards to raise six kids, you never forgot about your real home. You always wanted to get back to the farm, to the woods, to the land.

On the occasional day off, we would drive into the rolling hills of Western and Central New York, away from the smokestacks and gray right angles of the city. You were looking for that place: just twenty acres or so, half-wooded and half-pasture, a house and a small barn, maybe a stream with some trout swimming in it. Something simple; nothing grand. "No Ponderosa," you would say. "Just a little place in the country."

The powder is a full four feet deep here, and the dog gracefully dolphins forward, cutting a trail for me. I wonder how long she can maintain this pace, and I wonder about me, too, as the sweat comes down my face and freezes in my beard. We won't make it to the top today, but that's not why we keep going. The sunlight sparkles through the airborne ice crystals. Deer and snowshoe hare have left trenches perpendicular to ours, and I can see deep into woods that are dense with foliage the rest of the year. It feels good just to go, so I go, like the dog, just lapping it up.

You've retired now, and you still haven't found your place. Those places never turn out as described in the real estate ads, nor do they happen to fit the picture in your head. But when you visit in the summer and see what I have here—the gardens, the woods, the ponds, the mountains—I know what you're thinking. This is your Someday Farm, your place with the wild blueberries and big trees. And it seems so easy and so happy. And mostly, it is all of that.

Except, though, on some days, when you're a long-distance phone call away, the truck doesn't start, the pipes freeze, the sun cannot break through a month's worth of clouds, the snow drifts up to the window sills in March, and the paychecks are half of what they ought to be. Or you lose your temper and kill the family cow. Or crack a distributor cap.

Find that new home fast, so you will see that you can taste and hear and smell and touch it all without the thin gauze of memory dulling the immediacy and joy and pain of the whole show.

Like when you break onto the shoulder of a snowy mountain with your dog and catch your breath and spit and watch it freeze on a tree's bark, and you have to squint with the sweat and glare from the snow and blue sky, but you can see down into the valley and maybe catch a glimpse of the place where you live, there in a clearing surrounded by tall white pines.

My place. And yours, until you can find your own.

Neighbors

The Minnow Man

Mary Blake

The minnow man was part of our growing up summers on the St. Lawrence River. He was as much an element of the scenery, of the memories, as the river, the towering pine, and the cottage.

Tall and solid to a child's view, Walt Plantz was gentle and kind—the type parents could trust their children with. He always looked old, as old as the boathouse where he repaired his nets and tied up his water-worn skiff.

He was a fisherman, a catcher of sturgeon, a stripper of roe for the appetites of downstate city people. These people wouldn't have recognized or even welcomed him in their world—a world Walt never experienced—but they trusted their blond-haired, blue-eyed children with him during their relaxed holidays on the river.

Now, on the St. Lawrence, vacationers wake to the sound of fifty-horsepower motors revving up to take L.L. Bean-clad, over-fed bodies to a few hours of fishing. Gone are the times when the minnow man would wake us before dawn with the sound of his oars squeaking in the ungreased locks of his weather-beaten boat, as he pulled away from shore and headed toward the channel and its teeming fishing beds. Gradually, the sound would fade as the current carried him farther toward the cold, swift waters where sturgeon lay waiting to be fed a barbed breakfast.

Walt was always back by early afternoon, or at least in time to sell "minnies" at five for a penny for our own fishing adventures. There were always four or five minnie buckets hanging from the dock supports. Sometimes as we watched, he'd pull up one that had caught a snake, and display for us the glistening silver scales that looked like sequins sewn to Mother's green evening dress.

Put to music, the minnow man would have been a campfire tune sung at the end of the evening: nothing too fast or bouncy, but one that moved along deliberately; never in a hurry, and never, ever impatient with the children who came to buy the minnows he always had for them. For those he liked, or those who were his best customers, he always threw in an extra one for luck. He said it was the one that would catch a fish large enough for supper.

Walt's baggy pants had started life as brown, but had grown so dark they bordered on black. I imagine they would have stood by themselves at night. His shirt was flannel, frayed at the collar and cuffs, the fuzz worn off from years of wear and the once-bright plaid now devoid of colors. His jacket was patched and worn from the weather, and the hat, an ancient brown Fedora, was, like his face and his boat, weather-beaten.

His face and hands were wrinkled and brown. His eyes, river blue, crinkled at the corners from long days on the water without sunglasses. The open palm he held out for our penny was glove leather and firm, but not rough. I tried for years to get an outfit as worn and as comfortable as his.

Walt Plantz was a good man. Unschooled and unlettered according to the world at large, a vagrant with no ambition by high society's determinations, he loved what he did and treated the land, the river, and people with respect.

The minnow man was a successful human being.

The Amish: Quiet Immigrants

Betsy Tisdale

Who among you is wise or clever? Let his right conduct give practical proof of it, with the modesty that comes of wisdom.

James 3:13 New English Bible

It is a quiet affair, this slow-paced immigration to the St. Lawrence Valley that began somewhere in the mid-1970s. Amish farmers and their large families have bought up abandoned, exhausted farms and have been hard at work coaxing a living from this recalcitrant land. In the farmland around DeKalb, Heuvelton, Rensselaer Falls, Depeyster, Lisbon, and Norfolk, road signs warn drivers of horse-and-buggy traffic. Windmills tower over farmhouses.

Crudely lettered placards advertise "Eggs for Sale," "Custom Planing," "Firewood," "Strawberries," "Vegetables," "Homebaked Pies and Bread," "Maple Syrup," "No Sunday Sales."

Men with wide-brimmed black hats—straw hats in summer—stand on wagons behind teams of workhorses, plowing, cutting, and turning hay, going for firewood, taking a cow to a married son or daughter. Smart-looking Morgan horses proudly pull black buggies on errands to the nearest village. Mailboxes advertise names like Yoder, Miller, Shetler, Zook, Gingerich and Swartzentruber. Children play tag outside one-room schoolhouses, sometimes running barefoot in October and April.

When the aisles in Canton's P&C are filled with an entire Amish family, which often means eight or more children, their dark, long dresses, black bonnets, black pants and suspenders, black boots and somber faces provoke sidelong glances from fascinated "English," as the Amish call the rest of us.

If you drive along Route 812 from DeKalb to Heuvelton in the early evening, you will see the soft glow of kerosene lamps lighting farmhouse windows. One of these houses is new, with a long porch across the front, facing south. Fourteen cows occupy the barn along with several pigs. Six children are in the barn at dusk finishing the milking—by hand, of course; the Amish have foresworn electricity. A nine-year-old girl named Rachel moves from the barn to the hen house to collect the eggs. Her little brother Moses, six years old, quietly follows her. He says to Rachel in Old German, "Look, somebody English."

Having pulled into the driveway, I get out of the car and ask the boy if I can buy eggs. Moses eyes my red ski parka for a second and then looks to his sister.

Rachel replies, in English, "You may go into the house. We have some, I think." Then the two children disappear into the hen house. Moses wonders when he will learn enough English at the schoolhouse to answer the questions from the English people who arrive in their cars at the farm. He knows he is not supposed to stare at their brightly colored clothes, jewelry, watches, purses. But it is difficult to hold in his curiosity.

I cross the yard, greeted by several kittens, and climb six wooden steps to the high front porch. Seven white caps hang from a clothesline strung between the porch posts, their strings blowing gently in the evening breeze. Four feedbags of seed potatoes hang from the porch rafters. A few pairs of muddy boots sit by the front door.

I knock on the solid wood. After a minute, the door opens and a round-faced Amish mother wearing wire-rimmed glasses politely asks me to go to the back door. "Oh, what a mess we have here! We are just finishing oiling the floor. It would be better for you to go around to the back, if you don't mind," she says.

Walking behind the house, I notice a large two-story shed, with an outhouse attached. Anna Miller greets me at the back door. She offers a warm welcome. "Please come in. We are glad to have a reason to stop."

"I'm sorry to interrupt your work. I just want to buy a dozen eggs."

"Actually, we are just finished," Anna replies cheerfully.

Two teen-age girls smile as they put away their oily rags. The wooden kitchen floor is gleaming. Each girl lights a kerosene lamp: one is for the long trestle table with benches, the other goes into the living room.

I smell bread baking in the giant black wood cookstove. A dry sink sits below a window; a white pleated curtain on the wall above the sink sets off a row of ladles, spatulas, and large spoons. A pantry table is filled with pies and jars of pickles. A large calendar with big numbers for the days and no picture hangs near the stove. On the wall over the table, a Regulator clock ticks a steady cadence.

"Lydian, please go to the cellar for the eggs. Elizabeth, you may start the potatoes for supper." I don't understand these orders given in German.

I study the line of black hats and heavy black bonnets on hooks along the wall of the mudroom. Behind me, the door quietly opens and soon I realize that six pairs of eyes are shyly scrutinizing me.

"Well, I guess they've finished their chores," says Anna.

Rachel and Moses disappear into the cellar with a basket of eggs.

"Levi, wash your hands good," says his mother in German. To twelve-year-old Mattie, she says, "Help Elizabeth with the potatoes."

Levi goes to the sink and pumps water to wash his hands.

Without a word, Mattie joins Elizabeth in the kitchen. Rachel, Levi, and Lydian emerge from the cellar after a few minutes. Rachel joins her older sisters in the kitchen. Lydian hands me a box of eggs.

"How many children do you have?" I ask.

"Ten," answers Anna with a smile. "The house seems a little empty now that Lena and Joseph have married. Malinda has been staying with Lena to help with the new baby, but now she is home. Gideon and my husband should be home soon. They took the butter churn to Lena this afternoon."

Through the doorway, I notice a quilting frame in the parlor. "Do you make quilts to sell?"

"Yes, we have been very busy here with quilting. In Ohio, we might make one a month just for some extra money. But the farming here is a little harder, so the quilting comes in handy."

Two girls are setting the table. Two more are peeling potatoes. Elizabeth is taking loaves of bread out of the oven and setting them on the shelf above the stove.

"Here they come," says Anna. In the deepening dusk, a black buggy pulled by a sleek black Morgan horse draws up to a new machine shed behind the barn. Presently, Jacob, Anna's husband, comes in the back door. He is a powerfully built, compact man in his early fifties with twinkling eyes, red cheeks, and a graying six-inch beard. Gideon, seventeen, is unhitching the horse, putting away the harness.

"What took you so long?" inquires Anna.

"We helped Noah with the new staircase to the loft. We will go back tomorrow to finish it. He will come to help split firewood next Saturday."

This and other news are spoken in German, so I feel left out. I watch nine-year-old Rachel at the table, cutting up potatoes with a paring knife. She looks quite adept. But there are black spots in the potatoes. Why isn't she cutting them out? Doesn't she notice them? Her blonde braids are tucked neatly up under her white cap. Her creamy, healthy complexion glows in the lamplight. Momentarily, Malinda stands next to Rachel and quietly cuts the black spots from the potatoes. Elizabeth then cuts the potatoes into small pieces. They have formed an efficient assembly line in total silence.

The house is as quiet as a church, yet there are ten people here. They speak softly to each other. No television, no radio, no furnace, no refrigerator humming, no vacuum cleaner, no washing machine. No telephone to disturb the serenity. Another kerosene lamp is lighted by the woodstove as Malinda starts to fry the potatoes.

I pay Anna a dollar for the eggs and thank her. As I leave, Anna points to the shed behind the house.

"If you think this house is crowded, you should have been here when sixteen of us lived in that shed for six months while the house was built. We slept upstairs and cooked and ate downstairs. My father and uncle and two nephews came from Ohio to help."

I leave the Miller farm with more than just a dozen eggs. I leave with a dozen pictures in my mind as well. Like little Moses, I have stared at a different way of life. I know I must go back.

Driving home in the dark past other Amish farms, I think sadly of my frustrating job as a schoolteacher. My students in a rural high school are often lazy, resistant to learning. My dream of opening the fascinating world of literature to them is crumbling. For parents' night, only twelve parents came to my classroom. My ninth graders are reading at a sixth-grade level.

One of my honor seniors turned in an obviously plagiarized report. When I confronted him, he denied it. I couldn't prove it because I didn't know what book he had used. But the writing style was far better than his ability indicated it should be.

My superintendent once gave me advice about discipline: "They should always be a little afraid of you." I remember fearing only the teachers I had hated. I remember learning from the teachers I had loved. The best was a Quaker teacher who taught creative writing.

The Amish children seemed busy and content. Was this an illusion? Were they putting on a harmonious show for me? I felt like a cynical spy. I knew I had to return to the Miller farm to learn more.

From books, we learn that the Amish are part of a conservative Christian denomination that adheres to a strict way of life. They are pacifists; during wartime, the men serve alternate service for two years as conscientious objectors.

They first arrived in Pennsylvania in the early 1700s from Switzerland and southern Germany, fleeing repressive state religions and the violence following the Reformation. With related groups of Mennonites, the Amish have prospered in America. The Pennsylvania Amish have lush farmland and are well established. Virtually every other farming state has Amish communities. They pay their taxes, although they do not pay Social Security, having proven to the federal government they will never use it. The Amish take care of their own, from cradle to grave. The cradle (or more likely, an oak crib made by an Amish woodworker) is filled nearly every spring. Ten children in a family is common; eighteen or even twenty is not too unusual.

Before schools were centralized, Amish children attended small country schoolhouses with their "English" neighbors. But Amish parents do not abide their children riding on a school bus, wearing a gym suit, or attending health classes, which include sex education. Amish fathers went to jail in protest in Nebraska, Iowa, Kansas, Illinois, and Wisconsin. The Amish do not believe in litigation, but their brave and quiet protest attracted the sympathies of some Midwest lawyers, who took the case to court in Wisconsin.

Finally, in 1972, the Supreme Court ruled in favor of the Amish on the grounds that their unique way of life was indeed threatened by compulsory education in centralized schools. Even with the ruling, most of the Amish left Nebraska because of the acrimony they endured throughout the legal battle.

Amish children speak German first, then start school at six years old and finish at fourteen, learning English and arithmetic. History and biology are ignored. At nineteen and twenty, a young woman will usually teach for a year or two before she marries. Lena Miller taught school to her younger brothers and sisters and cousins for a year before her marriage. Now her younger sister, Elizabeth, is teaching school. Children attend 180 days a year to satisfy the state, but have few vacation days so they can finish in the first week of May to help with planting.

I visit the new schoolhouse on a side road off Route 812. Built by the Swartzentruber family and two Miller families, it gives one the strange sensation of having just entered a Winslow Homer painting. Four rows of lift-top desks are occupied by twenty quiet children, the oldest in a row on the left, the youngest on the right. Shy smiles greet me as I sit in a chair by the wall.

Windows on each side of the room provide all the light. A wood stove in the back corner keeps the room warm. Lunches in black buckets and boxes sit neatly on corner shelving. A row of black-brimmed hats, bonnets, and cloaks lines the wall in the corner behind the stove, mimicking the rows in the Miller house. The door opens to the rear through a woodshed. At the front, the wall is covered by a blackboard behind the teacher's desk. Elizabeth is teaching eight grades, with two or three children to a grade.

Two second-graders, a girl and boy, are called to the front of the room to correct their math lesson. They sit on a bench along the side wall and exchange notebooks. Elizabeth quietly reads the correct answers. The little girl and boy stare intently at their notebooks, pencils in hand, ready to mark each other's mistakes with an X.

The boy has made several mistakes; Elizabeth tells him to rework the problems more carefully. "Don't be in a hurry, Dannie, just do a good job," she offers calmly.

Elizabeth tells the little girl to help Dannie rework his math. The two children return to Dannie's desk, where the girl stands beside him, patiently helping him with each of the sums marked wrong.

It is now her job to teach *him.* There is no shame.

The other eighteen students continue to work on their own. An eight-year-old deaf boy receives help from his thirteen-year-old brother. The silence is almost visible; it is overwhelming to me. The younger children color with battered crayons in their arithmetic books—four butterflies, five trees, six barns.

I help a fourth grader with this problem: "Father has picked 328 peaches. He takes 200 to market and leaves the rest with Mother to can. She puts eight peaches in each jar. How many jars of peaches will there be?"

The boys have taken off their boots; the girls kept theirs on. In warm weather, they all prefer to go barefoot and play fast games of tag at recess. Even then, they do not shout or yell. The girls can often run as fast as the boys; their stamina is incredible.

A pair of girls holding hands and running together slip in the rain-soaked schoolyard, covering their pinafores with mud. They pull each other up and run some more to tag another child. Then the pair split and the tagged child joins hands with one of the girls. This game will go on for a half hour, with no rest. Pairs of boys are tagging other boys. Pairs of girls tag other girls, who laugh in response.

When it is time to go in, all faces ar red, braids and wispy strands of hair peeking from skewed bonnets. Dresses and pants are quite muddy, and lungs are gasping for air. Each child washes bare feet and muddy clothes at a sink in the entryway to the classroom. There is no mirror for the girls to check their sweat-streaked faces and disheveled hair. The Amish do not use mirrors at all, interpreting strictly the commandment, "Thou shalt not make a graven image." The girls help each other with their grooming.

On the day before Christmas, the children in school are trying to memorize little poems Elizabeth has written for them on slips of paper. Parents and younger brothers and sisters are to come to this day of recitation at the schoolhouse. They will be given candy; there is no Santa Claus in the Amish way.

"Our Christmas is really the 6th of January," Anna explains. "We believe that's the original date before the Romans changed the calendar. It's a special day for the little scholars, but we don't have a long vacation or the presents like you do."

Church is held every other Sunday at a different house. Long, sturdy benches that fold for easy storage and transport are moved from house to house. The service is long and conducted in High German. Hymns are sung a cappella.

"There are probably seventy to eighty families here now in

our community," says Anna. "Most of us moved here from Wayne County, Ohio. But we have also lived in Canada, where my husband grew up. The men came here first on the bus to look at the land.

"Then we sold our farm, put the animals, furniture, equipment, and everything else on a railroad boxcar and moved here. The women and children came on the bus.

"We bought this farm, two hundred acres, for $45,000. The barn was here, but we had to build everything else. We brought the flooring and the clapboard from Ohio.

"But my goodness, it is cold here! And the land is in rough shape. We got more from our forty-four acres in Ohio than the ninety that we farm here. We grew equal amounts of corn, oats, wheat, and alfalfa there. We don't get half as much per acre here. It will take a while to build up the soil.

"In Ohio, we got eleven dollars per hundred weight of milk when we left three years ago. Here we get only eight dollars, but they're talking about raising it to nine."

Since they don't use electricity, the Amish don't have milking machines, or bulk tanks from which the milk trucks can pump. Milk cans are loaded by hand onto small trucks with hired drivers. A small cheese factory in Russell had been buying their milk, but since it started buying only from "English" farmers with bulk tanks and eventually closed, some Amish farmers have begun selling milk to the newly rebuilt Amish cheese factory in Norfolk, which is thirty-five miles away. It, too, is in danger of closing.

"Sometimes I wonder why we moved here," Anna says wistfully on a dreary March day. The fields are still snow-covered. The sky is gray.

Good farmland in Wayne and Holmes County, Ohio, is going for $3,000 an acre. There are 15,000 to 20,000 Amish there, the greatest number in any state—including Pennsylvania. Due in no small part to their prodigious birthrate, the Amish must expand their landholdings. In a recent twenty-five-year period, these holdings increased one hundred percent in Pennsylvania.

The Amish have accounts at banks, but they do not generally

borrow from banks. They pay no electricity bills, make no car payments, do not buy insurance. They have no credit cards. They do not go to Disney World or Club Med. They are strictly a cash-and-barter society.

Some of the large, young families in Ohio realized their children would be unable to acquire farms there with the crowding and high land prices. Their decision to move to St. Lawrence County in New York came from a need for land—and privacy.

Each time I visit a farm, I learn more. Once I saw a young and frisky horse pull off from its tether and run, pulling an empty buggy, four miles through Rensselaer Falls. Two people in cars tried several times unsuccessfully to force it off the road before it bolted through town and across an intersection. Finally, south of town, they forced it into the ditch where the buggy turned over, only slightly damaged.

Joni Yoder brought the buggy back to his farm on a big flat-bed wagon pulled by two Belgian workhorses. They were all grateful no one was hurt, and thanked the drivers for getting the horse off the road.

The wide roads and small dirt lanes in St. Lawrence County offer relative peace and quiet to the new Amish settlers. There is plenty of cheap, if not prime, farmland. However, life is still a struggle. Markets for farm goods are far away. Quilts are sold locally, but are also sent to Pennsylvania and Ohio. The federal government forbids butchering and selling one's own beef or pork. The market for milk is depressed.

The Millers pay a little more than five hundred dollars a year in property taxes. After the house and machine shed were built, the taxes rose from three hundred dollars. Their tax slip from the Town of DeKalb classifies their land as a "horse farm." A huge vegetable garden in front of the house and another on the side provide a great deal of their food. They also have raspberries and six hundred strawberry plants. In wet summers, they can harvest few strawberries to sell.

In the fall they butchered a cow for their own consumption. In January they killed two large pigs. They make their own bread and butter; flour, sugar, coffee, and spices come from the store.

Most Amish children look amazingly strong and healthy, although some obviously need dental care. Babies are usually born at home with the help of an Amish midwife or Angie Peacetree, a Seneca midwife who lives not far away. But if there are problems, they go to the hospital in Ogdensburg, Potsdam, or Malone. The Millers cared for a newborn baby girl recently after the birth had required a Caesarean section. To save the family money, the baby was taken from the hospital nursery to the Millers' home.

On a chilly October day, the parlor stove crackles to keep the room extra warm. A small oak crib has been moved into the room. Malinda rocks the black-haired baby and feeds her catnip tea from a bottle. Mattie and Anna hover nearby. Jacob comes in from the barn to warm up by the stove. His hands are huge and red as he holds them over the stove. Surveying the scene, he tells me, "Everyone is happy to have a baby in the house. That baby is never left alone. We are spoiling her because we all want to hold her." He smiles and then takes a pouch of tobacco out of his pocket to light his pipe.

Soon enough, these girls will be mothers themselves. They will help care for neighbors' small children and their married sisters' and brothers' first few babies before they marry. The Amish are extremely devoted to their children. Although households vary, in the Miller house, a harsh word is never spoken to a child. Looking like miniatures of the adults in scaled-down versions of the same homemade clothes, children do not watch Sesame Street, do not play with GI Joes or their mothers' make-up. Little boys wear dresses until they are potty-trained.

If they stood side by side in a line, the children in an Amish family would look like a set of steps. By the time a girl is fourteen or fifteen, she can practically run a household by herself. She can make a dress or pair of pants on the treadle sewing machine. She can do fine quilting. She can bake bread, black the stove, paint the woodwork gray, change diapers, work in the garden, do the laundry, and milk the cows.

She may also assist her father and brothers with light carpentry and sanding in the woodshop. Nine-year-old Rachel hands long strips of clapboard one by one over her head to her brother,

Gideon, who stands on a ladder as he nails them on the shed. Her arms are strong and tanned by the sun. Her wrists are not delicate, but thick and sinewy. The boys follow their fathers and older brothers around the farm, doing chores at a very young age. Jacob and Gideon take six-year-old Moses along on the bobsled pulled by a team of workhorses, across the snowy fields to the woods to cut firewood. Little Moses stands in the middle of the empty flatbed with his legs spread apart. He leans on the end of the handle of a huge axe, forming a stable tripod. His father drives the horses carefully.

At least five men in this Amish community earn their living from making furniture in their own woodshops: rocking chairs, straight chairs, dining room tables, picnic tables, bassinets, dressers, dry sinks, hutches. Their sons work with them. Menno Yoder runs his lathe from a diesel-powered engine, which is permitted in the culture. He makes dining room tables. Another man makes dining room chairs. He has a damaged eye—the Amish do not use safety goggles.

These men are booked a year ahead. Business is good. Their wives and daughters make quilts, aprons, potholders, pillows, and baskets. They do not advertise, but orders come in steadily, locally and from far away, even out of state. A shop in Canton sells local crafts including Amish quilts and dolls, and a restaurant outside of town has a shop where Amish crafts are sold.

Quilt dealers find the women who are the best quilters and send them steady streams of orders. The Amish buy plain, somber colors of polyester fabrics for their own use by mail-order from Amish stores in Pennsylvania and Ohio. Their quilts are often dark, but can include deep reds, blues, purples, and greens, but no pastels, no prints, no whites. If a customer provides fabric for a quilt order that is printed or brightly colored, they will use it. Piecing is done on a treadle sewing machine, usually by a window in the parlor. Quilting is done by hand on a frame that can be lowered from the ceiling and raised when not in use.

The Swartzentruber Amish, like the community in the DeKalb-Rensselaer Falls-Heuvelton area, are the most conservative in the country. They refuse to put orange reflective triangles on their buggies as a safety measure as requested by the county sheriff, although they have compromised by outlining the back of each buggy with white reflective tape. Their buggies are open, without glass enclosures to protect them from the wind and rain. They will accept a ride in a car only in a medical emergency.

The Amish in the Norfolk area are more liberal. Women commute to Potsdam in the cars of their "English" neighbors to work cleaning houses. Sometimes the men can be seen hitchhiking. Their children ride a Town of Norfolk school bus to their one-room schoolhouse. Some neighbors have complained that the Amish stop in often to use their telephones.

Lydia Gingerich grew up in southern Tennessee, picking cotton and tobacco with her seventeen brothers and sisters. Her father had moved his family from Ohio to Mt. Pleasant, Tennessee, when he became seriously afflicted with arthritis in his early forties. He knew his children would be able to support the family by growing and harvesting tobacco and cotton.

They also raised pimiento peppers for the National Biscuit Company in Georgia. Five acres of strawberries produced additional income. Her father took up woodworking and sold cedar chests by the side of the road. His arthritis gradually disappeared. The warmer climate, and doing woodworking instead of milking cows in a cold, damp barn, may account for his recovery.

Lydia, now thirty-eight, has moved with her husband to Heuvelton and is pregnant with her fifteenth child. She is clearly happy to have her father visiting, a long trip by bus from southern Tennessee. Her brother-in-law has come too, since he plans to move his family north to DeKalb in April and set up his business making tarpaulins for trucks and boats, as well as car upholstery. He has purchased 80 acres and will build a house. It seems that most young Amish couples in St. Lawrence County build tiny houses (fifteen feet by thirty feet) on land owned by "English" dairy farmers. The young Amish husband works as a hired hand and may do woodworking and have a maple syrup operation on the side. The young wife makes quilts and has a baby within a year or two. Can they save enough money to buy their own farm? Yes, and they do. The Amish epitomize frugality.

A retired dairy farmer who now works as a realtor is glad the Amish are moving into the county. "They're good, honest, hard workers," he says. "They're buying up land that none of us wants. They're willing to work hard and long to improve the land and build up their stock. They're good neighbors.

"At least a dozen farms in this area are owned by the Federal Land Bank because the owners gave up and left. The land is just sitting there. It makes me sad. But I won't bother to try to sell those federally-owned farms. The government won't give us any commission, so no one is motivated to sell them. Of course, local hooligans smash the windows, and next thing you know, the whole place burns down. It's a shame.

"The Amish pay cash for their farms," he continues. "Of course, just like anyone else, they don't want to use a realtor if it means the price will be higher. I'd say they're buying farms in the range of $40,000 to $70,000. They're buying the old Mom-and-Pop farms, the places that are marginal. They are incredible workers."

If you really want to see an example of "incredible workers," go to an Amish barn raising. Last spring a barn went up in one day on a farm along Route 812. The raising had been planned for the day before the roofing was scheduled to be delivered. Ironically, the metal roofing ordered from Canada did not arrive until a week later because the truck broke down.

Sixty-three men at one time were carrying lumber cut at the community sawmill, sawing, hammering, holding boards for each other. The cement foundation and beams for the doorways had been completed ahead of time. Horses stood in two circles around feed on wagons. Thirty buggies were parked in the barnyard. Dozens of barefoot children played in front of the house.

Inside, four huge tables were filled with individual dishes of food, in readiness for ravenous appetites at noon dinner: applesauce topped with marshmallow fluff, pies, cakes, cookies, jello, beans, potatoes, squash, and beef, pitchers of milk and coffee. Teenage girls held babies while mothers cooked and talked. A baby crawled happily under a table. No one seemed to be in a hurry, neither the women cooking nor the men building the barn.

All the work was evenly shared, so it seemed no one had to rush. The community worked like a finely tuned machine.

Everybody is taken care of, all needs are filled, all desires met. This is the Amish ideal. As with any society, there is a dark side to Amish life. A narrow gene pool causes a higher-than-normal incidence of dwarfism, deafness, cystic fibrosis, and "maple syrup urine disease," a form of mental retardation. A young lab technician at a nearby hospital to which an Amish couple has been brought has a sinking feeling in her stomach when she meets their young child. "When the kid pees in the cup and I see the urine is the color of maple syrup, I know instantly the kid is retarded and there is nothing medically we can do to improve the situation," she laments.

The eight-year-old Miller boy, one of fifteen children, probably has congenital deafness as a result of inbreeding. Although a local audiologist provided a free hearing exam and a very good hearing aid, the boy was confused by the sudden noise. Coming home from school every day with a headache, he gave up. The family was used to his deafness and was not motivated to teach him to speak.

Genetically induced kidney disorders have proven fatal to some children. In one such case, the county social services department and a doctor in Burlington, Vermont forced a family to accept medical services over the religious objections of the parents. The result was a storm of local protest. Another time, jars on bank counters and store check-outs were filled and refilled with loose change from "English" wishing to help defray the medical expenses of a critically burned teenage girl.

Another problem is increasing "worldliness." There are many different groups of Amish, ranging from the most conservative Swartzentruber group to the "beachy" Amish who drive cars. Some communities are more cohesive than others. The Norfolk community has certainly had its share of troubles. Their cheese factory burned to the ground eight years ago. Of course, there was no insurance. They decided to rebuild. They hired "English" managers who simply disappeared—with cash and cheese.

The Amish apparently do not check references. They also do

not go to a lawyer to sue for damages: that would be seeking revenge. They believe God is the final judge.

Their naivete in business matters also puts them in jeopardy with the health department when it comes to selling food. At the cheese factory, they have had to make some compromises by acquiring electric cooler cases and other equipment.

The factory sells excellent aged cheddar, jalapeno cheddar, garlic and chive cheddar, brick, and Monterey jack, as well as butter and eggs. If you stop in during the afternoon you can buy fresh warm cheese curds. But the factory is located on Plum Brook Road, five miles off Route 56, the main road between Potsdam and Massena. This is a remote place to do business, but it draws a good local crowd.

At least one Amish girl from the Norfolk community married "out," but her husband deserted her after a baby was born. The Amish community shunned her for marrying one of the "English," essentially excluding her completely. After her husband left her, she started working in a restaurant as a waitress. Later, the community accepted her return. Amish teenage boys have been observed using the pay phone on the main street of Norfolk. Whom could they be calling, some of the Amish girls who clean houses in Potsdam?

An Amish woman with a houseful of children had a nervous breakdown. That would seem completely understandable to most of us.

A horse collapsed while pulling a buggy a few years ago along Plum Brook Road in Norfolk. There was talk that the horse had been mistreated. A local woman who is a licensed wildlife rehabilitator went to see an Amish elder about the situation. He explained to her that the world expects perfection from the Amish, but unfortunately, they have problem members, too. He assured her that the matter of the abused horse was being handled within the community.

There are some serious questions to pose to the Amish. If they fled European governments that they considered rigid and totalitarian, how much freedom do they encourage among themselves? Can a teenager really make an informed choice to stay or to leave the Amish way of life? What about that young mother waiting tables? Is it fair to expect a wife to bear fifteen or twenty children?

By refusing to vote in our political system, do they forfeit their place in a democratic government? Do the elders always possess the necessary wisdom to guide the community? Is there room for any disagreement at all?

These are valid questions. Meanwhile, the Amish continue to work hard on their farms and in their woodshops. They adamantly refuse to be photographed; these would be graven images. But their influence is being quietly felt in St. Lawrence County.

One Potsdam couple hired a seventy-year-old Amish man to paint a small room in their house. He decided to reduce his fee from six dollars to five dollars an hour when the couple offered to drive him the fourteen miles to their house. They were concerned that he was hitchhiking at dawn when it was 15 degrees below zero, and then again after dark to go home.

They asked if he would like to stay at their house while they went to Philadelphia. He agreed, arriving with a suitcase and canning jars of peas and strawberries. He agreed that he would answer the phone when they called to check on his progress. He patched the plaster and painted the ceiling, walls, trim, two windows, and a door for $225. He learned how to use the vacuum cleaner. He brought in the mail and fed the cats. He worked slowly but carefully. At the end of the week he called the couple in Philadelphia and told them he was finished, then hitchhiked home.

In spring he will return to putty the windows of the house and paint the front porch. Another Potsdam woman is very fond of her eighteen-year-old Amish "cleaning woman." "Amanda is just like a member of the family," she says. "We love her. She is so mature compared to other girls her age. She's very practical, and wonderful with my children." Amanda is paid four dollars an hour and works once a week for four hours at a time. She works for five other families in town. Non-Amish neighbors and employers share the car-pooling.

On a cold winter dusk, several Amish women in long blue

dresses and black capes with black bonnets sit on a bench inside the Big M supermarket on Elm Street in Potsdam, waiting for their ride home to Norfolk. They smile shyly at people as they enter the store. Behind them is a video rental counter. Next to them is a pay phone. The checkout registers beep busily. Overhead are glaring fluorescent lights. Logging trucks, milk trucks, and cars rattle past outside the vibrating plate glass windows.

A cigarette hangs from the mouth of a gaunt woman in curlers as she yanks a shopping cart from a nested stack. She slings a two-year-old toddler roughly into the kiddy seat. Her four-year-old son begins to cry when she refuses him a ride in the cart. His nose is running. His jacket is grubby and unzipped, and a fat tummy peeks out below a dirty t-shirt. She smacks him hard on the rear end and yells, "If you don't shut up, I'll really hit you hard!"

Three Amish women by the window flinch almost imperceptibly and avert their eyes. During the past ten years, since I first stopped at the Miller farm to buy eggs, I have become a good friend of the family. I treasure my vivid memories: mental photographs of them working at the wood stove, at the quilting frame, in the garden and barn. My requests to take photographs have been politely but firmly turned down.

"We see them stealing pictures from the road when they slow down their cars, but there is nothing we can do about it," they say. I learned the children's names as quickly as possible. Joseph, the oldest son who married almost seven years ago, lives now on his own farm. His wife expects her fifth baby any day now. His sister Lena lives close by with her husband on their own farm, with four children so far. Lena makes butter with her family's churn. She has plenty of quilt customers since her mother taught her well.

Three more sisters, Elizabeth, Barbara, and Mattie, and a brother, Uri, are also married and have eleven children among them.

I have been buying and selling quilts, dolls (with no faces), aprons, potholders, and other crafts from the parlors and woodshops for eight years. My buying trips give me plenty of opportunities to observe the Amish way of life.

I admit to great feelings of pleasure while rocking a new Amish baby or sleepy child. The children look forward to receiving my son's copies of *Ranger Rick* and *National Geographic World* or pencils, crayons, and drawing paper at Christmas. A friend sent two huge boxes of books that would have been discarded by the Binghamton School system; she selected books on nature, social studies, and geography for the Miller school. Surprisingly, a biology book was greatly appreciated by Anna, for it explained why her dizziness last winter was caused by an ear infection.

On my weekly eighty-mile loop to Amish farms, I pick up thirty dozen eggs for the Potsdam Food Co-op, check on quilt orders, and buy maple syrup for family and friends, or vegetables, depending on the season. I enjoy seeing evidence of steady, quiet industry at the farms I visit—another quilt, another rocking chair, another wedding, another baby. I enjoy the red strawberries at the end of June, the aroma of freshly baked bread in a spotless kitchen, the sight of newly-made sausages going into the smokehouse on poles. These people are not "back to the land" farmers; they've been there all along.

I wonder if I might choose to come back in the next life into the Amish world. With farms failing across the nation, maybe the Amish low-tech method has something to teach us. With strong family structure, a pervasive work ethic, and plenty of chores to keep them in shape, maybe the Amish can teach us a few things about living the good life.

They've been working at it full-time for hundreds of years.

All Amish names, although typical, have been changed to protect each individual's privacy. A few other details have been changed for the same reason, but all essential information is true.

Wedding Day at Birdsfoot Community

Peter Van de Water

I wore a coat and tie to Steve's marriage celebration. Becky said I shouldn't, that I'd be conspicuous, but I told her I would feel more comfortable dressed that way. Besides, at Birdsfoot Commune, it was okay to be different.

Steve was to be married, but this wasn't like any wedding I knew. The weddings of my experience were in solemn churches, with demure brides in white satin, taffeta bridesmaids, and groomsmen looking like Antarctic penguins lined up to pose for some fur-hooded photographer.

We got to Birdsfoot, an organic farming community, a few minutes before the marriage celebration was supposed to start. The guests were working their way up the garden paths to an open hayfield. We followed. At the hilltop, the path led under an arch of cedar poles; on the ground, cedar chips slowly released their welcoming fragrance. Steve stood barefoot athwart a farm wagon, throwing bales of hay to the wedding guests who were arranging them end to end in a giant circle. Bright banners of cloth, like Tibetan prayer flags, fluttered from poles ringing the circle of bales. Druids probably married in such surroundings, I thought.

I wondered about what was to happen, and thought of the time Steve had hugged me. A conflict had arisen at an environmental meeting we were both attending, and afterward, I had been surprised by Steve's hug of understanding. If Steve was so warm in a political meeting, what would be in store for the guests at a wedding ceremony? Would we guests be required to take off our shoes and socks to get close to the earth, or chant some mantra while we gazed into the sun, or embrace those to the right and left of us as a symbol of international harmony?

The hour of the wedding came and went; no one seemed to care. People stood in small groups, whispering, waiting for instructions. A few latecomers hurried up the path. A robin called from a hedgerow at the hayfield's edge. Finally, we guests were told to sit in a circle on the bales of hay. Patreesha, gentle mistress of ceremonies, said we should be quiet and think thoughts of peace and love.

Steve and his bride took opposing places in the circle. The rippling breeze blew the cloth banners almost straight out, and the sun warmed us when it wasn't under scudding clouds. I peeked around. Women, mostly young and middle-aged, wore bright, embroidered shirts of cotton or silk. Some were barefoot, and most wore billowing skirts; I was momentarily unsettled by the sight of black hair curling on feminine legs. Bright vests, broad hats—raiment from foreign travels—distinguished the men.

Steve wore a fez-like felt hat, a multi-colored embroidered shirt, and black silk pants like those worn by Vietnamese peasants. When he donned footwear, he slipped into white fur boots which could have come straight from a "Dr. Zhivago" set. Steve's father, the only other one in a coat and tie, looked uncomfortable. I dipped my head in a sympathetic nod, wedged myself closer to Becky on our bale, and relaxed a little.

Suddenly Dulli, Steve's bride, a pretty, wholesome looking young German woman, leaped to her feet. "Steff, I luff you. I vant to marry you," she bellowed into the breeze. The ceremony had begun. Steve and Dulli, now in the middle of the circle of bales, exchanged vows they had written, and around the circle, each of us in turn spoke our thoughts to them. Wanting to be wise and witty in my oral offering, I failed miserably, and spoke instead some vacuous platitudes about health and happiness.

Then bride and groom read from each other's love letters, remnants of a long-distance courtship. A local minister pronounced them married; it seemed apparent her involvement was needed only to satisfy the legal strictures of the State of New York.

A great round of hugging followed the ceremony. It didn't seem to matter that men hugged men and women hugged women. Some of Steve's and Dulli's closest friends were crying tears of joy. It felt good to observe such happiness for the newlyweds, and it was obvious that the residents of Birdsfoot Community, past and present, shared a deep affection for each other.

I exchanged a few awkward hugs and kisses with other guests; then, shepherded by Patreesha, we wandered along the windy hilltop to inspect the house that Steve and Dulli were building together, and to hammer a few symbolic nails into the sheathing. The house turned out to be just what I expected: sturdy, unpretentious, and in harmony with its hilltop setting. The rough-cut siding was left unpainted to weather in the winds and rains. The floors were natural wood, uncovered by rugs or carpet, and the beams were left exposed. One beam in particular had gained local notoriety: a massive oak, it had taken the wobbly efforts of a phalanx of sturdy volunteers to place it firmly on the foundation walls. A wood stove provided the only heat. Despite Spartan furnishings, the effect was warm and inviting; the young couple would be well sheltered, I thought.

After the marriage ceremony, everybody was invited to a potluck dinner reception at the Community Center in Crary Mills: an old Grange Hall with a tin ceiling and, upstairs, a stage for the band and wooden floors for dancing. Three hours is about my limit for weddings and receptions, and this affair promised to be a marathon, so Becky and I deliberately arrived late. I was plenty hungry, but there wasn't much left. The remnants of salads, tofu in dozens of glutinous forms, breads, and fruits littered the banquet tables, but there was an untouched platter of sliced beef and ham, obviously shunned by the vegetarian crowd.

Hoping nobody would notice, I piled my plate high. Upstairs there was contra dancing, and Becky and Lee, my grandson, were stomping happily. I was a reluctant dancer, but once dragged into the circle, I found to my relief that contra dancing was little different from the square dances of my youth. Skill level didn't seem to matter anyway. Old and young, graceful and gauche, pranced and pirouetted, making circles of swirling color as the ancient floor heaved gently in time with the music.

It was all very jolly, but still a foreign world to me. When my three-hour time limit had expired, Becky and I left a party in full swing. We nodded good-byes to knots of more soberly dressed male communicants clustering just outside the entrance to the Community Center. Some were smoking, and all were engaged in serious discussion—probably, I thought, of seeds and mulches, hoes and scythes, or the latest machinations of the Bush administration.

It was easy to imagine the same scene set a hundred years ago: the stolid citizenry of Pierrepont and Langdon Corners and Crary Mills assembled for a harvest celebration, waxing enthusiastically over the amazing newfangled farm machinery just invented—mowing machines, corn planters, manure spreaders, cream separators, potato planters . . . *why, with his new machine, a good man could produce four times as much in a twelve hour day as his father could back in Civil War times!*

I wanted to capture the scene forever on daguerreotype or tintype. I wanted to compare my picture with the dusty scenes in the drawers at the St. Lawrence County Historical Society. These men, children of the sixties, had a connection to the traditions of the past that their counterparts on Wall Street and in suburban America do not.

Emotionally, I could relate to these quiet country people. I sympathize with their reverence for preserving the quality of earth and water and air. I'm an organic gardener, too; I produce vegetables in abundance, and apples, blueberries, raspberries, and maple syrup for sale. I like having calluses on my hands and garden dirt caked to the knees of my jeans. I value wholesome food and disdain the showy fruit and vegetable displays in the P&C. My gardener side comes from my father and, like him, I enjoy swapping ideas on seed varieties and growing techniques with the farmers at Birdsfoot.

Among ourselves, we gardeners affect a modesty about the fruits of our labors, but I left Steve's and Dulli's wedding glowing from knowing comments about a big bowl of shiny Harelson apples, my contribution to the gathering.

On the way home, Becky and I pondered our day. We felt honored to have been invited to Steve's marriage celebration. We knew we had been included in a world unknown to our usual professional colleagues. Did our new friends represent a nostalgic but vain attempt to return to a bucolic past? Would the sweep of progress bury their outdated lifestyles and crush their misguided idealism? Or were they, instead, a link with our forgotten forebears, a Biblical "remnant" clinging to the best of the past, preserving it for the modern world until the rest of us were ready?

Who were these people? I thought. Why were they here? What did I know of them, and should I know more? How did I, a middle-aged family man who had spent thirty years of professional life in responsible administrative positions, fit with them?

Thirty years ago, we would have called the people of Birdsfoot and their friends "hippies," or "drop-outs," or some similar none-too-flattering appellation. Now, if the setting were a college campus, they would be known as "crunchy granolas," or simply "granolas." The current generic is "counter-culture"—less pejorative, maybe, but nevertheless a term like "attention-deficit disorder" or "sight-distance limited" that attempts to mask something that could be unpleasant if faced squarely.

The "counter-culture" in the North Country isn't terribly visible. On Main Street in any North Country village, only a discerning eye would notice the difference between counter-culturists—CCs for short—and rural natives. Maybe there are subtleties of dress, such as the CCs' preference for wool caps (called toques in the North Country) rather than the lettered baseball caps of the natives, or plaid wool shirts rather than Carhart jackets. But CCs blend nicely into the North Country milieu, befitting people who shun ostentation and like to live lightly on the land. During my years as a college administrator, CCs played no role in my life, and I expect that was true as well for just about all businessmen and professionals in the North Country.

I had a fleeting acquaintance with two young men from Big Dog commune—men whose names escape me now—when they helped my father build a log cabin a mile back in our woods, maybe twenty-five years ago. My father admired these men for their gentle ways and self-sufficiency, but there was something dark and mysterious about them that caught my attention: the aura of free love, maybe drugs. Later, when Big Dog was abandoned, my curiosity got the best of me, and I hiked back in the woods near Russell along overgrown trails up a hill to a clearing and the biggest log house I had ever seen.

Why had it been abandoned? What went wrong here? Would others come back? I wandered around looking for clues, but only haunting images remained: a cultivator rusting in a forlorn, weed-choked garden; a wall poster with a big, yellow "happy face," the mouth of which had been repainted in a child's hand so that at the corners it turned down, sorrowfully.

Only in the last few years have I come to know more about CCs through our shared struggles to preserve the environment. Since 1970, we environmentalists in the North Country have won a few more battles than we've lost. When Horizon Corporation proposed thousands of second homes in the Adirondack Park near Colton, we stopped the Tucson developer until the Adirondack Park Agency set land-use controls.

We lost when the New York State Power Authority forced through the 765KV line to carry power downstate, but we chased the state away when it suggested a "low-level" radioactive waste dump, and we stopped the St. Lawrence County incinerator. Most recently, we convinced the Strategic Air Command to stop flying B-52s low over our homes.

Whenever there was an environmental crisis brewing, there would be meetings. The usual format was that some facile bureaucrat—replete with charts—representing one government agency or another, would harangue the unwashed, unlettered citizenry of the North Country about the merits of some disguised environmental debacle. Then, at least in St. Lawrence County—much to the astonishment of the government bureaucrat and his coterie—up from the crowd would pop numerous speakers to refute and rebut skillfully, with both emotion and evidence. Most—but not all—were men, and many of the men wore scraggly beards, overalls, plaid shirts, and hiking boots. My new friends: the CCs!

Through these loose environmental alliances, I came to know more CCs, to respect their feeling for the planet, and admire them for being willing to fight for it. Here, living quietly in the woods and on the fringes of North Country villages, I discovered a group of people who have infiltrated the established order of things with ideals of peace, serenity, harmony, and tolerance.

The CCs first came to St. Lawrence County in the 1960's and 70's. They were young and bright, often graduates or drop-outs from prestigious colleges and universities. The main attraction was the North Country's open space, woods and waters, natural beauty, and, perhaps most of all, cheap land. Like nineteenth-century immigrants seeking succor in ethnic neighborhoods, CCs clustered at first in communes with like-minded friends: Big Dog, Birdsfoot, Beaver Creek. Except for Birdsfoot—still a thriving community of a dozen people or so—the other alliances have disbanded.

The original CCs, escapists searching for something like the modern equivalent of early nineteenth-century Utopian experiments such as Brook Farm, New Harmony, or the Oneida Community, have long-since had youthful idealism rubbed away by the harsh realities of North Country living. Agrarian utopias are better suited to more southern climes, where the soil is deeper, the markets closer, the summers longer. But most of the people have stayed anyway, have built their own frugal farms and homes, have assumed their quiet roles in their own communities, and have attracted others like them to the area.

A number of CCs have even accepted positions on School

Boards and planning commissions, as their role has shifted from escapist newcomers to respected, responsible neighbors. But at reunions such as Steve's marriage, memories return. Shared dreams and the pioneering hardships of the past make greetings among long-time friends particularly poignant.

The CCs aren't an organized group in the usual sense. No letterhead proclaims, "Counter-Culture Society"; no Pennysaver picture announces new officers or regular meetings. Indeed, remembering that CCs prize individualism, it may be unfair to describe them in sweeping generalities.

But common values and a shared way of life say "CC" just as surely as a member button denotes the Rotarian, or a window sticker on the pick-up truck boasts "NRA." While not so obvious, CCs, like most groups, have subtle ways of signaling to each other. A battered car or truck with a bumper sticker proclaiming "Love Your Mother (Earth)," or "I get my energy from the sun," or "Make Peace Not War" is a dead giveaway that you are behind a CC—or at least someone who shares CC values.

Most CCs have little regard for money. It would be bad form to seek to accumulate wealth, or talk about it, or drive a car that showed you had it, or climb any kind of ladder to gain more of it. If one can find a job—ideally part-time—so that life's needs can be met, that is sufficient. Most CCs are well acquainted with Scott and Helen Nearing's book, *Living the Good Life,* a back-to-the-lander's "Bible" that exhorts true believers to devote half the day to "bread labor" and half to music, study, writing, travel, and social intercourse. The Nearings fled an "acquisitive" suburban society for the hills of Vermont, then Maine when Vermont became too crowded. For North Country CCs, like the Nearings, the ideal job has flexible hours and allows for self-direction with lots of time off.

In the North Country, the "helping professions" of teaching or social work come closest to the ideal, while farming in its various forms is appealing, though often hard with meager compensation. As a corollary to this philosophy of work, most CCs I have known are exceedingly generous. This year, for the first time ever, some of my root-cellar carrots became moldy. When I related this unwelcome phenomenon to my friend Patreesha, she replied instantly that Birdsfoot had plenty and that I should have as many of theirs as I wanted.

CCs embrace nature. Their homes are far back from the road, made of wood—preferably hand-hewn logs or rough lumber—and left unpainted, naturally. Clothes are nature's fibers: wool and cotton for work and everyday, and sometimes silk for dress-up. Machinery is too expensive, too showy, and just too agribusiness for the hobby and subsistence farms of CCs; horses are preferred, and hoes and hand-rakes that bring the wielder close to the earth.

Food is grown organically. Cover crops, animal manures, and mulches provide healthy soil for abundant crops of healthy vegetables. They shun commercial fertilizers, herbicides, and pesticides. The organic farmers of Birdsfoot have an enviable reputation for producing wholesome, appealing vegetables. Birdsfoot spinach, in particular, is prized in local markets. Even the Cornell University College of Agriculture, long addicted to promoting farming and gardening with chemicals, has begun to consider the merits of organic farming, and has invited one of the Birdsfoot gardeners to be a panelist at a forum in Ithaca.

At Birdsfoot, foods are preserved in root cellars and dried and canned rather than frozen, as freezers use too much of nature's resources in the form of electricity.

In fact, conventionally produced electricity is used lightly, if at all. Most homes are heated by wood—a renewable resource—rather than by oil or by electricity, which is usually generated by non-renewable oil or coal. Nuclear power, with its endless half-life and no safe means of waste disposal, is out. Solar and wind are the desirable energy sources, and photovoltaic cells, solar collectors, and windmills mark the homes of many CCs. Because energy is hoarded, and because much of television is only glitzy commercialism anyway, most CC homes do without it. Mention the choicest gossip from Rosie O'Donnell or Oprah Winfrey to a CC, and your reward will be a blank stare and a polite but perplexed shrug of the shoulders. Who knows? Who cares?

Even children are a luxury. Because humans consume too much of earth's precious resources, conscientious CCs are unlikely to have more than one or two children.

With the exception of environmental issues, CCs generally avoid politics. Some, with total disdain for "the system," refuse to register to vote. Yet in their own gatherings, CCs practice democracy in extremis: there is no president, chairman, or leader. Someone may be the "convener," whose job is to set the meeting place and time and, with others, set the agenda.

There is no majority vote. Instead, decisions are reached by "consensus," a lengthy procedure during which each person's viewpoint is sought and considered, and no utterance—however impractical or absurd—is rejected out of hand. Only when everyone in the group can accept a proffered decision is a consensus reached.

I remember so well my despair at the organizational meeting of the Coalition on Low-Altitude Flights. Fifteen or twenty or us, including many CCs, were trying to establish the procedures by which the organization would be governed. When it became obvious that "consensus" would be required on all decisions, I suffered inwardly, having already been the victim of too many lengthy meetings over too many years. Predictably, our meetings dragged into the night.

There are other ties that bind CCs: North Country Public Radio, with its classical music and special programs for jazz, African, and Gaelic music; "Seedcorn," a Potsdam-based group that promotes sustainable energy and other environmental causes; the Potsdam Food Co-op; Nature's Storehouse in Canton, a source of whole grains, dried fruits, and natural vitamins.

The CC world is not my world. Unlike Steve's house, mine has carpet and lamps and pictures and color TV and modern appliances and even some knickknacks on the bookshelves. I don't need all those things, but I like them.

I'm grateful, however, that for most of my life I have been attuned to the rhythms of simple country living. Most of my professional friends don't see what surrounds them. I learned this in 1976 when a mini-tornado smashed through Canton. My house in the village was in the eye of the storm, which uprooted four huge maples in my front yard and even more honey locusts in my back yard. We were then building a stone house in the country, so after I had hacked and sawed my way through the devastated yards, on weekends I began to haul loads of firewood through the village to my new home. I didn't give it much thought at the time, but the sight of a vice-president of St. Lawrence University, dressed in coveralls and mounted on an ancient John Deere tractor, towing a load of firewood piled high in a worn-out manure spreader, must have been incongruous to my college colleagues.

What I remember is that I chanced upon several faculty friends as my John Deere putt-putted by the college walks. I smiled and waved as always, and they looked right at me, but they didn't acknowledge me. They couldn't know me, and so they didn't see me.

I'm pleased I've been allowed glimpses into the lives of CCs. I'm glad CCs have found a home here. They fit well. They appreciate the beauty in their surroundings. They ask little of others, and are kind and generous neighbors. They live lightly. They have a lot to teach others about the methods of organic farming, ways to dry and store vegetables and fruits, and threats to the environment.

They have much to teach others, too, about respect and caring, not only for the land, but for people of diverse backgrounds and differing ideals. Now that I know a little more about CCs, I feel comfortable with them. I hope they feel comfortable with me. If I keep my eyes and ears open, I expect I can learn a lot from my new friends. Oh, I'm still going to paint my house every few years, and keep my lawn trimmed. And Becky likes lots of lights, especially during the holiday season.

I guess that's why I wore a coat and tie to Steve's marriage celebration.

Katie

Karen M. Johnson-Weiner

When I first met Katie, she was sitting in a rocking chair in the middle of a crowded little room. It was maybe 12 feet by 20 feet and the small space was all there was in the little house for her five small children to play. It was late fall and already cold, but the big wood stove kept the room very warm. Her children stared at me. The oldest, six, wasn't in school yet; the youngest, a one-year-old, snuggled in Katie's lap.

I really didn't know what to say to Katie on that first visit, so I asked her about her children. It was a good move. We began comparing childbirth experiences and moved on to discuss feeding and clothing babies. Her children quickly accepted me, and in the weeks and year that have followed, my Pennsylvania German has improved as I have drawn endless pictures for them of "shayas" (barns), "galies" (horses), "metlies un buwas" (girls and boys), and "wawas" (wagons).

Understanding the Amish way of life has been my goal for many years. I wanted, at first, to study Pennsylvania German, an unwritten German dialect, but it didn't take me long to decide that the grammar of the language was not nearly as interesting as the people who were using it. Why and how, I began to wonder, did the Amish continue to maintain a separate language, and the separate, archaic lifestyle that went with it, two centuries after the first Amish arrived in North America? And so I began to explore the North Country Amish communities, discovering a new culture, a way of life grounded in belief in God and dedicated to following Christ's example.

The Amish came to the North Country in the mid-1970s, and there are now two distinct communities. The largest is the Swartzentruber settlement, founded by Amish from Holmes County, Ohio. One of the most conservative Amish groups, the Swartzentruber community has grown steadily in the past twenty years. I first made contact with the Swartzentruber at the local farmers' market. After several encounters there, Katie invited me into her home.

Katie was not the first Amish person I met, nor even the first Swartzentruber Amish person. There are Amish women I have known longer and others I visit more often. Yet, when someone asks me what the Amish are like, I think of Katie first.

Katie is my age, but otherwise we are very different. I have a Ph.D., and she has an eighth-grade education. I show up in jeans, and her dresses are ankle-length and dark. I teach full-time and rely on day care; Katie cleans, cooks, and sews, and has never had a baby-sitter. I am a TV addict and Katie has never lived with electricity or indoor plumbing. Yet, she has become my friend and taught me about her world.

Were you to ask Katie to describe herself, she would look at you oddly, and then tell you that she's just a wife and mother. Pressed to go further, she would sigh and say there was no more to say. Asked why, she would tell you, "That's just our way."

Katie has become all she wanted to be, for she is a wife and that is *the* career goal for Amish women. It's what young Amish girls are raised to expect, and they prepare for it from birth. Katie is a good wife. She knows her place and her responsibilities. Among the Amish, descendants of sixteenth-century Anabaptists determined to live "according to evangelical truth and the word of God," men and women have clearly defined roles. Referring to the creation of Adam and "his mate," Eve, and their subsequent expulsion from the Garden of Eden, Amish writer Joseph Stoll argues that "scripture very clearly places the man in a position of responsibility as the head of the household, and his wife in a position of subjection." This power relationship is upheld, the Amish believe, by New Testament writings. Cited often in Amish magazines and stories is the fifth chapter of Paul's letter to the Ephesians, in which he proclaims, "Wives, be subject to your husbands as to the Lord; for the man is the head of the woman, just as Christ also is the head of the church. Christ is, indeed, the Savior of the body; but just as the church is subject to Christ, so must women be to their husbands in everything."

It is an order that places women at the mercy of men, a fact of which Amish women are all too aware. A short story in the Amish publication *Family Life* tells of a widow whose only daughter, Rachel, was "grown to womanhood" and yet continually rejected suitors. When asked why, Rachel replied, "I guess I'm just scared. It frightens me to even think of marriage. You know what the Bible teaches about the wife submitting to her husband. It says he is supposed to 'rule' over me. Why, I would be completely at his mercy! He could treat me any way he wanted to."

The woman's only protection is her husband's obedience to Paul's command: "Husbands, love your wives, as Christ also loves the church" (Ephesians 5:25), a command that, Stoll argues, "leaves no place for bossiness or a superior feeling and grants no right to be selfish or mean."

The Amish would deny that women are less than men. Indeed, many have told me that men and women are equal according to scripture. After all, one preacher insisted, "doesn't it say in Galatians 3:28, 'There is no such thing as . . . male and female, for you are all one person in Christ Jesus'." As Stoll writes, "Life is full of authority. Being a woman means there is one more level of subjection than being a man. That is all. It doesn't mean that a woman is thereby being degraded, cheated, or despised. It is simply a fact of life, like being born a girl in the first place."

To the Amish, what is important is to fulfill one's God-given role in life. A woman is expected to keep the home, help her husband, and teach her children. Katie knows her place. John is the head of the household. Yet Katie and John are partners who are both needed if the household is to function. He takes care of the farm and she takes care of the home. John makes the final decisions, yet he defers to Katie's expertise. She is the quilter, for example, and she sets the quilt prices. She is in charge in the kitchen. John reads the Bible, but Katie sets the girls and the younger boys to their tasks. She takes care of the "house garden" and she sets the canning schedule, which guides much of the household activity in the late summer and fall. Katie makes out the shopping list that John takes into town.

Responsible for maintaining the house, Katie is thrifty, as, indeed, she must be with so many children. Nothing is wasted. Her letters to me come on half sheets of paper or even on the back of my letters to her. The mix of colors in the quilts she makes is often determined by what scraps of cloth she has left over from the clothing she has been sewing.

One day last spring I took my children, another friend, and her two sons out to see the new calves at Katie's farm. We found Katie and most of her children sitting on a huge pile of clothing back behind the house, next to the garden patch. "The rag man's been," Katie said. As she explained it, someone visits thrift shops or clothing outlets (she wasn't sure), picks up unwanted or surplus pieces of clothing, and sells the clothing by the truckload. Katie had just gotten a load.

It was easy to see that many of the items were quite serviceable. In fact, my friend's five-year-old found a sweatshirt bearing a likeness of Batman that Katie cheerfully gave him. Nevertheless, they were certainly not Amish clothes. "We get them for the buttons," said Katie. And that's what everyone was doing—twisting the buttons off the strange mix of trousers, shirts, blouses, and sweaters. Katie's littlest ones tried their best; her bigger girls sat with huge mounds of buttons in front of them. Some of the buttons were too fancy for use on Amish clothes.

Katie examined any that seemed questionable, separating them into those useful for dresses and pants and those good for threading on strings for baby toys.

Stripped of buttons, most of the items were useless. Yet serviceable tee-shirts and thermal underwear were set aside to be washed and used, as were plain, dark-colored shirts that could be altered to meet Amish standards. Other solid-colored pieces in browns, blues, grays, dark greens, and black were saved to be ripped for cleaning cloths. Anything in bright colors or patterns or "silky" material was set aside for burning.

We worked together quietly on that pile of old clothes. My children and those of my friend ran and shouted in the fields, played in the barn, and fed anything they could find to the pigs and cows. For the most part, Katie's children watched them curiously, too bashful to join in with the strange "English" children. Eli, Katie's oldest boy, was the exception. Eli has been my son's favorite ever since he showed Seth the chicken coop and, as part of the tour, put a chicken on his (Eli's) head. Seth has admired Eli ever since, an adoration that shows no signs of fading, for Eli patiently lets Seth "help him chore" whenever Seth comes out. The friendship is a mutual one. Eli has confided to me several times that he "just likes the way Seth talks."

I worry about the effect my children will have on Katie's. The Amish attempt to live a life separate from the world, and Amish children, especially Swartzentruber Amish children, have little contact with those outside their Amish community. Katie's children learn English when they start school at age six or seven and, even then, don't speak it much unless an outsider is present. Katie told me once that she doesn't mind if the children speak English around the house, but "if they do it too much, we make them stop." My visits, especially when my children come with me, bring the outside world into Katie's home. Once I heard one of Katie's boys ask if he could have "englishe henshing"—"English" mittens. I haven't worn brightly colored gloves since, but I know that I can't eliminate the rest of the world's influence so easily.

Katie doesn't seem to think I'm a bad influence, and she welcomes my children (although she has asked them to leave their tape recorders at home!). Certainly, having two more children around the house doesn't faze her in the least. Children are always everywhere. In fact, I've never seen Katie alone. When I first met her, she had Jonas on her lap. He was a year old, one year younger than my son. In the years that I've known her, I've had one more child and she's had five, for a total now of ten. For the Amish, a baby is a gift from God, and, as Katie is the first to say (in a variety of intonations), she has certainly been blessed.

One would think that school would also be a blessing to a mother at home with ten children. Katie, however, looks forward to the end of school in the spring and dreads the end of the summer break. "I lose my help," she says. In fact, school plays a marginal role in the Amish community: the important lessons—how to manage the farm and the house, how to care for children, how to work hard—are learned at home.

When an Amish child is born, it is born into the community and treated as a future member of the community. John Hostetler, a sociologist who was raised in an Old Order Amish community, notes that the child may be referred to as "a new woodchopper," but never "the little stranger." The parents have an obligation to train the child so that it does, indeed, become a contributing member of the group. Yet, although the parents act as a unit in raising children, each has a particular role.

In his letter to Titus, Paul charges older women to "set a high standard" and to "school the younger women to be loving wives and mothers, temperate, chaste, and kind, busy at home, respecting the authority of their own husbands" that the word of God "will not be brought into disrepute" (Titus 2:3-5). Katie instructs her children by example. Rather than telling her daughters how to make a pie, she hands them dough, and they copy her actions, the four-year-old banging her lump flat and the thirteen-year-old duplicating Katie's twisted crust edging. Katie is unfazed by the flour flying everywhere. Cleaning up is another chore to be shared, another skill to be learned.

Indeed, every task, from frying chicken to sorting potatoes for sale, is a family task. Now, Katie's oldest daughter, only a year away from her eighth-grade graduation and the end of her formal education, can easily handle the house in her mother's absence. All of the children help; the four-year-old washes the face of the two-year-old, and the five-year-old brings in wood.

My arrival is an occasion for Katie to take a break, but while we sit talking and rocking, her children stay busy with their tasks. I have never heard her raise her voice, nor has she ever had to ask a child more than once to do something. And the older ones anticipate the orders. By involving the children in daily tasks, from fetching a washrag for the baby's face to weeding the strawberries, she not only teaches them to do the task, but also makes them responsible for the family's well being.

The responsibility each child has to the others is reinforced in a variety of ways. Older children are expected to stop what they are doing to assist or comfort a younger one, something even the toddlers have picked up. When the baby—now almost a year—cries, the next oldest, himself only two, runs to her aid. The children learn early to give not only their time but also their possessions. I have seen Katie take a cookie away from her five-year-old and give it to her three-year-old, and the five-year-old does not cry.

Before I met any Amish, I believed in the stereotype of the orderly, spotless "Pennsylvania Dutch" home, in which the children were always scrubbed and well behaved, and the floors were so clean one could eat off them. I have never found such an Amish home. In fact, with ten children, each child learning by doing, Katie's house is sometimes in chaos. Yet, I have never seen Katie—or any other Amish mother for that matter—lose her temper or even become outwardly impatient. It is an acquired calm, and Katie teaches it to her children as she teaches pie making and housecleaning.

During prayers before and after meals, for example, she holds the baby's hands together, immobilizing it and calmly shushing its whimpers, and when it is old enough to sit by itself, the gesture and the silence that goes with it come naturally. Katie braids her daughters' hair—a long process, as, following the advice in I Corinthians, Amish girls and women never cut their hair, and not even the littlest girls can let their hair down. Each takes her turn climbing up on the high stool in the kitchen and sitting patiently while Katie first makes two braids and then twists them elaborately with string so that they won't show under the cap. She pulls the hair tight, but the girls don't complain. A hard candy helps the littlest make it through; by the time a girl is six or seven, she no longer needs or gets the candy, and, by the time she is married with children of her own, her hair, thin from constant twisting, will hang below her waist, her hairline will have receded from being pulled back so tightly, and she will be able to put it up in under five minutes.

I watch two of the little girls distract the baby with a string of beads to keep him from crying. They are keeping him busy while Katie sews and talks and their big sister washes the kitchen floor. The infant is also their entertainment. Their "job" is to make him laugh. For these little girls, and for the Amish community, there is no sharp line between work and play. In fact, a gathering to accomplish some job is called a frolic. Like weddings, frolics are occasions for families to come together and enjoy themselves.

By chance, I arrived one day when Katie's brother Amos and his family were butchering hogs. Helping him were Katie and John and brother-in-law Pete. Everyone was in the cellar, Pete stirring frying fat in a giant kettle to render it for lard, John up to his arms in ground pork, mixing in spices for sausage, and Katie and Susie, Amos' wife, busily pulling cooked meat off the bone.

Most "English" people have never seen a gathering like this. It wasn't preparation for a big dinner; it was filling Amos and Susie's cellar so they could eat throughout the winter. The week before, the three families had met at Pete's house to fill his cellar, and the week before that, they had met at Katie's.

As I joined Katie and Susie to pick the bones, Susie welcomed me by putting a little pile of salt by my place. "We like to eat a little too," confided Katie, dipping a small piece of pork in the pile. John had his hair and beard wrapped in a "kopduche," a head scarf, causing great hilarity and many comments about the new "woman in the group." He also put up with much criticism from his female counterparts about the spices he was adding and his mixing techniques.

At a break, we ate mounds of half-moon or "schnitz" pies, turnovers with a filling made from dried apples, tasted "balogna" made at Pete's the week before, and drank hot coffee. Amos' oldest boy refilled the woodbox so that Pete could keep the fire going under the kettle of boiling fat. Amos's oldest girl fried up a bit of the sausage John had mixed so that everyone could taste it. Katie and Susie pronounced it flat and sent John back to mixing.

Throughout this time, Katie's five youngest children and Susie's four or five pre-schoolers played under the supervision of Susie's older girls, who were also busy doing the daily cooking and cleaning. The cousins reveled in the chance to play with other children, friends they didn't get to see often enough. The bigger ones sat on the cellar stairs, fascinated by the activity and anxious to be able to run errands.

In short, frolics are parties at which a lot of work gets done. Cousins, who only get to see each other at church when there is little time for running and shouting, play tag outside while their parents stuff sausage. Silo filling means a day off from school. At barn raisings, the young boys watch the men build the barns and count themselves lucky to have a role passing nails. And while the younger children watch their fathers, their mothers socialize in different groups inside, some cooking, some quilting, and some—a mix of the newest mothers, grandmothers, and adolescent girls—gathering in a back room to nurse babies, change toddlers, and just mend clothing. Work and play are inseparable.

Katie's oldest daughter is nearly old enough to join the "young folk," those aged sixteen and older who meet to socialize until they marry. Frolics are an important part of the young folks' social calendar, along with hymn sings, suppers, and skating parties.

When Ruthie goes to her first hymn sing, Katie's role changes quietly but dramatically. Unlike younger children, young folk have a social life with each other distinct from family activities. Young folk are able to spend time running around before settling down, being baptized, and getting married. In other Amish communities, young folks may buy forbidden objects such as cameras, radios, or even cars and store them at the homes of "English" neighbors. Katie's community, however, is one of the most conservative; Swartzentruber young folk don't visit "English" restaurants, hike their skirts higher, turn up their hat brims, or go on shopping trips to the nearest mall.

Ruthie won't be able to run too wild. Nevertheless, she will be managing her own life. If all goes well, she will choose to become baptized, marry a baptized Swartzentruber Amish man in good standing, and begin to raise her own family according to the teachings of her community .

The community is the church. Indeed, the Pennsylvania German word for church is gmay, from the standard German *Gemeinde,* which means community. For the Amish, the "church" has nothing to do with a building in which one meets, or even the meetings themselves; it is, rather, a redemptive community formed of those dedicated to putting the teachings of Jesus Christ into practice. Katie, like other Amish adults, joined this community by becoming baptized. Baptism is, for the Amish, a covenant with God. Only adults can make a commitment of such importance, and they are urged to think carefully before taking such a step.

If Ruthie chooses to become baptized, she will be bound to maintain the discipline—what the Amish call the "Ottning," from the standard German *Ordnung* or order of the community. Encoding the community's beliefs, the Ottning governs most aspects of Amish life, from the length of one's skirts and the width of one's hat brim to the use of tractors for belt power. The Amish refer to the Ottning as a "Zaun," a fence that unites the individual to the larger community and protects the community from the outside world.

Katie will be sad if Ruthie chooses not to become baptized, but there will be nothing she can do about it. Ruthie's decision will not be Katie's failure or success. Baptism is an individual choice; researchers suggest that anywhere from one tenth to one third of all Amish young folk ultimately decide not to be baptized. If Ruthie does not join the church, she will not be encouraged to stay in the community, but she will certainly not be thrown out. If she does become baptized and then violates the Ottning, she will be excommunicated—placed under the ban and shunned.

Shunning is community-wide tough love. Katie will shun a disobedient church member, even—or perhaps especially—a child, because she has no choice. The Bible says to "root out the evil-doer from your community" (I Corinthians 5:12-13); following the biblical command that one neither eat nor keep company with those expelled from the church (I Corinthians 5: 11; II Thessalonians 3:14). Shunning requires members of the community to cease all social and business relationships with the excommunicated person.

We see shunning as cruel. I cannot imagine willfully cutting all ties with a child of mine. For Katie, it is an act of both necessity and love, for not only will shunning protect the community from the wrongdoer; it may ultimately convince the one shunned of the error of his ways and bring him to repentance.

Katie doesn't appear to worry about what her children will do in the future or, indeed, about the future at all. Katie's approach to life seems to be to simply do the best she can and accept what comes. She has, as the Amish say, "given up." Resignation is not highly valued in my "English" world, but, for the Amish, to be resigned, to conquer one's will and submit to God's will as expressed in the Bible, is to achieve "Gelassenheit," a term that, according to Sandra Cronk, incorporates the personal attributes *of yieldedness* and *powerlessness.* To achieve Gelassenheit, to trust in God so completely that one questions nothing that befalls one, is the ultimate goal of every Amish individual.

Indeed, Hostetler and Huntington, in their 1971 study of children in Amish society , argue that "True education," according to the Amish, is "the cultivation of humility, simple living, and resignation to the will of God." This is expressed repeatedly in Amish publications. In an Amish children's story, for example, a little girl complains about not being able to make pictures as pretty as those made by some of the others. Her mother leads her, through gentle questioning, to the lesson of the story: "If we do our best with the talents God gave us, He will be satisfied." Or, as a story in *Family Life* ends, "Carry your cross for Jesus cheerfully, and your reward will be great. Carry it begrudgingly, and you will break down under the load." In one Amish poem, the author describes an infant lying trusting and secure in its mother's arms and wishes likewise to rest "trusting in my Father's will." Another reads, "We just can't know what lies ahead, . . . We just can't know the reasons, why sorrow has to be. . . . We just can't know, but we can trust."

Katie trusts. She gives herself up to the life she believes God wants her to live. Consequently, she doesn't worry now about the choices her children will make in the future. Her concerns are to raise her children and fulfill her own role in her immediate family and her community, the church. As long as she is resigned to her role as an Amish woman, her immediate and extended family and her church will provide her the support to face all that life will bring.

Katie's role as wife and mother is mirrored in the way she serves the larger church community. Like all other church members, she has vowed to maintain the discipline of the church, a promise renewed at communion twice a year. Although women cannot be ministers, they are responsible for preparing the home in which the church service is held. Church, held every other week, rotates from home to home, a practice probably traceable to the sixteenth century when Anabaptists had to gather in secret. To prepare for church, Katie will clean her house from top to bottom. She will line cupboards and drawers with new shelf paper and paint the downstairs rooms. She will scour pots and pans and wash all of the dishes.

And just as she must feed those in her immediate family, Katie must feed the larger church family she welcomes into her home—perhaps as many as thirty households. The supper served is the same from house to house, and each Amish community has its own standard meal. One group may serve sandwiches and Jell-O salad. The Byler Amish of Pennsylvania are known as the "Bean Soupers" for their custom of serving bean soup after church. In Katie's community, the meal is soup, bread, beets, pickles, and coffee, with pies to follow. Katie bakes dozens of loaves of bread and numerous pies.

Of course, Katie doesn't do it alone. Beginning the Monday before service is held at her home, Katie's sisters and mother come to help, reinforcing the bonds that keep the community together. I have seen them together, four or five women, all dressed alike in the manner prescribed by the church discipline, humoring the young children, nursing the babies, and supervising the "big girls," who are learning by doing to prepare their own homes for church.

The house will be as clean as new when everyone arrives for Sunday services and mountains of food will be prepared. Katie doesn't do this in the same spirit with which I cook and clean before a visit from relatives; she's not worried so much what people will think, nor is she hoping to "show off," and she certainly does not resent the extra work. Instead, she is preparing her home to welcome friends and family to share in worship. Her hard work is done gladly in her devotion to the Ordnung and to the church; that others have shared in it is a sign that the community is intact.

Katie's actions reinforce a way of life that has been shaped in response to persecution, one guided by a commitment to serve God. We look at their buggies, large families, lack of electricity, and strange clothing, and we speak of them as unchanging; yet, the Amish change. Their communities have evolved. Some now permit indoor plumbing and flower gardens; the Swartzentrubers don't. No two Amish communities have exactly the same discipline because no two communities have faced the same set of circumstances. Yet, all are guided by the conviction that the practices of the surrounding society will not please God. They must be in the world, but they will not be of it (John 18:36). Katie lives her life by this belief; it is, she says, "just our way."

I don't want to be like Katie. I don't want a life of unquestioning submission—not to my husband, nor to my community, nor even to my God. Nor do I wish such a life for my children. Yet, I envy Katie her security, her piece of mind, and her faith. I envy her life of seasonal ups and downs that continues unaffected for the most part by the events of my world. I retreat to her kitchen and sit by her stove, and our talk about quilting, farming, baking, and babies brings the stress and disorder of my life into new perspective.

As I sit in one of Katie's hickory rockers, I watch Ruthie, who at thirteen has already learned from her mother to manage the household, prepare meals, clean, and garden. She is very bright. When I first met her, she had not yet started school and spoke very little English, but she pestered me to teach her the "ABCs" and "1-2-3s." She and her brother started school together, but she was soon a grade ahead, making 100s on her spelling and arithmetic. Seven years later, Ruthie no longer climbs on my lap and asks me to draw pictures of "a barn with a silo and a wagon and a horse." Now she smiles and talks softly and shyly. She is not many years away from having her own home and has already ceased wearing the pinafore apron of the little girl and adopted the cape of the adult woman; she appears to be playing dress-up. Slender and tall, Ruthie moves quickly while her mother lumbers.

The community hopes that, twenty years from now, Ruthie will have at least five or six children and be a duplicate of her mother. Katie's a big woman, shorter than I am but about twice as wide. Nine months pregnant, she looks about the same as she does in between children. She wears dark dresses that are usually stretched tightly over her more-than-ample frame and, in winter, heavy, black high-top shoes. From April to October, she's more likely to be barefoot, and she has huge, wide feet. Her hair is pulled back and hidden under her white cap, making her round face even rounder. She had her teeth pulled sometime back and often doesn't put in the false ones. In short, she's hardly what we "English" would call attractive. But, she works hard to support her husband, and she teaches her children to work hard, be patient, and yield to the church.

If Ruthie becomes like her mother, then, in her Swartzentruber Amish community, she will, as well, be the ideal woman, as beautiful as they come. For it is with women such as Katie that Amish communities have survived for 300 years.

A Fred Exley Fan's Notes

Peter J. Bailey

It seems inevitable that as Fred Exley's death in 1991 recedes deeper into the past, we will come increasingly to confuse the Watertown, New York native and longtime Alexandria Bay resident with the self-named protagonist he created in his *Fan's Notes* trilogy. Fred quite intentionally created this problem, of course, his trio of fictional memoirs *(A Fan's Notes, Pages from a Cold Island,* and *Last Notes from Home*) deliberately blurring distinctions between author and character Exley, the protagonist being consistently portrayed as someone possessed of dramatically inflated versions of Exley's own vices, excesses and deficiencies. Complicating matters further, I should acknowledge, is the fact that to know Fred personally was regularly to see the distinction's validity challenged. Whereas it was an utterly sober, highly professional writer who invited me to work with him on turning his novelistic trilogy into a one-man stage play, it seemed to be the protagonist at his most anxiety-plagued worst who would occasionally call in the middle of the night to inform me of impossible literary projects he was undertaking in the morning, of writing rivalries in which he imagined himself embroiled, or of national magazine covers his picture was scheduled to adorn. To know Fred's work well, I've decided, is to understand one of the basic truths dramatized equally by his fiction and by his life as well: that in human beings, virtues and flaws—idealism and cynicism, sensibility and vulgarity, profundity and triviality—are too inextricably linked to be separated. With Fred, even more than with most of us, you regularly got the whole package.

I met Fred through a student enrolled in my Contemporary American Fiction course at St. Lawrence University in 1987. One day in class I compared Truman Capote's novelistic treatment of actual events in *In Cold Blood* to Exley's *A Fan's Notes* experiments in autobiographical fiction, and Kathleen Henry came up after class to say she and her husband, owners of an Alexandria Bay grocery store, had known Fred for years. Later that week she took an offprint of an essay I had recently published on Exley's novel and Frank Conroy's *Stop-Time* to Fred in the Bay as a token of my esteem. Fred decided that I'd appreciated his purposes in the novel better than other commentators had, and he soon began calling me from Watertown bars or from his Wellesley Island apartment at all hours of the night, generously rehearsing the article's virtues with me, and urging that I seek a larger audience for the piece than the academic journal in which it appeared had afforded.

Soon he and I had worked out the details for him to give a reading at St. Lawrence in the spring of that year, and once the date was set and the publicity distributed, I learned that, due to imbibing to mitigate pre-reading anxieties, Fred had failed to get through his previous appearance at the university ten years earlier. So Ms. Henry and other Alex Bay friends drove Fred to Canton one afternoon in late April, and we all took him to dinner at the University Inn, each of us attempting to distract him from ordering drinks and encouraging him to eat his prime rib instead. My introduction to his reading emphasized what the essay had: the absolute distinction between author Fred, the novel's all-controlling literary imagination, and protagonist Exley, the hapless inebriate dreamer whose story Fred's books portrayed fictively as his own. Those few in the audience who could follow the art-and-life contrasts I was describing probably doubted, once Fred began a reading which can best be described as shaky, whether character and author were as distinctively opposite as I'd argued. No matter how often Fred moistened his thumb, the pages of his manuscript resisted turning over; he seemed progressively to rely on the podium to support himself, and I realized halfway through the reading that an additional cup had appeared on the lectern next to the water glass I'd filled for him. The audience's applause at the reading's conclusion seemed to resonate with relief. That Fred had chosen to read to an auditorium of St. Lawrence students and faculty a chapter graphically describing his protagonist's sado-masochistic sex play with Robin Glenn, the love object of the then novel-in-progress, *Last Notes From Home,* was testimony either to Fred's artistic integrity or proof of his utter obliviousness to the issue of audience. Probably it was both.

I'm not sure where the idea for a theatrical version of Fred's trilogy originated. He had friends at the Guthrie Theatre in Minneapolis who expressed interest in the project, and Richard Gilman at Yale Drama School had been encouraging as well; Fred also knew William Devane, who was at that time appearing on the prime time soap, *Knots Landing* (to Fred, *Knothead's Landing),* and who'd expressed willingness to play Fred if a good script was developed. Why it occurred to Fred to entrust the task of transforming his books into a stage monologue to an academic who'd never even contemplated writing a play, I'm not sure, either—his selection may say something about the intensity of his interest in the theatre. He was reading proofs and making final changes in *Last Notes* at the time, for another thing, and I suspect he didn't much relish the idea of imaginatively revisiting and restructuring paragraphs which had already cost him years of effort and misery to produce. And, he clearly liked the terms in which I'd interpreted his work, the ironic distance I'd posited between him and his protagonist flattering both his actual life and his capacity for crafting novels.

When I received his letter proposing the project, I jumped at the opportunity, partly out of sincere respect for Fred's work, and partly out of an optimistic conviction that the best of his sprawling fictional memoirs could be somehow distilled into a compelling hour-and-a-half soliloquy. What I hoped the play could accomplish, I see now, was to recapitulate on a stage the process Fred had described in *A Fan's Notes* in having his protagonist imagine the salutary effects of unburdening himself to a psychiatrist: "I wanted to lie hour after hour on a couch pouring out the dark secret places of my heart—do this feeling that over my shoulder sat humanity and wisdom and generosity, a munificent heart—do this until that incredibly lovely day when the great man would say to me, his voice grave and dramatic with discovery , 'This is you, Exley. Rise and go back into the world a whole man.' " What I hoped the play could do was to materialize before the footlights somewhere a "whole man" Exley who understood from personal experience the human ills so unsparingly dramatized in his trilogy—mental derangement, drunkenness, violent impulses, ungratified sexual longing, despair—but whose transcendence of all of these is attested to by his ability to stand onstage and articulate his having survived all of them. (Few graduate students who, like me, completed graduate degrees in English in the 1970s emerged from their programs without having mastered the rhetoric of artistic salvation, the Modernist discourse of literature-as-the-redemption-of-shapelessly-raggedy-ass-human-existence; Fred's protagonist's human existence seemed to me about as shapelessly-raggedy-ass as it gets.) I wanted what I designated *The Exley Play* to dramatize not the writer who clung for dear life to the podium as he stumbled through public readings but the one the existence of whose books epitomize a literary discipline and self-control the trilogy's terminally disarrayed protagonist is incapable of achieving. What I'd neglected to notice was that the process hadn't worked for Exley's protagonist, who is never remotely transformed into the "whole man" of his psychiatrist fantasy.

I spent much of that summer cutting out and pasting together xeroxed passages from *A Fan's Notes, Pages From a Cold Island,* a few of Fred's published essays and excerpts from the *Last Notes From Home* manuscript he'd copied for me. The first realization I came to was that my task was complicated by the idiosyncratically intuitive structures of Fred's novels. Each book proceeds according to an oddly achronological, associative logic which often left me wondering how, in a few pages of *A Fan's Notes,* for instance, the narrative quite seamlessly shifts from a discussion of the idealized Exley created by Exley and his USC chums for his employment applications to a detailing of Exley's father's death in Watertown to a fond reminiscence of the final days of New York Giants coach Steve Owen's NFL career. The job of reorganizing material the original organizing principles of which were, at best, oblique proved daunting, the effort at points making me admire the more the novels' architectures, at other points prompting me to wonder whether I hadn't overestimated the artistic calculation expended in the books' construction. Once I'd gotten to know Fred better that summer by talking to him at some length, I understood that the structures of his novels replicated exactly the way his relentlessly analogical and restlessly combinative mind worked. However much I wanted Fred to be Joyce's detached, godlike artist, "indifferent, paring his fingernails" as he produced his impassioned prose, Fred had struck his literary pact with the devil's party of Henry Miller and an aesthetic which insisted that literary intensity is inseparable from self-indulgence and self-exposure.

Fred allowed me complete freedom as to what episodes from his work to use in the project. His only suggestion was that, were *The Exley Play* staged relatively quickly, its concurrence with the publication of *Last Notes From Home* would make it a useful promotional vehicle for that book, and, consequently, including a goodly portion of the novel might be advisable. The ninety page manuscript I ultimately spliced together attempted to dramatize the Exley protagonist's fiercely ambivalent relationship with America—which usually meant the Exley protagonist's relationship with American women. Adhering faithfully to the trilogy's own structure, I began with the opening scene of *A Fan's Notes* in which Exley's protagonist experiences his imagined heart attack in the bar of Watertown's New Parrot Restaurant, the epiphany it inspires revealing to him the inextricable connection between his self-hatred and his loathing for the country of which he is so markedly a product. The playscript culminated in the *Last Notes* closing admonition to Robin Glenn, "I shall in the end defeat you, Miss America, shall defeat you, learn to live with you and make you mine." In between these substantial monologues I used what I considered some of the most effective and evocative prose passages in Fred's work relating to the theme. I chose the expression of Exley's love-hate bond with Giants star Frank Gifford and the national celebrity he exemplifies; Exley's confrontation with the Kodachrome Americans whom he detests because they confer the very fame he covets; the sour acknowledgment, prepared for by enormous rhetorical momentum, that it is "my fate, my destiny, my end to be a fan"; the deeply moving *Pages from a Cold Island* eulogizing apostrophe to Talcottville resident Edmund Wilson as the epitome of American artistic integrity. By late August, I was ready to travel the sixty miles to Wellesley Island and present Fred with our play's first draft.

I had a number of reasons to be uneasy about this trip. There was, first off, the very real possibility that Fred wouldn't like the job I'd done, it having occurred to me at an advanced stage in the process of construction that no writer could fully approve a reconceptualizing of his novelistic visions, even if they'd initiated it. Then too, I felt a real reluctance to visit Fred at home. However confident I was of my analytical character/author dichotomy, I was nonetheless aware that some of the pain which breathes through Fred's work is the product of personal experience, not merely novelistic contrivance, and I'd have preferred to let the locale of that despondency remain the invisible background of two a.m. phone calls rather than becoming a place where I'd be spending an afternoon. I had somehow mythologized Fred's apartment, I understand now, into a kind of cave of sorrows, sorrows of a distinctly non-literary sort: entering that cave threatened to nullify my cherished belief in the difference between art and life. I also worried that he'd be drinking, a circumstance which would be unpleasant in itself, but which must also serve as a mirror reflecting back to me that I'd been doing my share of that that summer as well. And finally, I was deep enough into the project to be quite certain *The Exley Play* was never going to work.

Wellesley Island is a sparsely-settled member of the Thousand Islands, and the weirdly middle class apartment building Fred inhabited, the only such structure on the island, seemed, in its utter detachment from all other topographical features, an architectural caricature of the conditions—"apartness, confusion, loneliness and work, and *work, and work*"—which Fred ascribed to Edmund Wilson as the source of his literary greatness. Fred's apartment, the windows of which looked out pleasantly over the Lake of the Isles, embodied the very same values: it was a neat, cheerfully sunlit place whose only disproportion was the rows of books covering nearly every horizontal surface in the living room. Fred looked comfortably rumpled in his cardigan sweater, khakis and bedroom slippers, his friendly informality lapsing only when he slipped into his old habit of calling me Dr. Bailey. We talked some about the football Giants' preseason performance, about Frank Conroy, William Styron and other writers I admired whom he knew, and about his meeting with Diane Sawyer, whom Fred had described rapturously in an *Esquire* "Women We Love" entry. Our vaguely nervous conversation competed with *Out of Africa,* the video which I somehow remember screening on Fred's TV for the four or five hours I was there. But "work, and *work, and work*" was primarily what Fred and I did that afternoon, he intently evaluating *The Exley Play,* I reading revisions of *Last Notes'* closing chapters in manuscript. Occasionally he would look over his half-glasses and ask me in a characteristically slurred voice which had nothing to do with boozing, "Say, don'cha think'd be better if . . .? ," and because he was usually right, I'd make note of the change; he was also quick to recognize the transitional sentences between scenes which I'd written, asking me politely if it wouldn't be a good idea to make them sound more like him than like "a goddam college professor." Otherwise, we did what you do in a room full of books: we read.

And one of my clearest memories from that amiable visit is of the good laugh Fred and I had over the pertinence of his *Last Notes* description of the Paris friendship between Joyce and Hemingway to our afternoon's activity: "Hemingway had only to read a single paragraph of Joyce, Joyce reciprocate, to understand that Joyce and Hemingway were bound together by being on the same arduous, near-reverent pilgrimage, that is, of what the French call 'breaking the language,' of doing nothing less than taking the language and making it their very own." So pleasant was the afternoon, in fact, that neither of us felt compelled to acknowledge sardonically that those "breaking the language" at the moment were not Joyce and Hemingway, but Exley and Bailey. It didn't seem to matter.

The letters of the following fall and winter I have from Fred are strangely silent about the reasons that Gilman, Devane et al gave him for not wanting to involve themselves in *The Exley Play.* My recollection is that, like most failed enterprises, our project ended not with a bang but a whimper, Fred and I gradually losing touch with each other as the fruit of our collaboration continued to attract neither a welcoming theatre nor interested actor. But a mid-December letter from Fred does acknowledge that most successful one-person stage plays have two characteristics which ours lacked: "the personality is invariably dead and has become a part of American myth or legend, whereas Exley is not only very much alive but his books have sold poorly and the Exley character is virtually unknown to the public." In a late-October interview with the Rochester *Times Union,* Fred, addressing the utter bomb which was the film of *A Fan's Notes* produced in 1970, had anticipated another reason for *The Exley Play's* failure when he suggested that, "They never should have tried to film *A Fan's Notes.* It's an exercise in prose, really, and that's not translatable to the screen." Nor, we were to find out, to the stage. At one of the Flower Memorial Library events in Watertown commemorating Fred's career in 1993, John Golden, a *Watertown Times* columnist, offered a still more precise explanation for the untranslatabilty of Fred's novels into other media. So candid are the works' self-revelations, Golden suggested, so intimate the relationship established between narrator and (presumably male) reader that transforming them into the media of more public ceremonies nullifies the primary appeal of these novels. The emphatically male slant of Fred's books on the sins to which Exley confesses—drunkenness, sloth, incessant lustfulness, misogyny and masculinist self-pity—may well elicit guilty identification from the reader in the solitude of his living room; in a more communal setting, however, that same reader will need to repudiate the Exley on screen or stage lest he risk exposure as the inveterate sexual dreamer and wastrel Exley depicts himself as being. It takes a kind of courage not many of us have, I think Golden was arguing, to publicly acknowledge in ourselves the depths of decadent masculine self-absorption which Fred routinely attributed to the protagonist who bears his name.

The Exley Play manuscript gradually made its way from a pile of papers on my office desk to a folder in a file cabinet, the text, I had decided, doomed never to be illuminated by footlights by the discursiveness of Fred's prose and by my inability to imagine a structure for his paragraphs compelling enough to transform their discursiveness into stage drama. My disappointment at the failure of my personal Fred Exley reclamation project was tempered slightly, I should admit, by the fact that I hadn't much liked the Robin Glenn material which comprised the coda of *Last Notes,* of our script and, as it turned out, of Fred's literary career. (The pulmonary problems which lead the Exley protagonist to fear he's suffered a heart attack at the beginning of *A Fan's Notes* killed Fred in the summer of 1991: so much for the absolute distinction between art and life.) Robin, I agreed with a number of *Last Notes'* reviewers, was a dismally ineffective plot device, a Miss America fantasy too transparently embodying a misogynist construction of the desirability and corruptness of American womanhood, and the fact that the Exley protagonist treats her so badly throughout their improbable wedding scene makes the novel's resolution difficult to admire. Perhaps what I couldn't forgive in *Last Notes* was the fact that Fred had exceeded my willingness to recognize myself in Exley's excesses, had written a novel, consequently, whose author I felt no real impulse to attempt to redeem through literary criticism or theatrical translation.

The Flower Memorial Library committee which, in winter, 1993, developed the series of events celebrating Fred's career—the American premiere of the *A Fan's Notes* film, a discussion of the movie and novel I moderated, and a lecture on Fred's work by *Book Week* critic and soon-to-be Exley biographer Jonathan Yardley—designated one program, "We're all from Watertown," borrowing from *Last Notes* a line initially intended, I'm convinced, as less than a compliment to either "we" or to Fred's hometown. (So intimately was Watertown intertwined in Fred's self-perception, in fact, that it invariably partook of his contradictory congratulatory and condemnatory impulses toward himself. "When those harbingers of fall signaled my immanent departure from Watertown," he wrote in *A Fan's Notes,* "I became very distraught because I knew that where other men look home with longing and affection, I would look home with loathing and rage, and that that loathing would bind me to home as fiercely as ever love does.") Rereading Fred's books in preparation for that series, I re-encountered the excesses which had discomfited me in preparing *The Exley Play* six years earlier. Although I still found some of them regrettable—the unreflective misogyny in particular—I appreciated more clearly than I had previously the extent to which excess in Fred's fiction, rather than being mere self-indulgence, is a manifestation of his artistic integrity, an affirmation of his basic literary honesty. In *Pages From a Cold Island,* the protagonist recalls advising a would-be writer taking a class from him at the Iowa Writers' Workshop to "Do what I say and not what I've done"—that is, not to let 'alcohol, fatuous dreams and disappointed life too dearly sap his youthful literary ambitions.' If he lives a life more disciplined than that which his teacher had chosen, Exley promises the student that, "like Edmund Wilson, he would in the end hold up to America a mirrored triptych from which, no matter in which direction America turn, she would—to her dismay, horror, and hopefully even enlightenment—be helpless to free herself from the uncompromising plague of her own image." And the student's artistic project would be effective, Fred's *A Fan's Notes* trilogy clearly demonstrates, in proportion to the extent to which the image emerging in the young writer's mirrored triptych closely resembles his own face.

Doing Time in the Adirondacks

Joan Potter

The last time I saw Randy Jackson, he was standing on the sidewalk in front of the shock camp in Moriah, waiting for a ride to the bus station. Tall and broad-shouldered, he was wearing a stylish black shirt and gray pleated pants instead of the green state prison clothes and the painfully starched white shirts that had been his uniform for many months.

I was watching Randy from the window of my car in the visitors' parking lot across the way, thinking it was the first time I'd seen him alone and relaxed, not one of a group of prisoners with shaved heads and rigid military postures. He was gazing into the blue Adirondack sky, the sun shining on his smooth, coffee-colored skin and blissful smile. I watched him until the black state station wagon pulled up and he tossed his duffel bag on the back seat and jumped in after it.

Randy was one of the most prolific writers in the workshop I led in the early 1990s for inmates of the boot camp that the New York State prison system had set up in the Adirondack settlement of Moriah. The young men serving six-month sentences there were mostly low-level drug sellers in their twenties. The rigorous routines at these prison boot camps, labeled "shock incarceration facilities," were intended to "shock" inmates out of their criminal lifestyles.

Randy and the other prisoners in the writing workshop were enthusiastic students. They told me how much they enjoyed being able to relax, laugh, and tell stories while escaping for one morning a week the marching, shouting, calisthenics, and physical labor that filled the rest of their days. And I enjoyed the young men that I taught. They brought me a sense of life, energy, humor, and imagination that I hadn't experienced since I left New York City.

When I made plans to move with my husband to the tiny mountain village of Elizabethtown, I didn't include getting involved in prisons, even though I knew they were proliferating in the North Country. I wanted to move away from my criminal justice experiences in the New York City area, where I'd spent years reporting for newspapers and magazines on men and women locked up behind the walls and bars of places like Sing Sing and Bedford Hills.

I'd had enough of trudging along cellblock walkways, notepad in hand, while silent inmates gave me needy glances. I was tired of sitting in shabby, smoke-filled rooms, listening to sad women in ill-fitting prison uniforms recount their histories of poverty and abuse.

In my new North Country life, I thought, I would become a different person—learn to garden, ride horses, and hike trails through the woods behind our log cabin. I would subscribe to nature magazines, follow animal tracks, and set up feeders to lure birds to our yard, where I would identify them in my Audubon field guide.

Moving to the North Country was basically my husband's idea. He loved the Adirondacks, and when we had a little money to spend, he thought it would be fun to buy a few acres. On a trip up north one fall, we picked out a wooded spot on a dirt road, four miles outside of Elizabethtown.

Over the next six months, while I commuted from the suburbs to Manhattan, where I worked in the criminal justice program of a large foundation, my husband, who had taken early retirement from his publishing job and was now doing free-lance writing, spent his time reading countless books and magazines about log cabins. Every evening, when I arrived home tired and grouchy from my one-hour commute, he showed me sheets of graph paper covered with his newest log cabin designs. I didn't express much enthusiasm, but I didn't discourage him, either.

And then, almost before I knew what was happening, I had left my job, sold our house, held a tag sale to get rid of years of accumulated stuff, packed up what was left, and headed north—for good.

On my last day of work at the foundation, my friends there gave me a farewell party with food and drink and lots of clever presents. Afterward, heading for Grand Central, I inhaled the smells that rose from the line of carts offering hot dogs, burritos, falafel, egg rolls, Philly steak, and sugar-coated peanuts. Entering the station, I exchanged a smile with a young man wearing dreadlocks and a bright African shirt.

"Oh Lord," I thought, "I won't be seeing people who look like that anymore." And I was right.

We arrived in late November. The oak and maple trees on our land were bare, and the ground was already frozen hard. We were greeted by our closest neighbors, a retired minister and his wife, who'd settled into a rambling old farmhouse. He was a non-stop talker who loved to tell stories about killing animals. His favorite, often repeated, was a detailed recollection of the sixty porcupines he'd shot and thrown into a big hole in his back woods.

His wife was a kind, modest woman who seemed content to spend bleak North Country winters planning her summer garden and hooking rugs. I think she saw right away that my jumpy New York City personality was not going to fit with the slow-moving local ways.

Three days after we'd moved into our house, snow fell all one night, leaving our driveway impassable. By 9:00 the next morning, even though I had no place to go, I was frantically awaiting the arrival of the man who was supposed to plow. I finally pulled on my boots and stomped down the road to the house of our neighbors. The kindly wife met me at the door.

"Why hasn't Jim gotten here yet?" I demanded. "He said he'd come first thing in the morning."

She regarded me with pity. "This is the North Country," she said. "You have to learn to be patient."

Like this woman, most of the people who lived in Elizabethtown seemed friendly and generous. They mostly talked about the weather—comparing this year's cold and snow to that of seasons past—or animals they had spotted. Black bear sightings caused the biggest stir. But I was used to the discussions I'd had at work, which were usually about city things: some political scandal, or a new theater production. I tried—without great success, it seemed—to match my conversation and my behavior with that of the local community.

One day several weeks after my arrival, I was browsing in the local bookstore when I heard a woman excitedly recounting her new adventures as a literacy volunteer at the Moriah shock camp. "I love it," she raved. "The prisoners are just young kids. They're adorable."

I couldn't share her enthusiasm. The prisoners I'd seen over the years, mostly poor young African-American or Latino men and women from hopeless urban neighborhoods, had always struck me as neglected people who'd never had a chance to make good use of their intelligence and creativity. I knew that when they got out of prison, most would eventually flounder and sink back into the chaos of their earlier lives.

The bookstore owner turned to me. "Why don't you volunteer at the shock camp?" he asked. "You said you were involved in prisons before you moved up here."

I raised my hands, waving the idea away. "No, no, those days are over. I've started a new life."

But my new life in Elizabethtown hadn't been going so well. I still wasn't fitting in. That became clear to me one day when the guy who owned the gas station ambled over to the pumps after ending a lengthy chat with a plump woman in a Jeep Cherokee.

"Fill it, please," I said. "I'm kind of in a hurry."

He and I had also had our long chats, so I guess he felt he knew me well enough to say what was on his mind. "You're always in a hurry," he said. "Someone just told me the other day that he thought you were kind of pushy."

It is true that in the months after we had settled in, I tried to push my ideas on people. I urged my new neighbors to help organize a book group, and then a women's issues discussion group; we managed to get them going, but both soon fell apart.

After those disappointments, I started to rethink my attitude toward volunteering at the shock camp. I missed the lively people I'd known back in New York. Maybe I even missed the prisoners I'd spent so much time with. So I decided to push my way through the barriers set up by the state prison system—references, regulations, TB tests, ID cards—and got myself accepted as a teacher of a writing workshop. My students, all required to have high school diplomas, would be writing true stories about their lives.

The shock camp was located in two old buildings that had been owned by Republic Steel before the iron mines were closed down. The buildings—vacant since 1971—had been refurbished and outfitted with dormitories and classrooms.

Most of the 250 young men incarcerated there were African-American. Their guards, known as drill instructors, were almost all local residents. When I was teaching there, all the guards—except for an African-American captain who'd transferred from downstate—were white.

The guards didn't know just what to make of my writing workshop. The shock camp program was based on discipline, and the security forces were in charge. I saw guards standing nose-to-nose with prisoners while bellowing abuse—just like in the movies—and prisoners falling to the floor to perform endless push-ups as punishment for some violation of rules. Every prisoner had to maintain a rigid posture; every utterance had to be preceded and followed by "Sir, yes sir," or "Sir, no sir."

The first day I walked into the classroom, the twelve young

men standing at rigid attention behind their desks shouted at the tops of their lungs, "Ma'am, good morning, ma'am!" and then looked at me with little smiles to see how I'd react. I felt right at home, but not because they had followed prison protocols.

I quickly dispensed with the "ma'am's," and we got down to work. Every Tuesday morning, the students would read aloud the pieces of their lives they'd written about during the week. Their stories were frightening, tragic, touching, and funny. We all discussed everybody's work; there was a lot of laughter and lively debate. From time to time, a guard would appear in the classroom doorway and stand there silently, or sometimes march around the room and yell at a student who wasn't sitting up straight enough. The guards didn't understand what was going on in the workshop, but they sure didn't like it.

Three times I was reported to a supervisor for infractions of the rules: I had handed a note to a student ("Contraband"); I had related a story that featured my son ("You are not allowed to mention members of your family"); and I had defended a student who was under attack by a woman on the prison teaching staff ("Never disagree with a prison employee in front of an inmate").

After sternly lecturing me, the prison supervisor admitted that the writing workshop was a godsend for the teaching staff, who knew how to run a high school equivalency class but had little to offer prisoners who already had their diplomas. From then on, I made sure my desk faced the classroom door so I wouldn't miss any eavesdropping guards.

Although most of the young men in the workshop came from urban areas—New York City and Long Island, mainly—a few had grown up in smaller upstate towns. But their stories were remarkably similar. Two or three claimed they came from stable families, but the others recalled fathers who were hard-drinking and brutal or else totally absent. Several said their lives had started falling apart after their parents split up.

Troy, a pale, bony twenty-year-old, wrote that he'd been in foster care from the ages of seven to sixteen. He'd lived in three foster homes, one shelter, and one juvenile institution. He and his brothers and sisters were beaten by a stepfather who eventually went to prison—along with Troy's mother—for sexually abusing one of the girls.

Another student, Andre, said his father had left the family years earlier. "Whenever I went to visit him," Andre said in class one day, "he'd end up telling me I was a worthless piece of crap."

For Andre, his brother, and two of their cousins, drug-selling was away of life. One day an argument over drugs led to a violent family fight, and one cousin was badly beaten. A week later, the four met at a local YMCA, where they played a pick-up game of basketball. "After the game," wrote Andre, "we realized that we cousins were not the enemy of one another. It was the cocaine that was the enemy."

Most of the students recalled that they'd begun getting into trouble in junior high school, and had eventually drifted into using and selling drugs. Their rationale for becoming drug pushers was very clear: they made a lot of money. They wrote in glowing detail about their BMW's, fancy clothes, gold jewelry, and expensive girlfriends.

One student, Anthony, described his profession this way: "The type of work I was doing wasn't honest work at all, it was the illegal selling of drugs. My position was guarding the money and protecting the people that did hand-to-hand selling. My conscience bothered me doing this type of work but the money was greater than my conscience."

A poetic twenty-five-year-old named Vincent was already the father of two sons and a daughter. He wrote: "I'm incarcerated for possession of a controlled substance (crack). Being in jail for me is an experience that I shall not go through again. It takes away a lot of love from your family to you."

The students were interesting and appealing in different ways—some for their charm and humor, others for their touching seriousness. But Randy Jackson had a combination of qualities—intelligence, dignity, and good looks—that made him stand out. At twenty-nine, Randy was the oldest in the class, and the only one with a college education. He wrote that he'd started drinking and smoking marijuana in high school, and in his mid-twenties, had taken up cocaine, soon becoming a regular user. He left his regular job for a life on the streets, and became addicted to the thrill of committing crimes.

"At first," he wrote, "I was doing crimes because I needed drugs, but in time it reversed and I was doing drugs so I could keep doing crimes." After his second robbery arrest, he was sentenced to shock camp.

Randy wrote lengthy essays about his childhood in a loving home, his adolescent adventures, and his gradual slide into a criminal life, relentlessly examining his failures and vowing to become a new and better person. The other students respected Randy's honesty and ease with the written word. They seemed to look up to him as a sensible older brother.

For a class assignment, "A Person I Admire," Anthony chose to write about Randy: "Sometimes I wonder how a person like that could end up in a place like this. I think that this person just got bored with his everyday living. He wanted excitement in his life and sometimes, like a lot of us, negative is more fun than positive." Anthony was sure his friend was now "ready for society," and wrote: "He's going to be somebody, somebody that I will be very proud to say that I know."

Shock camp prisoners were required to attend drug treatment sessions and to participate in a behavior modification program. They devoted hours to military drills and exercises. And they spent several hours of each day away from the prison, working on community projects. Each morning, squads of green-clad prisoners piled into vans that sped along wooded roads to their worksites. Supervised by guards, they cut brush, sawed logs, painted public buildings, and cleaned up golf courses, parks, and cemeteries.

I was curious to know how this alien rural territory appeared to city dwellers who'd rarely been north of the Bronx. I asked my students to describe their impressions of the region. "It's not that I don't like it up here," wrote a husky, sad-eyed young man named Frederick; "it's the fact that I'm up here for all the wrong reasons. But if I would look at it from another point of view it would bring nothing but pleasure to me."

Frederick said he had sometimes wondered how it would feel

to be close to nature, and wrote that "the rivers, lakes, and small streams excite me, and the mountains and nature make me feel closer to God."

He concluded: "If I could dream of someplace where I could walk for hours on end and hike without fear of being followed, or sit with my kids and tell stories of things that happened in the past, I would be sitting and walking and hiking up North."

Many of the students described new, fascinating experiences: "My favorite job was building a rock bridge through mud that will last far past my lifetime."

"I even learned a little bit about the American Revolution when I worked at Crown Point. We saw people ice fishing, just like Eskimos."

Most wrote about the startling beauty of their new surroundings; perhaps they thought that was what I wanted to hear. But William, who came from Queens, was struck by the isolation and lack of opportunity. He wrote that, to him, Adirondack communities "are very quiet, small, and there's very little to do." He wrote that he hadn't noticed any clubs or movie theaters, and while riding in the prison van, he might "see nothing but plants, mountains, and rivers for at least half an hour."

Many remarked about the surprising friendliness of the community residents they encountered on their various jobs. "I found that everybody I met did not look down on us for our being convicted felons but rather looked at us as human beings instead," wrote Michael.

Raymond, a husky young man with a sweet baby face, recalled the time he and another prisoner were in Elizabethtown, the county seat, painting the trim on the courthouse. "It was around noontime and we had just finished our lunch break," he wrote. "We were walking toward where we were working and there were about eight or nine women sitting on the bench smoking cigarettes, laughing and talking.

"Now I had to go over there and work on a ladder about two feet away from where these ladies were sitting. I thought they were going to get up and go inside or say something nasty but to my surprise they stayed right there, laughing and talking away."

I asked Raymond why he thought the women might have insulted him. He hesitated, then stammered, "Well, because we're inmates, and because, you know, our dark skin."

That dark skin wasn't totally ignored by all local residents. One of my students reported being called "nigger" by a town highway department worker who was supervising him on a job. I related this incident to a man I met at a rather classy party. The man, an avid Adirondack mountain climber, had worked with some inmates clearing trails. "It doesn't hurt them to be called 'nigger' every once in awhile," he observed, widening his pale blue eyes. "They have to remember that's what they're going to hear when they get back to the city."

I'm not sure how the friendly local residents would react to seeing these young men return to the community as vacationers, which several said they would like very much to do. One of the older students, Allan, wrote that he had started smoking and selling crack when he got out of the army in 1986, and eventually "got hooked on drugs bad." But he was hoping that the shock camp program would "change my life for the good."

After his release, wrote Allan, "I would love to come back and visit some of the places up here, knowing that I was a part of it for a brief moment."

I know that someday I would love to bump into Allan, that tall, lanky fellow with his cynical smile and sharp sense of humor. It sure would brighten my life to be wandering through Elizabethtown and meet up with Allan or any of my other ex-students, wearing t-shirts and jeans and showing off the town to their wives and girlfriends, just like they said they wanted to do after they graduated from shock camp and got their lives together.

I don't expect to see them in the Adirondacks, though. Sometimes I think about running into one of them on the street when I'm visiting New York City, having a cup of coffee together, and reminiscing about the other guys in the workshop, laughing over some of the wild experiences they'd written about. I'm hoping I won't see any of them on the New York TV news, in handcuffs, being shoved into a police car.

At the shock camp graduation, I felt a motherly pride sitting in the audience, applauding as each young member of the writing class strode eagerly to the front of the room and shook the hand of the superintendent. Randy Jackson, the leader of his platoon, was one of the first whose name was called. He beamed at his fellow prisoners, who were still clapping energetically as he walked back to his seat.

Afterward, over refreshments, I gave a good-bye hug to each of my students, met the relatives who had managed to make the trip up north, and told them what a talented writer their son or brother or husband or boyfriend was.

Out in the parking lot, heading for my car, I waved goodbye to Randy Jackson as he waited for his ride to the bus station. In one of his last essays for the workshop, Randy had written about his upcoming graduation from shock camp, how he and his platoon would perform their last complicated drill, how he would embrace his friends and tell them to stay strong. He envisioned himself on the bus to Buffalo, having a conversation with a woman in the next seat. He imagined their words as they arrived at the depot:

"Well, ma'am, this is where we part."

" 'May God bless you and good luck,' she says as she offers me a smile and her hand to shake."

" 'Thank you,' I say, and nod my head in response to her kind gesture. I walk to the front of the bus to exit and look over my shoulder and smile my good-bye to her. As I climb down the steps to a world long gone, yet eagerly sought, I ask myself if she will remember my face when my deeds and efforts take me to fame."

Reading his words now, I miss Randy and wish I knew how he is doing. I'm thinking, "Maybe you haven't reached fame, Randy, but I'm praying that you've survived."

Taekwondo and the Prison Guard

Constance Jenkins

Irony can be especially cruel in a small town. Gouverneur is so small that Jeff Forsythe can stand in the parking lot of the place dearest to his heart and look across the road at a place that changed his family's life forever.

As in any small town, you meet yourself coming and going in Gouverneur. Neighbors' dogs run through your yard; neighbors run through your personal business. Integrity generally rises to the surface, but when it doesn't, a small town can be suffocating. Add in the isolation and lingering poverty of this region, and you have a tough place to live.

It got tougher for Forsythe and his family in 1991. That's when his sister-in-law, Krista Absalon, was transformed from a small-town single mother to a poster girl for women's rights after a hellish night at the local Casablanca bar and restaurant. Trying to drink away a miserable day, she passed out from massive intoxication and later learned that five local oafs, some of whom she had considered to be friends, were bragging that they'd had sex with her that night.

As word of the event spread throughout the town, nasty, often preposterous rumors circulated while area women chose up sides, either to lobby for justice or to question whether the unconscious woman had somehow been a willing participant.

Deep furies festered, then intensified in 1993. After pleading guilty to sexual misconduct, the Casablanca men were sentenced to mere $750 fines by the local male judge. New court proceedings followed, but in 1996, the case was dropped with reluctance when two of the defendants were found not guilty.

All Forsythe will say now is that he mistrusts the media and hates gossipers. Family members "know who has lied," he says, but the Casablanca is along the main street of their small hometown. When they walk down the street now, there's a mental tally of who said, or didn't say, what. And ironically, one of Jeff's proudest achievements, his own martial arts school, is separated from that site by just a thin strip of waving cattails, rusting railroad tracks, and the dark macadam road.

Forsythe, though, has struck a deliberate philosophical balance with his North Country hometown, melding his dreams with his roots through the ancient Eastern art of taekwondo. In his roles as husband, father, son, brother, neighbor, corrections officer, and martial arts teacher, he consciously strives to be a person whose impact on others is positive.

Although he works each day in one of the county's three prisons—Gouverneur Correctional Facility—the gentle 39-year-old remains calmly centered because of his martial arts training. He speaks enthusiastically of Korea's national sport, admiring how well it encompasses the physical, the mental, and the spiritual. "To really bring your life into focus, you need all three," he affirms.

That steadfast focus—that clarity—has sustained him from his formative years, through the turmoil of the Casablanca years, and to the present when he goes to prison every day. "Sure, it's a depressing environment and it can catch you if you let it," he admits. "You have to use your outside time to offset the prison atmosphere." His decade-old martial arts school, Master Kim's

Olympic Taekwondo Center, is located strategically between his home and the correctional facility. The school is clearly the realm of his dreams, and of his heart.

Slim, with an athlete's compact build, Forsythe is deeply serious about things that deserve it. He waves an arm to point out the other businesses that surround his own in the small shopping plaza: a Chinese restaurant, a credit union, a can redemption center, a fishing and hunting shop, a hair/tanning salon, a thrift shop, and a cleaning service. "In the past ten years, all kinds of places have come and gone. Who would have guessed that a Korean martial arts school would still be here?" he muses.

"I opened this business because I want to help people, and because I want to be remembered for something," Forsythe says. Area people have responded heartily to his offering: six days a week, men, women, teens, and children flock to his school. Some aim for fitness, others for self-defense skills. The inherent self-discipline and dignity of the martial arts form allows them to blossom. Families, especially, are drawn to the classes.

The school does seem rather incongruous for the area. A granite-colored wide spot in the road, Gouverneur is a small village of about 6,000 residents. Founded in 1805, it sits mostly unnoticed in the southwestern corner of the largest county in the state.

According to state figures, St. Lawrence County brings in $60 million in tourism annually, but while it is rich in history, Gouverneur is not a tourist town. To the contrary , its commerce is based on iron and steel fabricating, dairy farming, talc and zinc mining, a cogeneration plant, and the prison. The per-capita income for county residents is a dismal $13,000.

In many ways, Gouverneur is neither this nor that. Located a few miles inland from the St. Lawrence River, it is a few miles outside the Blue Line demarcating the Adirondack Park, a few miles north of the sprawling military complex at Fort Drum, a few miles southwest of the college towns of Canton and Potsdam and the thriving industry of Massena. To many, its main claim to fame is that it is the birthplace of Edward John Noble, master marketer of that quintessential American candy, the Lifesaver.

Until the Casablanca case, many people had never heard of Gouverneur. After the case, many were sorry that they had.

For Forsythe and his wife, Clover, however, Gouverneur is their hometown and their chosen place of residence. It is where they come from, and where they came back to after some initial exploration.

Born on Valentine's Day 1958 on a U.S. Army base in Germany, Jeff Forsythe is the oldest of the four sons of an easygoing mother with native-American roots and a strict Scots-Irish State Trooper father. "They really were like yin and yang," Jeff reflects. In many ways, he displays that dichotomy. A true study in opposites, Forsythe is a mellow, gentle man earning a living in a gritty world. A small-town American boy, he has embraced the exotic Far East. When pushed to lash out, he pointedly selects the high road.

"I don't ever want anyone to assume that we were abused, but our family was strict and we were well-disciplined. I thank my dad for it. Life would be a lot tougher now if not for what he taught us," he says.

Touching briefly on two childhood stigmas, he mentions living in a trailer and being a favorite target for criticism because he was "the son of a Trooper." As the oldest child, he says, he felt an extra responsibility to live beyond reproach; he chuckles almost admiringly at the memory of a fun-loving younger brother—unburdened by insecurities—who arose early one morning, smashed eggs along a hall floor, then dove atop the mess only to slide into the legs of his curious father, who had heard the commotion. Suffice it to say that the youngster was punished.

Quick to explore new worlds, Jeff avoided cliques in school. "I hung around with all sorts of people—not just jocks and not just rebels," he recalls with satisfaction. Remembering the comparative gentleness of high school days in the 1970s, he adds that the main recreations were driving around and drinking—often simultaneously.

The Forsythe family's moral code is typical of this straightforward region. "All of us boys knew we were not to get into trouble, and we were to stick up for weaker people. We always tried to help, and we stayed together," Jeff says. These values are also a precursor of the five tenets of taekwondo that guide him today: courtesy, integrity, perseverance, self-control, indomitable spirit: What's the hardest for him? "Probably self-control," he decides.

The path to taekwondo was laid down early for him. It was a movie that caught his attention. "I saw a Bruce Lee film and couldn't think of anything else," he says. Soon after, the teenager and his mother began traveling to Canton for weekly martial arts lessons.

He rounded out his high school days with baseball and wrestling, then headed south to visit friends in Georgia after graduating in 1976. "I was ready for some independence," he notes. In fact, he was ready for adventure, and easily agreed to join the Army if the recruiter would guarantee a Korean tour of duty.

He laughs, "No one wanted to go there, so I had no problem." At age 19, he was delighted to become a tank driver in Korea. During his 13 months there, he lived off base and soaked up the local lifestyle. "Their culture is over 2,000 years old; they're really onto something," he marvels.

His next assignment was also tempting to him. He grinned. "I couldn't pass up Colorado Springs. The ratio of women to men at the time was three to one." Jeff did enjoy the beauty of Pike's Peak, too.

Fifteen months later, he found himself completing a circle in his life when he was stationed in Germany. Although he liked his time as an adult there, Jeff was hampered by a growing uneasiness. "People were just drinking all the time, and I wanted to get out and do something in life. I knew I needed to find a career, because except for the Army, who would hire you to drive a tank?"

So, a week after returning stateside to Gouverneur, a restless Forsythe again went south. This time it was to Florida, to sell air conditioners with a friend. He was the delivery guy. After a while he met Clover, who had traveled from Gouverneur with another friend to vacation in the sun. They eventually began dating seriously, and when they found they really missed the seasons, they headed home to family, friends, and the changeable weather of the North Country.

Without a regular job in sight, Jeff tended bar, lived in a trailer with his wife and small children, and drove a junker car. "It was tough," he says simply. Dad gave him a welcome shove into respectability by getting him into the painters' union after pulling strings with a friend.

A little embarrassed by the story, Jeff says, "He got me a break. That's what friends are for—around here, anyway."

Jeff worked hard and traveled downstate as well as to New Hampshire for jobs. At one point he made $26 an hour, amassing an incredible $60,000 in nine months. The tenet of perseverance was very clear to him. "You've got to be good at something up here, or you'll suffer," he says. "You've got to be good, and you've got to stick with it. I knew a painter's job was not permanent, so I was always looking."

His alertness paid off when he took the test to become a corrections officer. Nearly two years later, he was called for a job. He worked at seven sites, including Sing Sing and Dannemora, two of the oldest prisons in New York.

Meanwhile, new prisons were going up all over the state, many of them in the North Country. "I was patient and they built one here, ten minutes from my house," he says. "I can earn a good living and support my family right here."

Despite their general uneasiness about becoming a dumping ground for downstate criminals, it didn't take a lot to convince Gouverneur residents of the benefits of this new injection into the North Country economy. The area correctional facilities offer a tantalizing chance to grab apiece of the American Dream, because salaries for the 350-or-so employees at each site surpass thirty thousand dollars.

Some people complained when the village won the prison, Forsythe remembers, "but only if it was close to their house. They don't have to worry about anyone escaping, because it'll never happen."

Gouverneur's correctional facility houses nearly 900 inmates in an open dorm setting. Tied to the tedious routine as much as the inmates are, Forsythe starts the day at 7 A.M.., moving his men through breakfast. He is stationed in the activities building, which houses a general library, a law library, and a barbershop. Services for all major religions are held there. Although rare in the non-prison population, Muslims predominate at the prison services, he says.

Despite the soul-stealing regimentation, Jeff sets his schedule around the demands of the job. "I've learned where to expend energy and were to slow down. I've gotten smarter," he realizes. "I think I've lost my temper twice in nine years. There's a lot of stress here if you're not careful."

Forsythe, obviously, is careful. Still, the nature of corrections feels contradictory to him because he is convinced that it's too late to turn around the inmates by the time they land in prison. "Most will come back," he realizes. "Some smarten up and don't, but most will return." Unlike many officers, he chats with his charges and tries to figure out how they see things. It seems logical to him that because the inmates come from brutal and impoverished backgrounds—and more often than not return to the— they would choose violence over reason.

"It costs over thirty thousand dollars a year to keep a person in prison. I'd rather see him get a thirty-thousand-dollar job and do something for the community. And pay taxes. Wouldn't that be better?" Jeff wonders. It may come to that someday, he reasons. He says he feels the system is changing, because the nation can't just keep building more and more prisons.

The inmates are allowed to "circulate" only at pre-set times, so Jeff must watch over them as they move from place to place within the prison grounds. Head counts are taken twice each day, and unless something goes wrong, Jeff leaves work at 3 P.M.

That's when his real day starts.

Acknowledging that he and his family live there, he is determined to improve a little corner of life in Gouverneur. He says he is distressed to see the prevalence of "poor, unmotivated people with three or four generations on social services" in his hometown. "I didn't open the school for the money; I make good money already. If people can invest in themselves and in their kids instead of in VCRs or TVs or three-wheelers, it'll come back to help them in the end. People learn that here. If you can make 100 lives work, you can change the face of the country."

Sharing lunch and Chinese tea next door, Jeff says he was more or less goaded into opening the school by his friend, Master Kim, who carefully brought up the possibility and accused Jeff of being "scared" to begin his own school.

"That really lit a fire under me," he asserts. He scrambled to get together his finances and business details to start his school. Since it opened, it has just kept prospering.

Shaking his head at his master's sly push, Jeff says, "He knew that would get me going."

Arriving next door at his school, Jeff points to an empty bookcase. "Someone broke in last night and stole my cassette player. Can you believe it? The only thing of value, and they found it." Holding up a tape of Korean music, he giggles. "They took the time to leave this behind, though."

An adult student who is first to arrive checks over the door with Jeff to make sure the new lock will hold. "Do you think it was one of your prisoners who did it? Anyone out recently?"

No pause; Jeff is sure. "No. None of them would have done this. Some of them know I have the school, but they wouldn't break in. It must have been a kid." Shaking his head, he wonders aloud, "How long would it take to work to be able to buy a cassette player?"

Jeff's school, Master Kim's Olympic Taekwondo Center, is open six days a week. Adults and children receive their instruction in a clean, open, and unassuming space nestled between the Chinese restaurant and federal credit union in the small shopping center, next to rusting tracks where a few freight trains still clatter by. After greeting one another, the students change into their "toboks," loose-fitting pajama-like outfits. Seeing me, a visitor, they are infinitely polite. It's rather unnerving to have people bow before me, but it seems like second nature to them.

The name of the school is not just a high-sounding title. This place actually is training prospective Olympic contenders, taekwondo having been added to the list of official Olympic sports.

The sport made its debut in the summer of 2000. Korea, the United States, Spain, Germany, Egypt, and England all sent competitors. In all of St. Lawrence County, Jeff's school is the only one authorized to train athletes for the Olympics. Ogdensburg and Massena are next on his expansion list, so more students, young and not so young, will be able to experience taekwondo.

Thus, on this warm summer night, a typical scene unfolds. Students dressed in white uniforms with colored sashes bounce into place in the plain classroom. Their world of color extends from white to yellow, green, blue, red, and black to designate the level of training that they have mastered. Beginners start with white belts, then move up. Each color also has degrees to it. Jeff is a master with a black belt, but he still considers himself to be refining his skills.

Forsythe and an assistant bark out guttural commands in Korean to lead the students through their beginning exercises. Learning to move their upper and lower bodies as one unit, the classmates merrily slap high fives after completing a task. Jeff walks up and down the rows, quietly encouraging, praising, and correcting his pupils.

Each students then pairs off with someone roughly the same size to practice some well-padded sparring. Half the students immediately head to the sidelines to deposit eyeglasses, then face off for twirling kicks and punches. One wall is lined with mirrors to help them observe their maneuvers.

"Attack in sequences of threes or fours to throw off their timing," Jeff advises.

"Make them fight your fight. Attack the mind first, and the battle will be won, no matter what the level."

Later, Jeff divides the students into two long rows so they can practice their kicks. Students in each line take turns holding a thick paddle in the air as a target, thoughtfully lowering it a bit when a shorter classmate appears. The kickers strike swiftly, leaping to reach the paddle. Jeff is also in one of the moving lines. He repositions the target higher than his head, then smartly smacks it twice with his bare foot.

Over and over, the lines advance, re-form, and continue. The faces shift from male to female, grade school age to teen to adult, man to woman, white to African-American. Some of the students are breathing heavily, but they all are smiling.

"You can get a black belt in three years," Jeff insists, surprised at my doubtful look. "It's just a matter of going through the steps, but there's a system and you can do it in three years."

Taekwondo is not an aggressive posture. Its purpose is self-defense. By being able to defend yourself, you won't have to be aggressive, according to its philosophy. "In the end, it's humility that counts. Helping people is what matters, and you can't force yourself on people," Jeff stresses.

Always first to set an example, he speaks softly, is patient, and is willing to listen.

His school has no hidden agenda; neither does he. "Gouverneur is a hard place," he says. "That's why I opened the school here. We're for the community, and I want my black belts to be leaders.

"It's about respect. If you forget what you've been given, you lose respect. I could make a lot of money in another place, but you can't forget where you come from or you'll lose respect for your parents and friends."

His desires are simple. "I want to be a good son, a good example. I worry about what others think of me." He laughs. "I don't want anyone kicking flowers off my grave."

Firmly believing that each one of us is responsible for ourselves, he tries hard to instill a sense of capability in his students. "Move on after you make a mistake," he advises. "Learn and let go. You can make up for it by following with a good decision."

So far, Forsythe is satisfied with his decisions and with the balance he has struck with the North Country. Gouverneur is small, but he doesn't look across the road.

"I'm really content with my life right now," he says. "I'm right in tune. I have my family, a good job, the school. My parents are healthy. I'm very happy."

Ghosts

The Fair

Jonathan Mairs

The week's delights with all its sights
has glided by too fast;
The joys of taffy, pink and white,
are all too good to last;
The dust of swirling horses as they
round the race track's bend,
Has settled on the grassy plain,
too soon we've reached the end.

The kids are buying books for school;
they're flocking in at Bing's.
The farmer folk must wait to hear
the song that winter sings;
The carnival, with calliope,
has stilled its wheezing toot;
The wind whines through the shabby sheds;
a worthy substitute.

Excerpt from *The County Fair*
by Walter B. Gunnison

The autumn air is still brisk and cold from the night before as I walk toward the Grass River on Main Street in Canton, New York. Light pours upward from the eastern sky, forcing the morning stars to fade and disappear. Ahead is a traffic light and beyond it a dull, gray steel bridge spanning the river. I can hear the muffled rush of the current passing under the bridge. The ripples rise and pause for an instant before twisting and falling away.

At the traffic light I follow a side street to my right. A few steps later, I lose sight of the river as buildings come forth to channel me down the street. Now named Riverside Drive, the desolate asphalt I walk was known for years to Canton residents as Water Street. A few old-timers still refer to the street by its original name, but most people today, even gas station attendants, don't know of the old Water Street.

On my right, I pass Canton Auto Supply, dark and deserted, with red gas reserve tanks and dull yellow gallons of antifreeze displayed in the front window. Directly across the street, North Country Auto Supply features the same red plastic tanks and antifreeze stacked neatly in the window. Each store has a blue and yellow NAPA sign that juts out over the sidewalk. The storefronts stare blankly at each other, waiting for the routine of the day to begin.

The sound of the river filters over the buildings. I cross the street and keep walking. On my left I pass a low brown building containing a bar whose windows are boarded up from the inside. A poster tacked against the painted wood siding advertises appearance dates for traveling comedians. Booking agencies out of Syracuse and New York send the performers upstate to bars, clubs, and restaurants. Under the scrutiny of the morning sun, the empty bar hardly seems a promising destination.

I pass State Street as it angles up the hill on the right. The Grass River Apartments rise high above the street and are surrounded at their bases by full parking lots. A light is still on over one of the main entrances, gathering mist. A car coughs, puncturing the sound of the rushing river. The car coughs again, its engine refusing to turn over.

Past the apartment complex, the buildings on Riverside Drive thin out as downtown recedes behind. The river is again visible. Houses are set back from the street, weathered and modest. The sidewalk ends and I step onto moist, grassy lawn, the river down a steep bank beside me.

As Riverside intersects Fairlane Drive, the houses become more modern. Split-level homes with garages sit neatly in front of well-kept lawns. The streets become more ordered and squared. It is at this intersection where the main gate to the St. Lawrence County Fair stood for more than eighty years.

The fair was established in 1852 by the St. Lawrence County Agricultural Society (SLCAS). It was held, at the discretion of the organizers, every year during the second week in September. The residents of Canton marked the arrival of the fair each September as the official onset of autumn. It was a celebration of the summer and the successful harvests with attractions featuring agriculture, livestock, and crafts.

That first fair lasted just two days, but the crowd that assembled on the grounds along the Grass River was supportive and hopeful for its future. Almost four hundred exhibitions of crafts and livestock were presented during that 1852 event, and approximately three hundred dollars was paid in premiums to the winners from each category. Gate receipts rose steadily in subsequent fairs and the fairgrounds were leased during the month of September for the next five years.

As the merits of the fair became more widely recognized, the entire community began to anticipate its arrival at the end of each summer. That enthusiasm resulted in more varied exhibitions and expanded premium divisions. Additional lands adjoining the existing grounds were leased in 1856 to match the growth in attendance and participation, and two years later E. Miner and L.E.B. Winslow purchased the lands for the SLCAS. The fair now had a permanent home.

With lands now secured, the SLCAS began to build permanent exhibition halls on the thirty-eight-acre plot. A wooden fence, painted white, was erected to enclose the grounds. The centerpiece of the fairgrounds was the grandstand, which could hold up to three thousand people and was said to be one of the largest in the state. The stands were partially covered by a large overhang so that races and games could be viewed during inclement weather. Spirited betting took place among the onlookers and crap games were held covertly in the shade below the bleachers, out of sight of the women. It is said that in one afternoon's gaming a young gentleman won enough for his fall tuition at St. Lawrence University.

Directly in front of the grandstand stood the judge's booth, which faced the race track and infield. The track was ringed by a low fence, also painted white, which opened at one end, where horses could enter and exit. The half-mile course, set in fine clay and meticulously groomed, was, in the opinion of the locals, "one of the best in the state." A dirt baseball diamond was stripped out of the infield and games were played by teams from county towns such as Norwood, Raymondville, Brushton, and Harrisville. The races and games would take place simultaneously, and when the judges rang a bell to signal the start of a race the baseball players would pause and watch as the horses sprinted around the track to a crescendo of cheers and whistles. At the finish, the players would return to their contest while the crowd settled up bets and refocused their attention on the game.

The exhibition halls were designed to present the varied produce and crafts of the North Country for competition and show. Floral Hall, a two-story octagonal structure, was the most elaborate of the buildings. Inside, watercolors and oil paintings, woven coverlets, knitting, embroidery, and other homespun goods were hung from the pillars that supported the top floor. Colorful quilts were draped along the upper mezzanine, and dealers showed off the latest in domestic manufactures. Mechanics Hall was located behind the grandstand and featured exhibits on farming innovations, techniques, and new equipment. Similarly, Vegetable and Dairy Hall was filled with fresh farm produce of excellent size and color. For those fairgoers who desired a top-quality sit-down meal without leaving the fairgrounds, the Grange Dining Hall did a steady business preparing meals from area produce, including an array of fresh pies for dessert.

A two-story barn and several rectangular sheds were constructed to house the livestock on display for competition. Shorthorns, Holsteins, Ayrshires, Devons, Jerseys, oxen, steers, sheep, swine, and fowl all occupied the buildings in pens filled with hay. Room was allotted for participants and visitors to browse and admire. The barn housed horses for show and racing. Stallions, brood mares, colts, harness horses, and mules occupied the stalls with their names and farms chalked proudly onto the wood.

Money was also invested to improve the grounds. Graded walkways, watering systems, and shade trees connected the exhibition halls, grandstand, and midway, adding a peaceful and simple grace to the fairgrounds. In the mid-1880s, SLCAS organizers estimated the total worth of the fairground to be in excess of fifteen thousand dollars.

The fair continued to grow, receiving over two thousand entries for exhibition in its twenty-sixth year, 1877, and awarding $3,500 in premiums. The SLCAS was operating well into the black financially and it was evident that the fair had become a prized Canton tradition.

The day before the fair's opening was always a noisy one in the streets of Canton. Farmers bringing livestock would herd their charges through the roads and down Water Street toward the gate. Animals frequently broke from the procession and wandered into residential yards, trampling flowerbeds, disrupting woodpiles, and feeding on shrubbery. It had also became customary for Canton residents to receive visitors and relatives in their homes during fair week. The heightened carriage traffic did not mix easily with the parade of livestock and the center of town often became clogged with unruly animals and shouting men until well after dark. Most of the town and surrounding communities were swept into the gateway of the fairgrounds in a flurry of noise, commotion, and anticipation.

The old Saxon saying, "a little farm well-tilled, a little wife well-willed," seemed to be the underlying philosophy of the week's exhibitions. Indeed, the directors of the SLCAS had set about to create a fair that would showcase and highlight the agricultural community of the North Country. The fair had been allowed to grow slowly and expand according to input from its participants, and in so doing, the citizens of Canton and neighboring communities forged a close and personal relationship with the annual event. The fair was not just a week-long festival, but also a celebration of family and of life in the North Country.

The New York State Assembly issued grants each year to county fairs such as the one in Canton for the awarding of modest cash premiums. This amount, though nominal, was central to the continued operation of the fair. In addition to gate receipts, the SLCAS depended on the small entrance fees required of each exhibition to stay on even financial ground. The state grant had a stabilizing influence on the fair's budget, allowing the directors to guarantee prize money to each of the exhibition winners. Judging and awarding prizes to exhibitors continued throughout the four days of the fair, thereby encouraging attendance each day. Premiums were awarded for livestock, butter, cheese, grains, vegetables, fruits, mechanical work, innovative farming implements, flowers, painting, quiltwork, drawings, and other domestic manufactures. Discretionary prizes were awarded to exhibitions that did not fit any specific category or were completely new to the fair. By placing few restrictions on entrance qualifications, the directors encouraged the public to be less inhibited about their participation in the fair.

As expected, the competitions spurred friends and neighbors to strive for greater quality. Although the cash award for a winning exhibit was small, the brief bit of local renown was the real compensation for one's efforts. As one prominent fairgoer, the Hon. Calvin T. Hulbard, noted, the gathering of farmers engaged in similar fields of production seemed to open a new current of communication on techniques and improvements. In his address upon the closing of the sixth annual fair in September 1857, he was moved to remark that "the faculty of improving our knowledge by what others have known or done, has, by some writers been declared to be the trait which best distinguishes the human race from the animal creation." This noble sentiment may have been lost in the September breeze, but the fair's participants didn't need the Honorable Mr. Hulbard to understand the strategy of the exhibition hall.

The directors of the SLCAS did little to tamper with the basic formula of the fair. Horse races, baseball games, exhibitions, and various midway attractions were well suited to the temperament of the crowds. However, minor adjustments were made from year to year to liven the usual schedule of events. The New York State Board of Health was invited to sponsor an annual booth to raise awareness of health and welfare issues. Firemen's tournaments were held in some years, and balloonists were frequently hired to provide shows. Local marching bands performed in parades and other marching spectacles, and even the State Police Rough Riders from Troop D in Oneida made it to Canton one year, providing a thrilling act.

The directors made sure to place tight restrictions on the running of the midway attractions. Through the 1892 fair season, no games for money were permitted within the fairgrounds, and the sale of "intoxicating liquors" was also forbidden. Local merchants set up booths showcasing their goods, and confectioners sold cotton candy and hot dogs throughout the day to wide-eyed children. In his 1928 memoir *Coming Up the Road,* author Irving Bacheller recalled spending his allowance on the midway as a child: "I shot away my five cents and bought three peaches, a bag of peanuts, and a piece of gingerbread. My money was gone but I cherished the hope that my father would buy a glass of pop for me."

A modest number of sideshow attractions were permitted at each fair. Barkers shouted out fantastic claims in order to lure fairgoers into paying for a brief glimpse. The Living Skeleton, Wild Man of Borneo, Human Snake, and the somewhat less terrifying Fat Lady were all showcased over the years on the midway. The hooks in the advertising for these "freaks" took advantage of the provinciality of Canton by promising the exotic and never-before-seen. Magicians and "Mystique Krews" turned the eye and tugged at the imagination. The sideshows and their sights were a curious flip-side to the standard fare of the exhibition halls and attracted many onlookers, but few takers.

Professional entertainers were also brought in to perform a few shows during the week of the fair. Ramza and Amo and the Blondin Donkey Burlesque, Ladieux and Louise comedic tumbling and juggling, and the San Suo Duo Japanese acrobats all performed in front of crowds at the fairgrounds. The acts were booked from agencies downstate and traveled by train to similar fairs across the state. The performances were an entertaining diversion from the fair's routine and were well received by appreciative audiences.

The centerpiece of the fair was the fine display of horses featured throughout the week, both in the exhibition halls and on the race track. Horses played a central role in the agricultural and rural life of the North Country and their place in the fair was firmly rooted. As the sole means of transportation and an essential working element in running a farm, horses were widely revered for their strength and beauty.

The northern New York region was home to some of the finest strains of horses found anywhere. The Compte de Chaumont, the Van Rensselaers, the LaFarges, and other men of wealth and leisure who settled the area imported from Europe only the best strains of blood in both horses and hounds. These proud beasts were well kept and considered a source of honor for their owners. Over the years, the descendants of these grand animals were crossed with the renowned horses bred by Justin Morgan of Vermont and found their way into stables all over the North Country. Locally, John Newby brought in rugged work horses from the Dakotas for sale from his stables on State Street.

Exhibitions of horses drew large and eager crowds in every town. News of famous horses filled columns in local papers everywhere. In May of 1895, the front page of the *Waddington Recorder* carried a feature profile and illustration of "Aurelius," the show horse with long, groomed mane and tail. The horse, owned by L.A. Cole and J.K. Rutherford of Waddington, was purchased in Santa Anna, California, and was worth an estimated four thousand dollars. The Hambletonian stallion "Gold Dust," owned by E.A. and C.E. Carpenter of Fowler, drew a particularly large crowd in Gouverneur during an exhibition and spurred a number of instant cash offers. One article reported R.C. Smith of Gouverneur to be the fortunate owner of a three-year-old Morgan stallion sired by none other than the famous trotter "Flying Cloud."

In talk of the success of a particular fair, the quality of the track and of the week's races was inevitably noted. In the week prior to the fair, the *St. Lawrence Plaindealer* carried the placings and track times from the Watertown and Ogdensburg fairs. The races featured horses from around the countryside, a few of which would compete at the fair in Canton. The Pace, Trot, Named Pace, Named Trot, Trot and Pace, and Three-Year-Old Trot and Pace each carried fairly substantial purses when compared with other areas of competition. John Newby entered some of the horses from his stables, and local interest was piqued over the upcoming races, the results of which would be printed in the paper of the week following the fair.

At the turn of the century, as the fair began its sixth decade in Canton, the directors of the SLCAS faced tough decisions concerning the upkeep of the grounds. Each year, the fair operated on a minimal budget with help in the form of the grant from the state legislature. The fair was not designed to clear a profit, and very little capital was carried over from year to year.

The unfailing support of the people of Canton and the surrounding communities meant that problems such as early cold and frosts did little to hinder attendance. The aftermath of the Great Texas Cyclone in 1900 exposed Canton to rain and high winds all week. Severe weather again in 1901 meant that crowds were thin, but surprisingly steady gate receipts and a claim from Lloyd's of London taken out against inclement weather insured that the fair could survive a few lean years.

The crisis that did concern the fair directors was the deteriorating condition of the exhibition halls. The graying buildings were showing the effects of fifty years of exposure to the alternating extremes of weather in the North Country. Five months of ice and snow followed by summer temperatures sometimes nearing 100 degrees caused the wood to expand and contract. Floorboards sagged and wooden joints creaked. The halls were dimly lit, damp, and musty. During fair week, overcrowding caused people to hurry through the displays, turning attention away from the exhibition halls. Although the exhibits were still presented with pride, the quarters that housed them were less than appropriate.

Mounting frustration over the bleak condition of the buildings was unleashed in a front page article in the *St. Lawrence Plaindealer.* The poor condition of the buildings ushered in an underlying resentment of the fair's directors. The Canton paper said, "If thousands of dollars can be put into a race course and grand stand, if hundreds can be spent on special attractions, money ought to be obtainable for the erection of a floral hall such as the displays merit. . . . There should be a music room where rival dealers can fight it out. . . . There should be a dairy hall with refrigerators and power. . . ."

Over a half-century of successful fairs had firmly established a precedent for quality. Generations of families had put their effort and pride into the fairs, and a reciprocal effort from the fair directors was expected. The need to renovate and repair the exhibition halls was obvious, and the fact that the public needed to make such an appeal through the local paper was unfortunate. But with the state of finances constantly remaining at a subsistence level, the major renovations called for by townspeople would be impossible. The directors of the SLCAS were placed in a curious position: in order to preserve the original standard, they would have to tamper with the formula.

In 1908 the fair was suspended for unspecified financial reasons. That September in Canton was undoubtedly a lot quieter than usual. The children returned to school. Women saved their goods and crafts for the following year. Horse races held at other fairs could only be read about in the pages of the *Plaindealer.* Cattle remained in their pens and the high school football team began practices early on the infield of the race track. The first frosts arrived and it would be another long year before the fair would open in town.

That autumn, the business community complained vociferously about the lack of traffic in the streets of Canton. Merchants depended on the amiable disposition of the large crowds that accompanied fair week. The absence of the fair would strongly influence the year-end balance sheets of many business owners. An editorial entitled "A Losing Proposition" estimated that more than twenty thousand dollars in revenue for the community would be lost because of the fair cancellation. Restaurants and civic groups serving meals to fair visitors lost valuable business and fund-raising opportunities. The American Theater also lost income from what was traditionally one of its strongest weeks. Fares collected by townspeople for harboring the wagon teams of other travelers were also lost. The same article speculated that Canton residents would unnecessarily spend close to four thousand dollars at fairs in Ogdensburg, Gouverneur, Potsdam, and Malone rather than at home that year.

Although the author of the article raised some valuable economic points to consider, never before, at least to most fairgoers, had the event been evaluated on the basis of the number of patrons it drew. The Canton fair had a long history of hosting some of the finest exhibits in the North Country. However, the yardstick for comparison now seemed grounded in how that quality translated into gate receipts. An increase in attendance would raise funds desperately needed for upkeep, but the directors knew that drawing patrons away from other fairs would require booking more attractions. Though adding attractions would raise the price of producing the annual fair, the hope was that high gate receipts would more than offset the initial expense.

At the turn of the century, although travel by rail and river had begun to open the North Country, horse and carriage remained the predominant form of transportation. The fair was a reflection of that; harness horses were showcased in the stables, carriage whips were sold along the midway, and the streets were filled with carriages and buggies.

In 1906 a new attraction in the Mechanics' Hall promised to change all of that. Attendance at the fair that year was low due to poor weather and reduced premiums. Traditional exhibits in the Mechanics' Hall showcased farming implements and simple machines that usually attracted only a small number of people interested in the farming industry. However, not even those people who saw the particular exhibit could have imagined the impact the gasoline engine would have on the whole of American society.

Cars began to appear on the streets of Canton to fascinated stares. An icon had arrived.

To the farming community of northern New York, the invention of the gasoline engine was foremost an agricultural revolution. Applications of the new engine to farming techniques would increase productivity and force farmers to adapt along with science or risk being left behind. The first appearance of gasoline-powered tractors and combines in the North Country would command a great deal of attention from enthusiasts and skeptics alike. Gasoline-powered engines would give life to crude milking machines and grain elevators. Trucks would take produce straight from the field to market. Increased production would change farming from a way of life to a business. The mechanic would replace the veterinarian and the sounds of gasoline engines would fill the harvest air.

To the rest of the community, the automobile was a major advance in personal transportation. Whereas trains and ships were autocratic and limited by the boundaries of steel and water, the auto was individual and democratic. Whereas horse and carriage travel was tedious and slow, automobile travel was fast and efficient. The car did not run on a schedule, required no sleep, and was limited only by the condition of the road. The horse was destined to become merely a sporting luxury. The train continues to run through northern New York but its cargo no longer includes passengers. The station in Canton has long been a tavern.

In 1909, after a year's absence and under a new board of directors, the fair again opened in Canton. One attraction was an automobile parade featuring over thirty sizes and models. Local merchants enthusiastically joined the parade by organizing floats advertising their businesses. Though the automobile was not an item that was grown, nurtured, or even hand-made, a premium was offered for the most impressive vehicle. That year, the first premium was given to George Robinson for his seven-passenger auto.

The market for the fair grew wider as the automobile became integrated into North Country life. Canton was now within reach of more people than ever. Families of fairgoers could organize day trips to Canton in their cars, taking in the sights and returning home by nightfall. Few of these new patrons brought items for exhibition and even fewer made the trip in order to view fine examples of produce, crafts, or implements. Instead, they were drawn by flyers promising races, shows, and games. Residents of Canton were also free to make day trips to fairs in other towns; thus the fair benefited from comparison and competition with other town fairs. However, because families attended a number of fairs each season instead of a single festival, long-standing allegiances began to dissipate.

The automobile allowed showmen and their traveling acts much more flexibility in arranging appearances as their circuit grew larger. Fair week soon became choked with attractions. County fairs in rural locations became a growing business for these shows. Portions of an article in the *Rome Sentinel* were reprinted in the *Plaindealer* on August 10, 1909, reflecting on the newest trend: "It is well enough to have agricultural fairs where products of the soil may be exhibited and stock and farm machinery shown, but additional attractions are necessary in order to secure the patronage necessary for financial and social success."

Indeed, exhibitions and displays had ceased to be the main reason for organizing the fair. The acts, originally intended to add a small degree of flavor and excitement to the fair, became the focus rather than the complementary attractions they had been. Organizers now began to plan the fair around the booking of attractions and, in an effort to draw even larger crowds, lost sight of the reason why people had come in the first place.

Unfortunately, the fair also attracted a new and largely unwelcome visitor. Cattlemen and horse traders followed the traveling showmen's county fair circuit, sweeping in with champion livestock to claim the premiums. These outsiders, with faster horses and stronger steers, consistently won competitions against local farmers. Race officials checked constantly for ringers that were actually much faster than the track time prescribed to them.

Viewed collectively, the fairs represented a profitable path to easy winnings. As one fair closed these men would pocket the prize money and head off to the next one. Still, the loss of prize money to an outsider weighed little against the damage in pride sustained by local farmers and stable owners. Competitions that had spawned local rivalries lasting generations were disrupted and the look of the old fair was quietly changing.

Geneva Goulette grew up in Clare, approximately twenty miles from Canton on the edge of the Adirondack woods, and now lives in the Riverside Apartment complex. "On the morning of the first day of the fair, we would rise early and travel by horse and buggy to Canton," she recalled. The trip was slow and cumbersome, but her spirit was always high. A trip to town coupled with the arrival of fair week was quite an exciting event. Geneva was just a young girl in the mid-1920s and her family would stay with relatives in town while they visited the fair.

The fairs of that era featured an eyeful of attractions for every visitor. The midway was located just inside the gate. The rifle shot and ring toss offered prizes for sharp aim and keen sight. Barkers and salesmen gave competing pitch lines that hummed in the frenzied air. "One year there was a sideshow featuring a woman with two heads," Geneva recalled. Fast rides with flashing lights and carnival music were a thrill unlike any other. "It is impossible to sense the sheer delight a merry-go-round meant to children whose only motion thrill was furnished by a swing on the drive-floor of the big barn or sliding down Griffin's Hill after an ice storm," wrote columnist Georgia Lott Selter. The merry-go-round, ferris wheel, and tilt-a-whirl were all assembled for the four-day event, then disassembled and shipped to the site of the next week's fair.

The bright colors and fresh scents of the Floral Hall made it Geneva's favorite exhibition. "The different types of flowers were always so beautiful," she exclaimed. Her family enjoyed strolling through the exhibition halls, but turned their attention primarily to the races and ball games at the grandstand. Professional teams of "ebony gentlemen" traveled from places such as Brooklyn and

Havana to play a series of baseball games for the fairgoers. Although there were dark-skinned people in the North Country, two teams made up entirely of black men were certainly a curious and thrilling sight.

At noontime, Geneva's family would retire to the buggy in the field on the other side of the race track for a picnic lunch. From there they would watch the rest of the afternoon races.

The festivities did not end at the day's close of the fair. The Canton business community also planned annually for fair week with sales, specials, and parades. Each year the American Theater brought in a popular show from downstate. "I saw the play 'Million Dollar Baby' one year," Geneva said. The night before the close of the fair, it became the custom to light the Canton sky with fireworks.

The directors of the fair went to great lengths to arrange for an aerial demonstration at the fairgrounds in 1910. Similar flights had thrilled crowds in Boston and at the State Fair in Syracuse and it was expected that the plane would boost attendance in Canton.

The pilot and his assistant arrived in Canton on Sunday, with the plane expected to arrive on Monday. However, shipping difficulties delayed the plane until late Tuesday. By working diligently, the pilot and his assistant installed the engine by Wednesday morning in anticipation of an afternoon demonstration in the sky above the fairgrounds. Since the engine was new, the pilot set about to test the motor as a final precaution. Upon ignition, the motor kicked to life then cut out suddenly, sending a hollow boom across the fairgrounds. The pilot and his assistant were unharmed but the engine was broken. The damages were impossible to repair.

As had been the case before, the directors of the fair had put forth an untiring effort to bring prominence to the fair, only to see those efforts fade. Like the exasperated pilot, they struggled with new ways to make the fair a success, but in looking forward the directors had failed to look back. In striving to exalt and glorify the sky, they pushed the celebration of the earth from the forefront. The people who had been the lifeblood of the fair in Canton were slowly being blocked out. Their incentive to be part of the fair by displaying their own exhibitions was slowly being lost. The fair had been established as a celebration of people but had been transformed into a commercial event. The fair had become a carnival.

As fewer and fewer exhibits were entered for show, the fair lost important income from entrance fees. Despite the addition of lighting along the midway to present attractions at night, the fair slowly lost its ability to hold the interest of the people for all four days.

The 1929 premium listing contained an open letter to all fair-goers urging them to enter more exhibits. The request stated that the people of Canton "should have a little home pride and get their share of premiums. You might get a first premium occasionally and quite often if you made the effort, and at the same time you would help our exhibition which in late years at all fairs is fast becoming professional."

The directors did not understand that the reason for the citizens' complacency had little to do with money. But, unfortunately for the directors, all of the fair's other problems had everything to do with money. Although modest monetary gains had been made over the previous two years, the SLCAS listed the total operating debt in 1929 at $5,800. Also, with so many expensive special attractions, the threat of bad weather left the fair in an extremely vulnerable position that no insurance policy could fully cover. Further, since there was little hope that there would be a turnabout in the number of exhibitions, the fair would have to continue to rely on imported entertainment to lure crowds.

Then, barely a month after the close of the 1929 fair, the New York Stock Exchange plummeted, sending the United States and the rest of the world headlong into a depression. Economic retrenchment by the state legislature in Albany threatened to cut all funding deemed frivolous. Indeed, although not cut completely, the annual $6,000 grant from the state legislature was reduced. In the wake of the Depression, an editorial in the *Plaindealer* offered the following advice: "The one great lesson is that speculation does not pay for the 'small fellow' in any way. Do not buy unless you can pay for what you buy." This credo certainly would have been helpful in running the fair."

With entrance fees down, budget cuts, dilapidated facilities, attendance low, and deep debt, 1933 proved to be the last year of the fair in Canton. Stunt pilots and trick bicyclists performed to thinning crowds. It was painfully obvious that the fair would not be able to stand on its own without significant state funding. Early frosts committed farmers to the preparation of their land for winter and townspeople talked mostly of the upcoming high school football season. The event that had been so closely identified with local pride for eighty years now stood as an empty attraction. Instead of filling a central role in the success of the fair, the people of Canton and the surrounding communities were now simply asked to play host. The anniversary was remembered, but the occasion forgotten.

The following June, in a meeting held at the office of F.J. Wheeler in Canton, the members and directors of the SLCAS voted to incorporate the fair and merge it with the one held annually in Gouverneur. It is difficult to believe that the directors earnestly expected that the Canton community would share in festivities held in Gouverneur. By incorporating the fair, the SLCAS lost state funding and could thus offer the Gouverneur fair little more than an endorsement. There would be almost no public reaction to the move for another fifteen years. Sentiment tends to run low when one is caught in the throes of a depression. Three generations of Cantonians had poured their creativity and spirit into the fair, but now the grounds would be unoccupied. The fair was gone.

A few weeks later, John Newby, the horse trader, purchased the fairgrounds at public auction. They had been valued in excess of $15,000 in the mid-1860s, but lackluster bidding generated a mere $1,600. Almost unnoticeably, an era was over.

The fair is uprooted and heads along Water Street, against the current, toward downtown. Crossing the bridge over the Grass River, the fair turns left on the Canton-Gouverneur Road and is gone. *The week's delights with all its sights has glided by too fast.* John Newby takes possession of the land and hires temporary laborers to dismantle some of the remaining structures. The pieces of wood that are deemed salvageable are saved for other projects, but most is sold for kindling. The Floral Hall is stubborn, its eight sides holding fast against teams of grunting men. *The joys of taffy, pink and white, are all too good to last.* The entrance gate is pushed over, spraying dust and small pebbles on the autos parked by the edge of the road. Horses trot around the track in front of the dilapidated and empty grandstand. The property is posted against trespass. *The carnival, with calliope, has stilled its wheezing toot.* The midway is dotted with patches of worn earth and matted grass. The call of the barker has faded over the hill. *The wind whines through the shabby sheds; a worthy substitute.* Used ticket stubs, bleached by rain and frost, collect in the weeds at the edge of the grounds. . . .

I turn and walk back along Riverside Drive toward Main Street. The sky is clear on this early autumn morning and people are beginning to emerge from their homes. At Main Street I turn left and away from their river, up toward the Silas Wright Museum, home of the St. Lawrence County archives. There I will visit the fair through crusty premium lists and soft, crumpled articles printed half a century before my birth. I will see the faces of happy children in yellowing photographs and imagine they belong to young Irving Bacheller or Geneva Goulette. Recounting their words, I will walk with them along Water Street and feel the anticipation of the fair gather inside me.

Information for this essay was drawn from the archives of local newspapers and the St. Lawrence County Historical Association.

Last Day at the Mines in Moriah

Tom Van de Water

First light touches the top of the gray tailings pile by Mineville's Number 7 Mill, once the largest man-made mountain in the world. A car climbing from Port Henry on Lake Champlain winds its way up toward the mill.

On the rocky slopes of these hills, just east of the Adirondacks' highest peaks, the people of Moriah have breathed life and death into this rock, created their own mountains, and watched them crumble.

The car climbs past gray cement block tenements made of mine tailings. Broken windows mark the vacant rooms, and clothes hang limp on long lines across porches.

The early light paints the steeple of the Polish Catholic church, turning it yellow against a slate sky. The church sits behind the row of tenements on the left of the road, dominating them like a parent. On the right, a sign still announces, "Republic Steel – Harmony Mine."

Across the pit, where mine shaft towers once stood, the car

pulls up beside a pale green building that was once the Republic Steel mine office building. Geologist Chuck Harpur, the last employee of Republic Steel in Mineville—a town once ruled by magnetite, some of the richest iron ore in the world—walks up the crumbling steps of the silent building.

A vacant glass window greets him at what was once the reception desk as he ascends the long stairway to his office.

Today he will close the office for good, remove the last official maps and files, symbols of Republic's power in a town it once dominated, and leave nothing but the cluster flies that have begun to overrun the place.

At the desk where J.R. Linney once worked, Harpur spreads out a map of the Adirondacks. It is dotted with markers for the many mines that existed—and the few that still exist—throughout the North Country. Often, the industry discovered other places where it was cheaper to retrieve ore, leaving towns like Mineville to decay. To the northeast is Lyon Mountain, another Republic Steel town, just west of Dannemora where the prison was built to supply prisoners for mining ore in the nineteenth century. In the northwest is Star Lake, where the Jones and Laughlin Company pulled out, leaving asbestos-filled mine buildings, oil leaking into a water-filled open pit iron mine, and hundreds without work. In the middle, near Newcomb, is the abandoned titanium mine at Tahawus, open pit ilmenite mines and mills left by National Lead but originally mined for their iron in the last century. The railroad line that snakes across the map from Saratoga Springs to Tahawus is rusting, hardly visible.

On Harpur's map, the still-active mines appear scattered in the circle of unique rock that defines the Adirondacks—wollastonite mines west of Willsboro, garnet mines near Gore Mountain, zinc mines in Balmat and Pierrepont, talc mines near Gouverneur. Harpur glances out the big picture window at the town and mine sites and thinks about the connections between this town and so many others in the region.

Harpur turns his attention to his notes. They document one fact above all others: exploiting mineral wealth did not come without cost. When he interviewed Joseph Mandy last week, he heard about the Fisher Hill mine disaster of the '50s. It left Mandy plagued by nightmares and the odor of human flesh. Five young men were crushed and splattered against a concrete wall when the cable of the skip carrying them through a mine tunnel snapped. The reverberations of that horrible crash echo through generations in Moriah. The Fisher Hill mine is today a state "correction" department's "shock center."

Harpur is more hesitant to write of the number of miners and families who have talked with him about silicosis. When he was hired after the mines closed in 1971, this "white lung," a cancer caused by dust in the mines, was not acknowledged or discussed. Some of his recent talks with miners haven't been acknowledged either. No one, however, is looking over his shoulder anymore.

Harpur pauses and leafs through his notes, past the woman who lost three husbands to the mines; past World Series pitching star Johnny Podres' family's mining history; past the ore train wreck that killed three men when the brakes failed; to his notes from an interview with Dr. James Glavin, the company doctor who broke down in tears while describing a mining accident. Harpur reads:

> A car two-thirds of the way down the inclined slope of Don B. had wrecked. . . . The cable holding the carload of men had snapped and the car tore up the slope so no one could get up or down. Eleven people were hurt down there and there was no way to get them up. A few of us offered to try to reach the men by going down one of the old, abandoned mine shafts, the Clonan shaft. The shaft hadn't been used for five or six years and the winter's ice had blocked parts of it. It was March. . . . The man running the hoist had to drop and lift the cage to break through the ice. We went up, then he let the cables go and we crashed down, smashing through the ice. We had to hold onto each other to keep from being thrown all over. We went down it twenty times, lifting and smashing for 1100 feet.
>
> At the bottom, we walked half a mile until we came to another shaft. Johnny Murphy, one of the chief engi-

neers, was with us and hooked up the long-unused wires to run the car for this shaft. It ran. But about halfway down that slope the car started to get away from us. Somehow he got us stopped. Then we walked another half mile until we came upon the eleven injured men.

For the first time in my life, the men sent up a cheer for me. I gave most of them morphine and splinted the broken legs. Then men had to carry them back the way we'd come down. They had to use stretchers.

About halfway through, I figured I'd better get back to the surface since the other company doctor, Doc Cummins, was gone to New York City and I'd have to care for the men. When I finally came up the Clonan shaft around 5 P.M., everyone in town was crowded around the shaft head. Families and wives were all over. I stayed all night. My wife sent me up some supper around 8 o'clock.

Harpur recalls Glavin's frustration and anger at the tragedy, and remembers how the name "Moriah" fits this place. But in Genesis, in the land of Moriah where Abraham offered up his son Isaac, Isaac was allowed to live.

As former miner George Simpson said to him recently, "Maybe it's best that these mines closed." The mines of Moriah offered both life and death. For Harpur, they offer only isolation. The musty smell of these vacant rooms is overwhelming.

Harpur looks back at the geologic map of the Adirondacks, pulls out his files on magnetite, and hurriedly scribbles geologic notes while he still has the records and models together.

The mines, he knows, are the result of metamorphosis of some of the earth's oldest rock a billion years ago, and their more recent uplift to form the hundred-mile-wide dome known as the Adirondacks. The rock in the High Peaks once was a feldspar-rich fluid, mixed and metamorphosed by intense heat and pressure. It is a violent history, recorded once on the mineral grains and reflected still on the somber faces of those few who continue to walk the streets of Mineville.

There are traces of this violent history on the silent face of a young mother with a baby on her arm and a cigarette in her mouth. It is even more obvious on the faces of the old miners who stayed on long after Republic Steel left. Harpur had asked former miner Wesley Cembalski to come in today after noon for an interview. Wesley had told him, "Agh, I don't have anything to tell you!"

Maybe. For now, though, Harpur will look at the geology of the place.

Here were rocks once thirty kilometers deep in the earth. At that depth, some minerals flowed like toothpaste. The ancient gneisses may have spread along their mineral bands, yielding to re-melted feldspar-rich fluid. From what he'd read, he was sure this mass of feldspar—this anorthosite—must have flowed in, creating a huge mushroom shape. Then, it would have been disrupted by the powerful changes of the Grenville event more than a billion years ago, when two continents collided along the axis of the St. Lawrence River. Harpur once told a colleague, "I'm a catastrophist." Catastrophe was what created the rock and the ore here. It determined the course of geologic history. Perhaps that's what attracted him to Mineville.

Certainly, the history of Adirondack rock was catastrophic. Its beginnings could date back to that vast Precambrian time when the first crustal material was crystallizing on a condensing earth. Mineville was the edge of the continent, before the Green Mountains of Vermont were squeezed up during the collision with Africa.

It was all too far back, thought Harpur. This took place before what most people thought of as geologic time, before the Tertiary or Cretaceous, before the Jurassic, Triassic, Devonian, Silurian, Ordovician, or even Cambrian. And yet these miners who spent a lifetime in this rock were able to glimpse that eternity. Harpur remembers Mineville engineer Thornton Finkbeiner telling him once that good miners had an innate sense of the rock, better than any book-smart geologist. Those miners knew exactly where to drill next without being told.

Harpur looked forward to talking with Wesley Cembalski.

Here was the ore. He held a chunk of the dense black magnetite in his hand. That's what drove this town and made it more like Butte, Montana than any New York village, he thought. It created a frontier-exploiting mentality. It was minerals that made the money that brought civilization.

This was the true wealth, muses Harpur; it wasn't the people. These Adirondack ore deposits formed during the pressure and heat when elements migrated within the rock from mineral to mineral. Iron-rich concentrations formed magnetite deposits in hundreds of locations around the Adirondacks. Garnet-rich areas formed, and zinc was isolated in the mineral sphalerite.

Early settlers thought the farming terrible and left. Miners stayed, along with the loggers. For Harpur, mining was synonymous with civilization. "Natural resources are the true basis of wealth," he has always said.

From the files on magnetite, Harpur copies the information about one of the richest ore deposits first found in Mineville, an unusual body forming a massive sphere of high-grade magnetite, some of the richest in the world. On the three-dimensional model of ore bodies in Harpur's office, it shows up as a circular core, descending into the earth like a spinal column.

The model shows where they mined huge rooms underground, with four-hundred-foot pillars of ore left to support the roof. Bill Blomstran, past mine superintendent, told him recently how, during the Second World War, even the pillars were mined to recover the pure ore. The Republic Steel photo of the pillar recovery shows a massive pillar, with a tiny figure of a man clinging precariously to a long ladder on its flank.

Amazingly, even today, the roof still holds without pillars. The Number 21 mine extends under the Mineville Fire Department, under the office building where Harpur sits, under part of the town. Other pits nearby have filled with water and are gradually collapsing at the margins. Harpur has been checking the old pits before his transfer. Though he's not anxious to move on to his next assignment in Brazil, he won't miss this echoing building above the "21" mine pit.

Harpur hears again the creak of his chair, the buzz of a fly in the window, the hum of a distant motor. He feels the weight of being the last man here for Republic Steel, the last in Adirondack iron. He recalls five years with Republic as chief geologist in Liberia. He wonders what Brazil will bring. It will be hard to leave this place where the mountains rise westward, and ore and history define each step.

There may be no way to explain the magnetite here, he thinks with dismay. Some of these rocks show evidence of both shallow and deep metamorphism in the same place. "Nature will fool you every time," he says to no one in particular. But if he can gather enough information, it may make sense.

By the time Harpur has collected the files he wants and eaten the lunch his wife packed, it's one o'clock and he hears the bell down below. It must be Cembalski.

Wesley Cembalski comes up the stairs, back bent but solid of step. He coughs and finds the breathing hard. When he reaches out to Harpur, though, his hand is firm.

Harpur asks about earlier days in the mines, and Wesley describes mucking the ore underground, shoveling back-breaking loads of magnetite into ore cars. He recalls that when he arrived from Kalencyn, Poland, the Witherbee-Sherman Company people said they'd provide everything for him. He remembers labor riots, strikers getting turned out of their homes by Witherbee-Sherman Company police. He describes the slow growth of union strength.

"Sure, I remember that strike of 1913. My father didn't strike very long. He went back to work and kept his house. Others, the company told if they didn't go back to work . . . they'd throw 'em out. A woman cooking on a hot stove was thrown right out. They couldn't do that today. No way. Poor people . . . they had a rope around your neck and pulled it tighter and tighter 'til you couldn't breathe. Then they'd let up just enough."

Harpur asks about Cembalski's breathing, and the old man responds that it's just "the dust," silicosis, for which he now gets some compensation. After the dynamite blasts, the mines were filled with a fine rock dust. Everybody had "the dust" to some degree. Later on, the air was better and they used masks.

Cembalski tells Harpur of escaping Mineville before the Depression and working in the slate quarries of Vermont, then being forced to return to Mineville when the quarries closed. "I didn't want to come back here, but there was really no choice. The air was bad underground; I got the silicosis and now just about nobody of my generation is left. Maybe it was best I moved then. I got married in Vermont before coming back here."

He sits back in his chair and tells of trying to keep one of his sons from working in the mines. "I told him, if he wanted to work in the mines he could pack up right now and git out, 'cause they wasn't going to live in this house."

When his kids were growing up, Cembalski says, "I tried to teach them Polish, but when they had problems in school and the teacher couldn't teach them because they had different sounds for the same letters, I quit."

When Harpur mentions his move to Brazil, Wesley shakes his head. "I couldn't do it. A young tree you can transplant, but an old tree, you move, it dies. I'm like that."

As Harpur sees him out the door a while later, Wesley Cembalski turns and grins. "Not many of us full-blooded Pollocks left, are there?" Harpur nods, glad to have had a chance to talk with this man, sorry he'll not likely see him again.

Harpur gathers up his notes, collects the boxes of files and the geologic models to be sent to company headquarters, and takes them to his car. As he drives out, he passes the Witherbee-Sherman building where the fighting broke out in 1913 between strikers and company police. The bars on the company jail are still visible.

Taking the road toward the Barton Hill mines, he remembers this was where Robert Garrow came to hide the body of the woman he'd murdered in the 1970s. Garrow had been stalked all over the Adirondacks and was captured here in his hometown after a tense standoff while roadblocks surrounded Mineville.

Harpur decides to turn up the road toward Spanish Settlement and drive up to Belfry Hill for a last look over the town. On the way he passes Joe Posada, out walking with his wife. He had talked with Posada last month about early mining, and was amazed he still kept up with relatives in Spain.

Up in the abandoned Belfry Hill fire tower, wind whips through the empty windows. Harpur looks toward the High Peaks, about fifteen miles due west. The air passes through the Wolfjaws, by Gothics and Dix Mountain. It sweeps across the forests of land owned by International Paper Company. It drops over Belfry Hill into Moriah, where updrafts hold ravens aloft. The ravens flap silently below the lookout, breaking the silence with croaking voices before dropping out of sight.

Harpur climbs back in his car and heads down the mountain. He keeps telling himself that from the long view of a geologic perspective, the desolation of this place is only temporary. The mountains keep rising and eroding, but the suffering of people is momentary. Geologic time can offer that kind of peace; even the huge tailings pile is beginning to heal, with small poplar trees taking over the lower slopes.

Along the main street Harpur sees Frank Dembrosky, just returned from a trip to Lithuania. Frank once told him how his grandmother reached Mineville through Canada from Lithuania after being turned away at Ellis Island for an eye disorder. She was a midwife in town for many years, and delivered Frank in the house beside the Harmony Mine shaft. Harpur would have liked to spend more time here talking with people. Maybe it's the people that matter most, he thinks, not the mines.

The car heads down the hill, past the long rows of headstones in the Catholic cemetery, and turns the corner for Port Henry. The sky opens out over Lake Champlain. Down by the silent railroad yard built on mine tailings, at the edge of the lake, an old man stands bent over, stirring the waters with a stick. He looks more like a conjurer than a miner, peering through the murky waters for something lost.

The sun sets, casting long shadows across the land that shone moments before with a golden glow. Harpur looks back up into those shadows, to the silhouette of the tailings pile at the Number 7 Mill.

He heads home, haunted forever by the mines of Moriah.

Becoming the Past

Harry W. Paige

You see them scattered around the Northern New York landscape: reminders, things abandoned, things becoming the past. Homes, barns, cars, trucks, farm machinery, perhaps laced with early snows and waiting for the auctioneer, the bulldozers, the animals, picture-takers, junkmen, the movers, or the slow decay of rust and ruin.

Patience appears to be their only virtue. They wait for the reclaimers, the repossessors of what has been lost, the scavengers of people's lives. These things appear to have been left behind by an army in retreat, its terrible urgency spelled out in those patterns of panic and undisciplined abandonment that the military likes to call "strategic withdrawals." But no army or no solitary human heart ever withdrew with such a show of desolation and sadness.

Homes are the most painful to see deserted; they once echoed life in abundance, the temples of our little celebrations of life. More than houses, they earned the right to be called *homes.* Now abandoned, they stand like falling monuments to neglect or loss or absence, the windows staring darkly like empty sockets at what once was: somebody's home; somebody's dream; somebody's hope; somebody's future. A place where people were born and died; a place of happiness and sorrow; a place where children lived and played and grew up. A place busy with life.

I see a porous tire hanging from a tree, swinging like a pendulum in the easy wind, measuring the slow rhythms of memory, rhythms that seem to play a faraway tune like something heard from a distant carousel. I see a clothesline strung with sparrows; a twenty-year-old Ford car, fender-deep in weeds. I see toys half buried in the grass, toys that made a season come alive: a sled, a shingle used for home plate, a single ski, a wheel-less wagon. Now the wilderness is taking over, encroaching on the man-made patterns and manufactured things.

The little creatures have arrived to stake their claim, too: the mice, the insects, the birds. A bird plays on the television antenna like a harp. A cricket sings its cheerful song to an echoing absence.

What I don't see, I imagine: a barn turning in upon itself, surrendering a board at a time. Often the roof is first, a huge hole as though a bomb, unexploded, had fallen through, the daylight filtering in with streams of dust and sun. Then the wind tears at the edges of things, trying to pry them loose, peel them back. Then the spring and autumn rains. The winter ice and snow. The smokeless fires of decay. All the elements conspire against things left behind, like a gray and ghostly wolf pack attacking a straggler.

I remember the ghost towns of the American West, those boom and bust towns abandoned in desert and mountain places. A few were even for sale: church, school, saloon, post office, general store, livery, homes. Everything! Even the cemetery out behind the church, its fallen crosses like a random harvest left in the fields. A man once wanted me to invest in such a ghost town; it was to be a business venture, ghosts for fun and profit. He planned to create an amusement park on the scene.

The price was right, but the memories weren't mine to barter.

I didn't have the right somehow to stake a claim to other peoples' lives.

They have ghost towns in the East, too: everywhere there are those spiritual beings, spiritual geographies signifying loss. In the North Country they are everywhere, like signs that warn that a life in this harsh landscape may take its toll.

Sometimes there are people who still think of these ghost towns and intend to return, although they seldom do. They are relatives living in distant places, with no stake in the old homestead except money and perhaps childhood memories. They live so far away and are so busy with other things that they haven't shown up to inspect the property, or even to put it on the market. California is a long way from St. Lawrence County—and not only in miles, but in histories as well. And so there will be other things left behind: dishes, pots and pans, even journals and diaries in the attic, things waiting for moth and rust and vandals and thieves. The stuff of auctions that usually go for a dollar a box. Sometimes there are letters. All things private as pain, lyric as memory.

People usually have their own good reasons for leaving things behind. A home, a farm, is not easily abandoned. It is a hurtful thing to leave a place where you have put down roots. Usually there is a sickness, a death, a lack of heirs, a moving away, a tragedy of major or minor proportions. Sometimes there is no money for taxes. People have reasons. Yet the results are painful to see: a deserted homestead is a possibility unrealized, a chapter unfinished. And the viewer can only write the ending in the mind or the heart.

The one who surveys the scene can write a happy ending: someone returns! The house becomes a home again! The granddaughter comes back from the city and chases away the wilderness, cleans up the place with paint, love, and hard work. Then she sends for the children, and the place explodes with life and laughter once more. The farmer mends the barn, tills the fields. Everyone waits for the harvest. There are happy endings!

But happy endings are the exception; mostly, there is just the waiting and watching the tall grass encroach. The vines climb the walls like the wrists of invisible intruders trying to get in. Mostly, there is the wind wearing at the corners and singing its shrill song. Mostly, there is the crowded solitude and the loud silences of abandoned things, things left behind.

It is said that nature abhors a vacuum, and it is so. Humankind does, too: someone sees a harvest in fields that lie fallow. Someone sees a home in a clearing in the woods. Someone sees a future in the moment's pause. Someone sees a tomorrow in the horizon's altar light. It has always been that way.

Nature tries to cut down what rises too high, tries to build up what has crumbled. A delta forms at the river's mouth, an island from the lava flow.

Human beings will always stake their claims: in one way or another, we are all homesteaders at heart. What is there is for use, not waste. But time and circumstance will alter the earth's landscape, and the landscape of the heart as well. Promises, dreams, hopes—they sour with time. Things happen that are unforeseen, unforgiving. And finally the dream, too, is abandoned; the hope discarded; the plan altered.

It was so on the great Western trails—the Oregon Trail and the Santa Fe. There is a body buried for every mile along the way. There were the things that became too heavy or required too much precious space: the favorite writing desk, the spinet, the family portrait—things that had to surrender to a harsher necessity .

Homemakers are a hopeful breed; they have to be, in order to face the unknown, the unknowable. They are driven by some homing instinct shared by other animals. They seek to put down roots, to make a house a home, to carve out their little acre of land in all this plenty. But there is a temporary quality about their noble efforts and hard work. "This place is mine," they claim when the work is finished, and they accept the myth of permanence they have created in the excitement of their victory. But it is short-lived, this victory, this celebration. Time and wilderness are waiting just beyond the clearing.

We will go on with our plans, our journeys, our homesteading, our thinking in terms of lifetimes, generations, and years. It is the right and human thing to do; otherwise, we would be paralyzed with doubt and our horizons would shrink to only familiar borders. We would never set out for the hills beyond. But we must become used to the leaving, too: the things abandoned, the ghost towns, the graveyards, the little markers we suddenly come across along the trails. The arrowheads, the journals, the ruins. We must become used to the temporary, even in the illusion of permanence we have created.

We must become used to the broken dreams and tarnished hopes. They go with the territory. They go with our expectations. Even with the bones of our ancestors that lie unearthed, scattered in the overgrown fields next to rusting fenders, tractors, and toys.

Whistles in the Night

Arthur L. Johnson

I dip underneath the tracks through the underpass as I approach Canton from the east on Route 11. I pick them up again on my right as I roll toward DeKalb Junction. Occasionally, I see a Conrail blue diesel with a string of freight cars. There may be a switcher working in Gouverneur. I always hope to see a train, but rarely do; most of them travel at night on this St. Lawrence Valley line.

John R. Stilgoe, in a 1984 book called *The Metropolitan Corridor*, describes the railroad as a corridor of the city, an "urban spine" reaching out to the country, forever breaking down its isolation.

A century and a half ago, Henry Thoreau resented the intrusion: "The whistle of the locomotive penetrates my woods, . . . informing me that many restless city merchants are arriving within the circle of the town."

Nathaniel Hawthorne said the train whistle "gives such a startling shriek since it brings the noisy world into the midst of our slumberous peace."

These men felt about the railroad the way I feel about malls. However, for most in their time, the railroad represented progress. Today, the railroad seems a remnant of a comfortable past, certainly more a solution than a problem. But it brought a revolution; Thoreau and Hawthorne knew it. Nothing would ever be the same where its twin ribbons ran.

I think about these things when driving by the rail line where it parallels Route 11 between Potsdam and Watertown, or eastward along the abandoned grade of the Rutland Railroad's line from Norwood to Rouses Point. Almost 150 years have elapsed since the shriek of the whistle announced PROGRESS from two directions in the same decade, disturbing the North Country's "slumberous peace." The "Northern Railroad of New York" was built first, in the 1840s, to connect the New England lines with Lake Ontario via Ogdensburg. Segments begun at each end met in Malone on September 30, 1850, when the Locomotive *Chateaugay* chugged through with a train of yellow passenger cars, opening a service that would last 113 years.

The Northern was the first railroad to use refrigerator cars, reputedly invented in the Ogdensburg freight yard in 1851. Thus began the butter and milk trains, and the North Country's specialization in dairy farming. The steep grades in the White and Green Mountains prevented the route from becoming a major east/west link, but the company owned ships, based in Ogdensburg, that completed a line of transportation to Chicago and the Midwest. They could not, however, compete successfully with the New York Central's "water level route" in the Mohawk Valley.

By our standards, it was a long poke from Boston to Ogdensburg. In 1860, you could leave Boston at 7:00 in the morning and, by staying the night in St. Albans, be in "the Burg" by 12:40 the next day, according to an ad in the Boston papers. Portland, Maine was plugged into the system by 1870 with the Portland and Ogdensburg, supposedly completing "a union of the Great Lakes and Casco Bay."

One hyperbolic orator called this "a marriage more significant than the wedding of Venice and the Adriatic." Not quite, although it did add to the breakdown of the North Country's isolation.

The Northern ran from Ogdensburg through Lisbon and Madrid (our little Iberia) to Norwood, and east along the course of present Route 11 to Lake Champlain. It lasted a hundred years and ended its days as the New York Division of the Rutland Railroad, a Vermont company. If you look closely at the old coal hopper cars parked near the prison at Ogdensburg you can barely make out the "RUTLAND" lettering in the rust, perhaps the final fading remnants of a way of life fast receding into history.

The track in use today from Montreal to Syracuse was part of the Rome, Watertown & Ogdensburg Railroad, a system built by 1861, reaching north from the Mohawk Valley to Lake Ontario at Cape Vincent, the St. Lawrence River at Ogdensburg, and the Northern Railroad at Norwood. Little woodburning "pufferbillies" pulled three-car passenger trains, sometimes at sixty miles an hour.

Imagine what that meant to the communities along the way! Suddenly, what had been a week-long trip could be completed in a day or two. Potsdam got the *Watertown Times* on the day it was printed. Land values must have soared, as they do today along new interstates. But for a few, the news was not good: local shoemakers, for example, could hardly compete with cheap factory shoes coming off the train from downstate. Some small businesses with local markets suffered. Stagecoach drivers and the operators of roadside inns found that their businesses were ruined.

By the 1880s, the RW&O had expanded with a line into Syracuse, an extension to Massena connecting with the Grand Trunk to Montreal, and branches to Sackets Harbor, Clayton, Morristown, and into Ogdensburg from the west. At Ogdensburg, a ferry connected the RW&O with the Canadian railways at Prescott, Ontario. Between 1909 and the late 1940s, passenger trains also served Waddington, Chase Mills, and Norfolk on the Norwood & St. Lawrence.

The system was an immediate popular success. On a single ordinary day, September 3, 1859, the Potsdam station agent sold

805 tickets. Travel was possible as never before. At its height, the line ran three or four daily passenger trains each way, and several freights. All this traffic ran on a single track with occasional passing sidings. Every agent was a telegrapher, relaying messages to trains and setting signals. There were crashes, of course—a couple of spectacular ones—but the marvel is that there were so few.

The railroad was an employer of an army of men, and much of the work was dangerous. One young man was killed in the line's first year of operation, setting brakes on a freight train near Adams Center in 1852. Edward Hungerford put it quaintly: "These men of the North Country were learning that railroading is not all prunes and preserves."

Norwood was a busy interchange point. In the late 1800s, its two main lines cooperated in a through-express from Niagara Falls to Portland, Maine, called the White Mountain Express. This train, with nine sleepers, came up the RW&O to Norwood, where it made a breakfast stop, and then headed east on the Northern and the Portland & Ogdensburg. The entire trip took 24 hours.

Malone became a busy railroad town when William Seward Webb's Adirondack and St. Lawrence built through from Remsen to Montreal in 1892. The old Rutland station is still there, serving as a bank now, and the remains of the repair shops and rail yards can still be seen on the northeast edge of the village center.

The railroad held a monopoly over land transportation from the 1850s to the 1920s. Freight trains stopped at stations with package freight as well as cars for industrial sidings. Every town had a freight yard, and industries with their sidetracks were located near the mainline. The sporadic chugging of the switch engine and the clank of couplers formed the percussion in the background music of town life. Passenger trains carried express freight, and Railway Express was the UPS of the era.

The passenger cars, with their clerestory roofs, changed little in appearance until the 1940s, though the open platforms at the ends of the cars gave way to enclosed vestibules, and wooden cars to steel. The feel and smell of green or red plush seats were part of the travel experience; you could tell which was the "smoker" without seeing the signs. Not until the 1950s and the diesel era did the streamlined coach with its arch roof and wide windows become the rule, and not even then on branch lines like most of those in the North Country. By then, though, passenger service was losing out to the interstate highway and the airliner.

The prosperous RW&O became the St. Lawrence Division of the New York Central in 1891. RW&O President Charles Parsons caved in after William Vanderbilt threatened to build a competing line to the North Country. Frequent service continued, however, and got better. Even today, there are those who can remember boarding a sleeper in Potsdam and riding overnight to Grand Central Station, New York. Now we can drive down in seven hours and get there tired, or fly down and pay a hundred dollars a night for a hotel. But to board a sleeper in a North Country village and wake up in the heart of the city, that's the way to go.

Alas, no more. Instead of being a restful time in between things—a time when you gave yourself permission to sit and watch the scenery and think—travel is a nerve-wracking encounter with crowded airports or clogged interstates.

I miss meeting someone at the depot—especially at night. There's an air of expectancy as the station agent trundles the baggage cart up the platform under tall gooseneck lights and people watch up the track for the first sign of the headlight beam sweeping around a curve. There's a growing roar as the safety valve on the steam engine blows and the heavy wheels grind past, the brakes gripping, as eager passengers watch at various doors.

Back then, arrivals were charged with drama. Now, you wait under an electric arrivals-and-departures sign for someone to walk up a chute. You don't even see the airplane.

And there's departure: you settle in the plush seat and watch for the conductor to raise his lantern and start the slow forward motion. Trainmen walk alongside, jump up nonchalantly as the steps come beside them, and bang shut the doors. Speed increases as the engineer "notches out" the throttle and the scenery rolls by faster and faster Or seeing someone off: you watch at a window through which you cannot talk, and wave as the window slides away. The tail-end marker lamps on the last car disappear around a curve, the mournful wail of the steam whistle leaves you feeling empty and alone in the quiet of the platform. Steam locomotives had personalities. The boiler front was a face. The drive rods churned the huge wheels forward as though they were living beings. A freight engine toiled up a long grade, visibly and audibly strained. An engine slipped as it started on wet tracks, giving a roar like a curse. A fast express bore down on you like nothing else on earth. And they all spoke to you with the whistle: two longs, a short, and a long was for a crossing. It still is. The penetrating odor of coal smoke is something that few of us now remember. It was a good smell.

The railroads enjoyed a resurgence during World War II, but their decline resumed in the war's aftermath, hastened by the interstate highways and expanded air travel. Today's Amtrak lines are a mere remnant, serving only major cities. Passenger service on the Rutland disappeared by 1960, and the last "Beeliner" rail diesel car rolled south on the New York Central from Massena through Potsdam, Canton, Gouverneur, and Watertown in 1964.

Notwithstanding the nostalgic laments of some older folk, few rode the trains in their last years. There is no evidence that passenger trains could lure back customers from Route 11: North Country folks drive, fly, or take the bus. No, like Bonnie Prince Charlie, they will nae come back again—except for the occasional excursion, perhaps.

Freight service ceased on the Rutland, and in 1963, the company took up the rails east of Norwood. The Ogdensburg Bridge and Port Authority bought up the segment between Norwood and Ogdensburg and acquired the Norwood and St. Lawrence. The New York & St. Lawrence Railroad operates both lines for the Authority.

The closing of the pulp dock in Waddington ended service between there and Norfolk; that track has been taken up. Freight service continues on the old New York Central line, however, through a succession of owners: Penn Central, Conrail, CSX.

Daily through-trains on this route run between Montreal and

the great Selkirk rail yard south of Albany, serving points en-route, including Watertown and Massena. The line has been upgraded: welded rail has eliminated the rail joints and the clickety-clack, allowing freights to go faster with less wear on the wheels. All that is left of the Potsdam yard is a single siding used for car storage, or for putting the local "in the hole" for passing-through trains.

Some through freights are pulled by red Canadian National locomotives. Small local industries along the route are served by switchers like that based in Massena, which makes daily trips to Canton, setting out and picking up cars as needed. The branches are mostly gone; the Ogdensburg-DeKalb Junction branch was pulled up shortly after the last paper mill in Ogdensburg shut down in the early 1980s.

Some of the long freights are over a hundred cars long with several engines, but passengers and package freight are gone for good. This once-vital urban corridor, this central spine of an earlier North Country life, is now relegated to the edges of our awareness—the whistles in the night. But to this romantic, whose boyhood was in the days of the big Hudson and Berkshire steam locomotives of the Boston & Albany, the whistles will always evoke travel, mystery , and a kind of awe.

In my adolescence, I read a lot of the outpourings of Thomas Wolfe. He lay in bed at night and felt the locomotive whistle in his guts. Me, too. For those of us who grew up at the lingering end of the railway age, the railroad will always be the steel thread that tied us to places we could only imagine.

The whistles in the night comfort me with the thought that the railroad is still there.

A Girl in Winter

Natalia Rachel Singer

"To look at the snow too long had a hypnotic effect, drawing away all power of concentration, and the cold seemed to cramp the bones, making work harder and unpleasant. Nevertheless, the candles had to be lit, and the ice in the jugs smashed, and the milk unfrozen; the men had to be given their breakfasts and got off to work in the yards."

Philip Larkin

One January a group of colleagues from the university and I took a trip to the Adirondacks to spend some time discussing outdoor education. Our destination was the Sagamore Institute near Raquette Lake, where the son of a robber baron, William West Durant, built the first Great Camp which the great-grandson of another robber baron, Alfred Gwynne Vanderbilt, turned into the most luxuriant and well-staffed wilderness resort in the world.

I had been there one year before with mostly the same group, and we had enjoyed the well-groomed cross-country ski trails, the friendly staff, the lectures on natural history, and the delicious, healthy food. I was looking for some quiet, and I couldn't wait to slip on my snowshoes and leave the cares of the world behind.

On our way to our retreat, we hiked up Blue Mountain in order to have an authentic wilderness experience to reflect on later, around the fireplace. Stocked with notebooks, Polaroids, and Chunky bars, we skied up as far as we could, then switched to snowshoes. The sky was blue behind the line of iced firs, and the birches and pines were canopied with snow.

In my endorphin-induced euphoria, the trees looked to me like cheerful villagers piling white baskets of feathers on their heads. When we got to the top, we drank hot soup from our thermoses and peered down upon the world. There was nothing to see but sky and trees, and a thin strip of road wrapping itself around the landscape like ribbon. Civilization and its discontents seemed miles—lifetimes—away. As I slid my way back down, I realized that the exertion of climbing and focusing on each step had kept my mind clean of worries; it was as though an eraser made of snow had wiped my brain empty.

We would remember this moment as the high point of the entire retreat. On that same afternoon, we were to encounter a new and very public manifestation of everyone's most terrifying nightmare. Perhaps we should have stayed on top of the mountain a little longer, basking in our optimism.

Famished for dinner and eager to be warm again, my colleague Bruce and I drove to the Sagamore entrance only to be greeted by the state police. It occurred to us that they might be looking for someone—a fugitive—and that we'd taken the wrong turn onto someone's private road. When we made our way to the main lodge to check in, our hostess told us quietly and grimly that the police were here to dig for the body of twelve-year-old Sarah Anne Wood, the girl who had been kidnapped near Utica this past summer and whose eyes had haunted me from posters in every airport and post office I'd visited since.

We found out later that Sarah Anne Wood's father was staying at Sagamore as well, and as we sat together at meals in the day ahead, discussing our misgivings about the nature-vs.-culture dichotomy and post-modernism's impact on the topic, we furtively scanned the faces of the other lodgers for someone's downcast eyes.

The staff must have fed Mr. Wood privately in his room, because we saw no trace of him. We *did* see a lot of state troopers — a room full of them, to be precise—with badges gleaming, their guns bulging from their belts. Our conversations must have puzzled them, but no more than theirs puzzled us. They were waiting for the big machine to be shipped up from the World Trade Center to replace the more primitive backhoe as they sifted through the frozen earth in search of evidence.

Outside, the bent trees with their babushkas of snow assumed a posture of mourning. On skis, all I could see were human-like shapes in the wood, the heads bent in grief. At night, as we drank cognac shots and beer and discussed the tendency of some of us—especially this writer—to anthropomorphize what we see in nature, I couldn't forget that everyone in our group was a parent, and that somewhere, in the Main Lodge, a father was kneeling by his bed on the hardwood floor and praying.

The last morning before we left, I went for a walk alone and followed a ski trail where our informative nature guide, Shelly, had led us animal tracking the day before. Shelly's natural history lesson had actually been a social history lesson, because every tree she pointed out was second growth, or third. No one, not even the former owners of the Great Camp, had recorded what the Iroquois had seen in the forest before the mining and lumber and paper companies stripped ninety-six percent of it away.

I couldn't help but think of our connection to the natural world as the work of a team of serial killers: New York State government repaying its Oneida allies by taking the Adirondacks from them and paying them less than a cent per acre, loggers ravaging the forests and creating soil erosion and siltation of streams, the industries from the Gilded Age to the present leaving behind their legacy in acid rain.

I considered the Durants, the Vanderbilts; somehow Sagamore's rich and very American history seemed culpable as well. These robber barons were responsible for bringing the nation's first electricity to the Adirondacks, as well as train carloads of wealthy Manhattan men, up for "gaming" and smoking cigars. And yet as much as I wanted to condemn the mentality that has made the natural world an object of conspicuous consumption, it was hard not to be impressed with the men's ingenuity and optimism, their faith in technology, their sheer pluckiness. They built their lodges to look like Swiss chalets, always with the idea that no matter how many trees they felled, there were plenty more where that came from. How had our American aristocracy treated the Sagamore staff? Were they kind to those skilled craftsmen who built the fireplaces carefully stone by stone, to the daughters who folded laundry and monitored the ice house, to the caretaker's girls who studied spelling in the old schoolhouse? How had America's richest families treated their own daughters?

As I walked along the old logging path, I said a prayer for the family of Sarah Anne Wood, and for all the families who have lost their children, and for all the children who have been damaged by their own families and are still not protected by the law. The trail opened up to a large clearing where only one old tree stood watch. It was a yellow birch, its bark stripped along the base, and it stood as a lone parent among a batch of adolescents—some young maple, white pine, and stands of scrappy cherry trees, known for their ability to survive after a forest's devastation and the erosion of a forest bed. Perhaps I should have seen these young cherries as a positive sign, a symbol of rebirth after death, but all I could think of was how much prettier the trail would be if there were trees everywhere, and the empty spaces made me feel somehow afraid.

When we left that afternoon there were TV crews crowding the roads. I wondered what I would say if someone asked us to offer our opinions. The earth where the police were working was ravaged, churned up, the dirty snow piled in twiggy clumps around molding stumps of swamp maple and balsam, plucked free of their roots. It was snowing heavily, and the weather forecast promised more freezing cold. It struck me as a sad state of affairs that after one hundred years of preserving the Adirondacks, the wilderness was, on that particular day, nothing more than a good place to hide a girl's body. We drove home silently, watching the school buses drop off children and thinking how trusting we are just to leave our homes sometimes and walk in the open air.

The snow fell on the landscape indifferently—over the body of Sarah Anne Wood (if it was, indeed, in the vicinity), over the tracks I'd made that morning and the ski tracks up Blue Mountain—burying all of it, even our rich and complex social history, beneath its weight.

Skeletons

Blood Memory, Blood Ritual: The Jewish Incident in Massena

Heather Allison-Jenkins

Willie Shulkin dutifully swept the wooden floor of his father's store on Water Street in Massena. It was a balmy, Saturday evening in September 1928. The morning rush had long been over, leaving downtown merchants time to get their accounts in order and tidy up before closing shop. Willie was careful to sweep every trace of the day's dirt from the grooves in the floorboards. He took pride in his task, a daily ritual. His papa trusted him to do a good job, and he was happy to do it.

At twenty-two, Willie had come to be known in his home town as "simple." He was forever marching up to people in the street and talking their ears off about whatever was on the tip of his tongue. Residents referred to him as "the Shulkin boy," which was commonly understood to mean anything from "not playing with a full deck" to "nervous"—but certainly harmless. He had grown up thinking of all fellow Massenans as his friends.

For a moment, Willie leaned on his broom handle, gazing at the pretty colors of the leaded glass window that read, "nikluhS dna nivalS," from inside where he stood among the merchandise. Willie smiled a deeply satisfied smilc. IIe knew that from the street that sign read, "Slavin and Shulkin," and he was part of that.

Jacob Shulkin owned the business with his longtime friend, Samuel Slavin. In 1903, the two men had seen the opening of the ALCOA production plant and the digging of the St. Lawrence Waterway by the St. Lawrence Power Company as a good business opportunity. They moved to the North Country from downstate to make a living supplying the newly immigrated workers with clothing and other necessities. By 1928, they had done well and expanded to offer bottled gas and furniture, too.

Massena had become a true melting pot, due to the influx of immigrants who came to dig the canal and work in the pot rooms of the ALCOA plant. One old-time Massenan who was a young boy in 1928 recalls foreigners being "shipped in by box cars from Pittsburgh, Philadelphia, New York, Baltimore, and other cities," which had been their first homes after emigrating from European countries such as Greece, Poland, Russia, and Italy. Combined with the French Canadians who also crossed the border for work, very few Massenans in the early- to mid-1900s spoke English.

By 1928, the Jewish population in Massena, New York numbered about three hundred of its twelve thousand residents. The majority of these nineteen Jewish families had narrowly escaped Stalin's brutal pogroms in Russia just a few years before. In their mother country, they had seen their grandparents and infants murdered by Cossack soldiers—just because they were Jewish. Now they were holding their collective breath, hoping that the same terror could never befall them in the promised land of America.

It has been said that the old Anglo-Saxon Protestants of the area were less than thrilled with the influx of foreigners, especially Jews. Aside from a few Ku Klux Klan cross burnings in the 1920s, however, anti-Semitism and prejudice in the small town were kept below the surface—until 1928.

Four-year-old Barbara Griffiths was the darling daughter of one such old-stock Protestant marriage. Her father, David, was not a rich man; he worked hard for his modest salary as a laborer for ALCOA. He had witnessed the steady stream of foreigners who settled and often made quite a comfortable living in his little town. Any resentment he may have harbored, he never divulged. Instead, he turned his energies to being a loving husband to his wife, Marion, and father to his two children, little Bobby and Barbs.

Then one Saturday his little girl turned up missing, and the townspeople found a convenient and all-too-familiar scapegoat. The nightmare of Jewish persecution would come back to haunt the tiny congregation of Temple Adath Israel, as local fears and superstition about "those people" rose to the surface like chicken fat.

The Griffiths family's weekend had started routinely enough when Barbs went with her father to a Saturday matinee. They returned home to the Nightengale section of town in good spirits. After a peck on the cheek, Marion Griffiths asked her husband if their daughter had behaved like a lady at the movie. Marion was a tall, handsome woman with gray eyes and the typical chiseled features shared by everyone in her well-to-do Protestant Boston family.

David, whom Barbs had wrapped around her baby finger, beamed at his daughter and answered, "Of course! Always. Right, Barbs?" Barbs' blue cardiganed torso bobbed as she nodded her head in vigorous agreement from the kitchen chair she had climbed up on. Pleased but not surprised, Mrs. Griffiths told Barbs that Bobby and some friends were off in the woods looking for willow branches to make whistles with, and that if she fetched him, they could both have a sucker. Barbs was out the door like a flash, calling to her brother, looking forward to the promised sweets.

When Bobby Griffiths returned home just before dark with a handful of willows but without his sister, Marion Griffiths asked with alarm where she was. "I haven't seen her, Mama," he answered.

A grandmother herself in 1992, and living with her husband, Jack, thirty minutes from Massena in Canton, Barbara (Griffiths)

Kiemens chuckled during an interview about the night she spent in the woods when she was a girl. The couple sat in worn easy chairs amidst skeins of the colored yarn that had taken over their home during the annual spring yarn sale. Their house doubled as Barbara's business, the Yarn Shop, at 10 Church Street.

Mrs. Kiemens admitted she was oblivious to the chain of events she sparked when she lost her way and, growing tired as the daylight faded, decided to lie down among the fallen leaves. "All I remember was two girls with long curls," she said with a smile. She explained that when she woke the next morning, the first people she met while walking out of the brush were two young women. The curly-headed girls had joined the search for her after her parents had contacted the police to report Barbs missing the night before. "I wasn't hurt," she added. "They brought me home and were so nice to me." As inconsequential as the event was to Barbara Griffiths, it caused a stir in Massena that has been unequaled to this day. A search posse of townspeople was formed, and a state trooper named Corporal Harry McCann was called in to investigate the disappearance just hours after Barbs had been declared missing. The reason for such speedy action was unfortunately steeped in the ignorance that breeds prejudice, and in this case, anti-Semitic hysteria.

Just after dark the Saturday evening that little Barbara Griffiths wandered off into the woods, Willie Shulkin wandered into the Crystal Palace. The greasy spoon in downtown Massena was known among the local youngsters as "Candyland," because of the wide variety of sweets the establishment's owner, Albert Conmas, carried for them. Willie was a regular in the shop, and greeted Mr. Conmas from across the floor when entering. Like everyone else, Albert Conmas was patient with Willie's incessant nervous chatter about the goings-on in town, and he returned the greeting with some small talk and a half-attentive ear.

Willie bought a two-cent lemon sucker with the two least shiny of the four coins he had in his trouser pocket. His papa paid him regularly for his help, but hanging onto his newest and brightest coins made him feel special—like he had a secret. Willie left the store with the bittersweet lemon taste puckering his smile and his shiny treasures still jingling at his side. He was content. As usual, he did not hear Conmas's muttering once his back was turned—an inaudible mouthful of vowels in Greek. As always, however, the muttering ended with a word sounding suspiciously like, "Jew," uttered as if the man were trying to spit it on the floor.

Apparently, Corporal McCann was having his dinner in the Crystal Palace when Willie bought his candy, and he caught Conmas's slur upon Willie's departure. Conmas spoke with McCann while pouring him more coffee. Lingering with an elbow on the counter, Conmas found through conversation that McCann was in town to ask around about the missing girl, Barbara Griffiths. Had he heard anything?

Conmas glanced furtively around him, then leaned close to McCann. "The Jews are having a holiday," he whispered. "Maybe they need blood."

Conmas's roots were entrenched in Islamic and Christian European society, which had regularly accused Jews of such horror since the Middle Ages. Accusations were often made more from ignorance than reason. Christians were scared to death of the Jews who lived among them. McCann obviously knew no better either.

What had escaped the lips of one disgruntled shop owner then set off a horrifying chain of events, which began with McCann tracking Willie down on the street and pulling him into the police station for questioning. Willie readily obliged. Before leaving the Crystal Palace, McCann had a hunch that Barbara Griffiths was being held against her will in the basement of the synagogue, where the Jews of Massena were planning to ritualistically murder her and use her Christian blood for one of their secret ceremonies. He was bound and determined to shake the truth out of Willie.

Willie fidgeted in a hard wooden chair in the small, musty basement that served as Massena's police station. He had been sitting, answering what seemed to be the same, stupid questions over and over again for a long time. His eyes wandered to the stone slab walls and to the metal filing cabinet, which needed dusting. He was bored, and he did not like this man asking absurd questions about his religion, including whether he had heard of Jews committing ritual murder. The truth as Willie knew it did not satisfy the officer, so Willie allowed his imagination to guide him.

"Sure, we take a Christian kid every year about this time," he quipped, his simplistic sarcasm tragically taken as truth. The answer seemed to satisfy McCann, who promptly returned Willie to his home, where his family had begun to worry that he might have gotten lost.

Years later, Willie's sisters, Dora Cohen and Mimi Klien, recalled their shock at seeing their brother standing under the family's front porch light with his official-looking escort. Both women agreed that if McCann had known Willie better, he would never have bothered interviewing him. They described their brother as impressionable and open to suggestion, like a small child. In his written report of the interview, McCann described Willie Shulkin as being of low mentality and having possibly been influenced by rumors of an old Jewish custom of blood sacrifice. This opinion, unfortunately, did not stop the gentiles of Massena from being influenced by the same tales.

One Massenan who took Hebrew lessons from Rabbi Brainglass, the leader of the Jewish community at the time, described him as "small but spunky." So, when the five-foot, two-inch Rabbi heard through the grapevine that a mob was gathering at the synagogue doors that night, he rushed down and held the rabble at bay single-handedly. Thankfully, the scene did not turn ugly; the Rabbi was able to convince the crowd that little Barbara Griffiths was, in fact, not being held for ritual sacrifice in the temple basement, and not one member of the mob crossed Brainglass.

Although Barbara walked out of the woods unharmed near her home the next morning, the Jewish community of Massena never received an apology for the false and absurd accusation. And although there has never been a similar accusation in the North Country, members of the still-minuscule Jewish population of Massena say the anti-Semitism that spawned the incident still lurks unspoken.

Almost everyone of the aging population has been asked a question like, "Do Jews really bury their dead standing up?"

Even more unfortunate is that these experiences are not the exception in this world, of which the North Country is a part. Many who settle here come to escape the relentless pace and materialism of mainstream society. Most find what they had hoped for and stay.

I entered St. Lawrence University in 1988, intending to ensconce myself in its small student community and the surrounding countryside, hoping to find the same buffer for the same reasons. I found much peace here, yet am sad to say that anti-Semitism still exists in this beautiful place.

My grandmother on my mother's side, Sonia Abromowitz, arrived alive on Ellis Island from Poland as a small girl when Hitler wanted her people dead. My father's family could have been related to Marion Griffith's, in theory. For generations, they had grown comfortable in the upper-middle-class American status quo of Protestantism. Consequently, I did not have the privilege of being born with a Jewish surname. Because of this, the few slurs I have been subjected to have not been aimed directly at me. On the contrary, I have been invited to share anti-Semitic sentiment by bigots living among us here who did not know enough to keep their mouths shut.

The year I graduated from St. Lawrence with an English Writing degree, I went to work as a reporter for the *Daily Courier Observer* in Potsdam. One day in the fall, I traveled to a local dairy farm to interview the owner for a feature story about the use of BST bovine hormone, which is purported to increase milk productivity.

The pungent mingling of cow manure and silage filled my nose when I stepped out of my car into the muddy barnyard of the third-generation farm. A "Dairy of Distinction" sign—a local symbol carrying some clout—was proudly displayed out by the road. The farmer I had come to interview was of old North Country stock—quite respected in his town of Parishville, where he sat on the school board, was part of the volunteer fire department, and had been elected to the town board as well. He turned from the black and white cow he was milking to introduce himself and offered his manure-stained hand, which I shook politely.

When I asked the farmer what he did with his veal calves, he answered, "We send them down to the city and let the Jews eat 'em."

My ears flushed hot; I could not look into the man's face. For a few moments, I stared at my notepad and fought to catch the breath that had left me so rapidly with his comment. I wished I could disappear. Then my face slowly rose with a painfully blank smile to meet his sneer, a monumental effort. I wanted so badly to tell him that I was offended by his comments, but feared that doing so would have meant the end of the interview—and I needed the story. I choked on my silence instead.

I wondered, had he known that I am one of those Jews, would he have offered me a veal calf to bring home in the trunk of my car and cook up that night, or to send downstate to my parents as a gift? Would he have answered my questions differently? Would this bigot still have shown me the extent of his ignorance? Would I have still felt like crying?

I thought of Willie Shulkin and a wave of despair washed over me. I realized that some people's attitudes may forever be stuck in the Middle Ages, and feared that I would always remain mute in the face of such degradation.

In 1978, Willie Shulkin passed away an old man. He had married and raised a daughter and, as of 1992, his widow lived in the Rochester, New York area. It has been intimated that perhaps Willie never fully understood the meaning of the incident in Massena in 1928, in which he and his family and friends were accused of slaughtering a Christian girl for religious purposes. His daughter however, recalls a man who was both a loving father and husband, who worked and was lucid up until the day he died. According to her, he never once discussed the incident.

I wonder if Willie Shulkin ever remembered the incident, and if he ever felt like crying about it during all those years in which he kept it secret within his heart.

Coming Home a Stranger

Shirley McFerson

Adapted from an interview conducted by Joan Potter. Shirley McFerson, today the director of the Caldwell-Lake George Library, grew up in segregated hotels in Lake George and Glens Falls, where her parents worked during the Jim Crow era.

Lake George: it's become Coney Island with pine trees. It's that trashy.

Guiseppe's, across the main street here, used to be a white clapboard house. The street once boasted mostly private homes, but they were gradually changed over into hotels, bars, t-shirt shops, jewelry stores, tourist things.

When I was growing up here in the 1940s, my parents' hotel was two blocks over, on the corner where Ottawa Street changes into Disco Street. The building is still there. It looks much better than when my parents had it.

My mother was born in Glens Falls. My father came to Glens Falls because his uncle, Jimmy Richberg, had gone there to work as a bellman/porter at the Hotel Rockwell on Hudson Avenue. I was born in Glens Falls in 1934, and my parents started renting the hotel in Lake George for the summers, maybe in '35. The joke was always that they had me, and then they had the hotel.

I can remember going with my father when the rent was due to a Captain Lanphere. Captain Lanphere always struck me as being nine feet tall, with a cap on. I thought Moses must look exactly like Captain Lanphere. He was an absolutely fierce elderly gentleman. Probably he was in his early 50s, but to me, he seemed ancient.

Growing up black in Lake George and Glens Falls wasn't easy. Someone was always asking me if my skin were dirt, and would it rub off. That would either get my knuckles in their mouth, or something said to them that would get them running and crying and screaming, because I could go right to the bone.

The only African-American history I learned in school was that Lincoln freed the slaves. That was it. I never found out that one of the main branches of the Underground Railroad for people escaping to Canada went right through this area until after I left and came back. There wasn't any emphasis whatsoever on black history. To my teachers, I was either "a credit to my race" or "smarter than the average"—of course, I had no idea what "average" was—or, I was "headed for trouble with that mouth."

Two teachers treated me well: Hilda Hayes, who was an English teacher, and John Vanderwort. Hilda Hayes encouraged me to write, because that was going to be my escape. And John Vanderwort encouraged me to do theater, because *that* was going to be my escape. They didn't tell me about escaping; that was my own realization.

I didn't know I was going to come back, but I always knew that I was going to leave.

I didn't go to school dances, proms, or things like that. I wanted to, but I never got a chance. I don't think a white boy ever asked me out. There were a couple of black boys, but they went with girls from Saratoga, which had a larger black community.

My parents grew up around here, and they knew what people were like. But they never considered moving away, because

Glens Falls was my mother's home and Lake George was my parents' place of business. It must have been as lonely for them as it was for me, spending those winters in Glens Falls. They had no social life, no friends; they just worked at the Hotel Rockwell, my father as a bellman and my mother as a chambermaid, and my mother worked as a maid in some of the stores that were still on Glen Street before the malls came in. We went to the First Baptist Church on Maple. I was in Sunday school, and maybe the baby choir.

The first thing I remember about working in the hotel is getting the bread. As I got older, I had more work to do. I was a lawn person and a wood person—part of the place was heated by wood, so my job was to stack the wood. When I got old enough to type, I started typing the letters for the place. Then I became barmaid, bartender, waitress, chambermaid.

My parents' hotel was small. I think I could serve maybe 30 people for breakfast and dinner. Every once in a while there was a dance with musicians my father would hire. Or there were musicians who were playing at another place and staying at Woodbine, and they would play.

When you work 18 hours a day, you don't really think of it as a pleasant situation unless it's theater. I don't mind doing an all-nighter to put up sets or rehearse or something like that, because there's going to be something that comes out of it. But 18 hours of serving breakfast, cleaning up the breakfast, cleaning rooms, being in the office to write the letters, back and forth from there to the dining room if someone comes in for a sandwich, loses its glamor very quickly. It's drudgery.

I felt as if there was no way out. I'd look up and see other people enjoying themselves, but I never enjoyed myself. I felt invisible.

For fun, I wrote. I started writing stories while I was in elementary school. That's what got me through elementary school, junior high, and high school. I wrote when I was supposed to be paying attention in class. But class was so boring that I either finished what I was doing before anyone else or didn't bother to do it at all.

I was writing so I could earn paper. I used to let the kids read the stories I was writing, and they would pay to read them by giving me clean notebook paper. I don't think I bought a sheet of notebook paper from the time I was in junior high, because to read my stories you had to pay—maybe ten sheets of notebook paper, or fifteen sheets.

I did chapters, so there was always someone reading one of my latest marvelous novels that was right out of whatever I'd been reading. I might change the names or change the background, but I was always writing stories about London, Paris, South America, outer space, everything. It was a lot more interesting than stuff they had to read for class.

I didn't like those people when I had to go to school with them, but I couldn't quit school. Maybe they looked forward to my stories, maybe not. I had girlfriends, but then we got out of school and went our separate ways.

I went away to school in Albany and couldn't wait to get away from Glens Falls and Lake George. After Albany, I taught for a year in Lockport, then went back to Albany to get a master's in library science. When I got out of college, I said I wanted a small high school library 50 miles from New York City so I could go in and see plays. I got Peekskill, which was right on the train line, with a train going out right after school and one coming back at night. That was how I got to see a lot of plays.

I think I must have stayed there about ten years. It's all beginning to get hazy .

And then I said, "Okay, why bother going back and forth on the train? Let's move to New York City." So, I went to New York City and worked for the public library for about ten years. Then my mother got ill and I came home to take care of her. After she passed away, I stayed. I found out I could not work with my father, so when this job at the library opened up, I took it.

My father's still in Glens Falls, and wouldn't you know that the man I've had all this conflict with now has Alzheimer's disease and I have to take care of him? Life does not get better; it really doesn't.

My father had three sisters, traditional Southern-style women.

As I remember, two of my aunts must have weighed 400 pounds, although he keeps telling me, “No, they were just big-boned.” But what about all the fat hanging off those big bones, right? They were married at early ages, and had large families.

I think the only time I ever thought about getting married was when I was still in high school. Once I got out of high school and realized what was happening to the women who were older, married, and having babies, I said, “No way. Uh-uh. That’s not the life for me.”

This was during the Eisenhower ’50s, when you had a big wedding and immediately started breeding, went into a little house in the suburbs, only knew the other women who were also dropping a baby each year, and that was it. Now all those women I knew have been divorced, if they were able to escape with their lives. I couldn’t understand why they couldn’t see that these guys were going to do that to them.

My father wanted me to be that kind of woman. There was also the problem with my mouth. All you’d ever hear was, “And you’re a bigger one.”

You’d hear my father say to my mother, “Did you hear what she just called me!?” And my mother would say, “I told you to stay away from her.”

Other than writing, my one hobby, I think, was ping-pong. I had been taught to play ping-pong by some guys from Africa who were working at the hotel as bellmen. Africans play ping-pong the way they play cricket: they play to kill. Of course, being left-handed, I soon realized nobody could beat me. I went out one afternoon playing ping-pong with this guy who was “interested” in me. I came back in and told my mother I’d beaten him five games out of five.

She said, “Well, I hope you get a good job ’cause you’re never going to get married.”

I said, “Great. I wasn’t planning on getting married anyway.” So, that was that. My mother knew I had this attitude problem. There wasn’t any chance I was going to get married anyhow. There were always people around to meet, but they were here just for the season, and who knew when—or if—they’d come back.

I found out when I got away from Glens Falls and I was around more African-Americans or African-French, or African-Canadians, or straight Africans, that I had been raised as what's called an "Oreo." When the only thing you learn about your heritage is that Lincoln freed the slaves, you don't really have enough knowledge to be able to deal with things, and you see things from the point of the majority rather than the minority that you are. It's just the way you've been brainwashed.

It took me a long time once I got away to realize that the only thing that a white person does is copy black music, black-style; that's it.

I had no idea there were people like Faith Ringgold until years later. I had no idea that there had been a black woman sculptor in the 19th century who was famous in Europe. I didn't know about black opera singers who had toured in this area.

One of the people I knew as a child was Diahann Carroll, the actress. She used to come to Woodbine with her aunt, who was a well-known organist and choir director. Diahann knew it, even in the days when she was Diahann Johnson. She knew her heritage. She tried to tell me, but, you know, I wasn't interested.

I found out years later that I had known a famous black entertainer from Paris in the 1920s, the woman who was famous for teaching the original Duke of Wales the black bottom and the Charleston on the dance floor. Her name as an entertainer was Bricktop. I knew her when I was a kid under her married name, because she used to stay at Woodbine. When I went to see Josephine Baker in New York City and Bricktop introduced her to the audience, I looked down and saw this woman on stage and I thought, *Why does this woman seem familiar?* Then when I was reading her biography, I found out why: Bricktop was Mrs. Ducongy, who stayed at Woodbine for two weeks every summer.

My parents couldn't see why I wanted to leave. They couldn't see why I wanted to go away, because they'd been away enough to know that you can run, but you cannot hide. And what you're running from is what you take with you.

If there are other communities that would be a little easier to live in than northern New York's, I don't know where they are.

My parents were okay about my going to college, though. My mother had wanted to be a teacher. And my father had wanted me to be an accountant so I could do the books.

So, I went off to major in English and minor in history. That was a culture shock. I went from being in the top ten percent of my class in Glens Falls to where I was just another person. How dare they not realize McFerson had arrived? I spent all my time saying I was leaving, and I had to be reminded that I couldn't wait to get away from home. I must have started enjoying it, because I stayed for my undergraduate and graduate degrees.

I made friends, but I never went back after I graduated. The only good thing about the old days is that they're gone.

In college, my friends were people who drank as much as I did. There was a bar down the way from the dormitory, and that was where I seemed to make my friends. I spent a great deal of my time there. At that time, drinking and smoking were still the mark of a college person.

There weren't that many African-Americans there. Albany up until the middle 1960s was still a quota school: ten percent of the entire population was African-American.

After I came back to nurse my mother, I didn't want to go back to New York. I had done what I wanted to do in New York. Then, I was so wiped out by the death of my mother that I couldn't even consider going back, even though I was living with my father.

When I was trying to recover from the loss of my mother I started doing things in the area—community theater in Glens Falls, writing again, a playwriting workshop at Adirondack Community College. I just sort of settled in that way. Once again, it was the writing and the reading that got me out of the house.

Lake George is different now. It's just a feeling, but I've gotten used to it—if anyone can get used to the feeling of being a stranger in a strange land. In Peekskill, I was a stranger; in New York City, *everybody's* a stranger. I'm a stranger in the North Country, too.

People say it's beautiful, but I never noticed that when I was growing up. I didn't miss it when I left, and I don't notice it now.

Looking for Home

Tremolo

Maurice Kenny

In the beginning there was only the Spirit World high above dark waters. It was a beautiful and peaceful world, a world without sorrow, pain, or death. People were content until a virgin woman became pregnant. Nearing her term and while walking across the Spirit World, anxious and pleased, she happened upon a small hole in the floor of the Spirit World where none had been before. She stopped and looked into the hole, which grew wider and rounder as she peered into the emptiness of the abyss. She bent and looked deeper and as she did she fell, though there are those who say her impatient brother/husband, the Creator, pushed her and covered the hole with a great elm tree. She fell toward the dark waters. Suddenly water birds came to her rescue: mallard, crane, grebe, heron, and loon. These beautiful and considerate birds banded together and formed a blanket of wings to catch her fall. Slowly the birds brought her down to the

> dark waters and they called Turtle, listlessly waiting in the mud on the bottom of the dark sea. Turtle rose from the mud and surfaced to accept Sky Woman on his shell. Soon she gave birth to a girl child who in years to come gave birth to twin boys who together created all the beauty of this world on Turtle's shell. The water birds have been respected by the Turtle-people since then: heron, grebe, and particularly loon, whose tremolo is heard to this moment coming from across a wide lake, dark and smooth.
>
> (from the Mohawk Creation Story)

Listen! Hear the old coyote howl on the mountain; listen to the singing of the wood thrush; shiver to the hoot of owls; duck from swooping bats chasing blackflies. We in this northern clime are fortunate to live among the indigenous animals and birds who walk the dark of night and sun of day, to have the shine of fish in near-clean waters—salmon, pike, rainbow trout—and the beauty of water and air fowl—mallards, red-tail hawk, eagle, kingfisher—and listen to the cry of the loon.

I am Mohawk. I was born not far from the Adirondack Mountains, in the foothills in northern New York State, and came to know the privilege of this "forever wild," this paradise of ancient mountains, lakes, forests, and winters of brutal cold.

My father had been a hunter and a fisherman, and my sights were drawn early in life to the creatures of the woods and streams through the stories he told of the four-leggeds, the wingeds, and those of the waters, and how they all came to be.

As a boy, I canoed the rivers and lakes, trekked pine and spruce woods sighting red fox or raccoons, was overjoyed spotting a rainbow trout circling a shallow pool. I learned the verdure as well: wild iris, witchhopple, chokecherry, hemlock, hickory, blackberry, wild strawberry. Camping, canoeing, and swimming were the highlights of summer; sledding, skiing, and skating were the joys of winter. Traipsing through woods or trekking rivers, I early taught myself that killing the various creatures was not necessary. I hunted without a gun, fished without a hook and pole. My trophies came home in my memory or on a piece of paper, as a poem or the outline of a story.

Then, after high school, I left. My father repeatedly told me that there was no place in the world as beautiful as our North and our mountains. As a young man, of course, I didn't believe him. I traveled and lived in foreign lands and distant states, worked in large cities, went to college in the Midwest, and seemed to forget or ignore the North Country. In my exodus, I took for granted that life in that area would continue and be there, should I ever decide to return. The wing of the cardinal, the bellow of a moose, the howl of the wolf, the flight of the pheasant would always be there.

I fear I was not the only one to take for granted the North and its many creatures. People who lived there paid little attention to the birds, the fish, the animals, the greens, the cry of the loon—a sign that the bird was there breeding and hatching—or the vibrant, resilient waters of the Adirondack lakes, before acid rain took its tragic toll of water and plant life. They thought the loon, the red fox, and the beaver were as common as wood anemone or red trillium.

I left the North for college and then work. My sojourn was long. I returned to my natal waters only for weddings and deaths——beginnings and endings—not sufficient time to observe changes in the flora and fauna: death of the Dutch elm, demise of the magnificent salmon on which I supped many a night as a small child, slow disappearance of that gorgeous wild flower that some came to think of as the stink flower, the blood trillium. Living in Chicago or San Francisco or New York City, I had little thought of home, except that cousin George was recently married for the third time and Aunt Millie had passed the January before last, one night after the Christmas holidays. I returned for weddings and funerals, where conversations never rose above the din of laughter, the tears, or the bitterness, and never lingered long. I did not come back north for high school reunions, though I doubt anyone knew my address to post an invitation.

Then retirement began to loom in my fears. I began to wonder if the city was where I wished to stay. I began to hear the hoot of the owl and the caw of the crow in my sleep; the scent of milkweed and honeysuckle resurfaced from my memory. I pondered going home to the North, but could I give up Broadway shows? The Metropolitan Museum? Lunch at good bistros? Walks on the Brooklyn Heights Promenade? Friday night jazz concerts at South Street Seaport Museum? Was I ready to forfeit these humanities for country picnics, church bazaars, long and icy winter nights when it would be impossible to drive into town for a movie? Was I ready for shoveling snow and mowing lawns? Despite these misgivings, it became common to conjure dreams of home in the North and remember the potluck suppers, cross-country skiing, Winter Carnival in Saranac Lake, summer concerts in Lake Placid's band shell, the hike up Mt. Jo or Scarface, or that two-day trek up the beauties of Mt. McKenzie. I had forgotten blackflies, for sense has told them for centuries to stay out of big cities, something which they never told their cousin, the mosquito.

I'd forgotten when to water the tomatoes, let alone in which kind of soil they grow best, or whether they need morning or late-day sun. I had forgotten that the fisher had returned to its natural habitat, meadows and conifer woods. I didn't know the black bear could now be hunted, that deer carry Lyme disease, that the loon cries like a child, that eagles have been spotted on a high spire of a white pine shored on Lake Flower, that moose have come home to the Adirondacks.

It will take time to get back into the proverbial saddle, I thought. But the bags are packed, the house is sold, the cat is in her carrier. Friends have been warned to make sure the apple pie is in the oven, the chicken and biscuits ready for the famished traveler, a traveler who has decided that Broadway shows and bistros are not important to the good life.

I had a last Guinness Stout with the boys from the department. The university will run quite well without me; in fact, I could recommend a successor—an expert in Egyptology, or economics, or teacher arts.

I'm gone. Gone. Kissed old Central Park goodbye; leaned a tear against the old Heights brownstone, wondering if anyone will ever care to screw a plaque saying I lived there once, twenty years.

And the next thing, here I am on the peak of Mt. Jo, Heart Lake below, a jug of black coffee in my tote, field glasses hanging down my chest, resting on my middle-aged paunch, heavy breathing from the climb slowly changing into a deep, prolonged sigh at the sight of the sublime. Off in the far distance, my gaze embraces Indian Pass, Mt. Marcy, tall Algonquin, the other High Peaks bathed in a glow of falling sunlight and a pure haze that I had forgotten ever existed.

Suddenly the twilight is shattered by a weird, uncanny noise—a child lost in the woods or, perhaps, in danger on a mountain ledge. The cry tears the silence, invades the ambiance. What will I do? Don't panic. How can I help that child in such danger?

A moment later, I am chuckling at my own miserable memory. It isn't a child lost in the brush, caught on a ledge and thirsty. It is the wail of a water bird. Spring light is falling upon Heart Lake, and a final ray of sun clutches the head of a loon. It cries, calling out to a fledgling swimming a quarter of a mile off. It is time for night.

I gaze down at the black dot on the lake. Then, knowing it is time for me, too, to enter the tribal cave, I lope down Mt. Jo's rugged slope and go home to flames in the fireplace and a huge pot of stew.

Rediscovering the natal waters, reacquainting the memory is a delightful, exciting education—getting to know the blue flag, the rainbow trout; finding where the raspberries ripen on the bush, where bear has not eaten all the blueberries, the habits of grey fox, raccoon, woodpecker. Recalling where the lakes are, which mountain can be climbed in an afternoon, the best hiking trails. Watching for cardinals or simply listening for crows, trying to outsmart blackflies and mosquitoes. Making friends of old acquaintances.

I'm home at last in the North. From my sun porch window, I view Scarface, Haystack, McKenzie, with Whiteface towering beyond. Cousins have arrived with extended hands for shaking.

Friends stop off with rhubarb pie, or applesauce, or homemade bread, or casseroles of scalloped potatoes. My nature books are separated out from cookbooks, poetry, and fiction.

I have a new cat and long for a black lab. I settle in to listen for the old coyote singing on the hill. I watch for a wolf or bobcat scratching a beech tree, or perhaps a fisher hiding in the thick branches of a hemlock. I'm ready for a canoe paddle. . . .

August, Sunday morning. Bob lifts his canoe on top of his Isuzu. I pack a thermos of coffee. The scent of blackberries is in the air. Blackflies have gorged themselves with enough human blood to disappear for another year. The woods are noisy with kit raccoons trampling the underbrush, looking for robin eggs.

The sun stands momentarily behind Little Bum Mountain. The lake below is dotted with canoes and motor boats. Three young boys fish at the dam of Lake Flower, where beyond it becomes once again the River Saranac . . . Algonquian for "place of red sumac." The town is fairly still; few cars careen up and down Lake Flower Drive or Main Street. A few senior citizens wend their way down the street to church. No sirens blast the air. Packed and heading down the road, we are as excited as two kids going off to their first circus. The canoe travels well on the van's top. In glee, we spot waves of black-eyed Susans just off the road, and yarrow just beyond.

Other vehicles pass us with canoes or kayaks tied to the roof. They are in a hurry to get to their lakes of choice . . . St. Regis, Tupper, or Blue Mountain.

We head for Polliwog Pond, where Bob knows of a cranberry bog he needs to investigate. It's part of a chain; we'll have to carry the canoe from one pond to another to reach it.

Our first paddle is calm water, smooth as a field of new snow. We are alone. Bob calls out to keep an eye for water birds, especially loon. There isn't a bird in view . . . only a fallen log or two floating on the water.

We do hear the caw of a crow on shore in the deep woods. We see nothing on our several carries from one to another in our chain of ponds—not a fox, or skunk, or squirrel. We see few flowers blooming in this gorgeous August sunlight, only a few trillium plants that hold no blossoms.

We pause occasionally to glance down at mushrooms. We feign picking. We can only guess at the names of the mushrooms, the moss, and the growth on the various felled logs rotting into the earth of the forest floor. This would be a good winter study, we conclude. On our third carry, to Little Polliwog, we meet three women and a boy just touching shore. We greet them, and the women claim they spotted several loons. Bob and I grow excited. We ask if they have canoed through the cranberry bog. They shake their heads "no" in bewilderment, apparently not knowing it exists.

We lower the canoe into the warm water and push off. Off to the left, only a short paddle, is Bob's bog. We spend an hour paddling through, looking for signs of cranberries. We spot nothing, not a single berry ripening under what is by now a very warm sun. Neither do we spot any of the loons the women spoke of in such pleasure.

Our last carry is to Polliwog. Atop the esker that separates it from Little Polliwog, we discover a mountain bike trail. We pause to smell the marvelous scents of pine and spruce, and detect the smell of burning wood from a camp we cannot see.

A young man rolls out of the woods on a bike. He barely waves. Our comments are strong, bitter, political. We don't want wheels rutting these eskers.

"Well, if he can ride a bike across the rim of this esker, I can eat my 'Oh Henry' candy bar. He'll leave tracks, but I'll take my wrapper out," I say.

Bob nods in agreement, and we steal down the deep incline to the pond. Bob stops and lowers the canoe down gently to the shallow waters. As if to say "be still," he puts a finger to his lips. He hears something that I do not. "Hear it?" he whispers, barely audible.

Yes, I do—a wail, the sound scientists say loons use to announce their location. It penetrates to the soul, the very essence of being. We could have heard the wail from a mile distant had we been attuned. It is intense.

We stiffen, anticipating revelation. Apprehensive but calmed by silent determination, I step down the bank. Fortunately, I do not trip on a root or over a rock, but position myself next to Bob, who has sprouted a hundred ears. I am breathless. Our hearts have ceased to beat, though the sugar from the candy bar rumbles in my belly.

"There it is," Bob undertones so quietly I can hardly distinguish his words. "Where?" I ask. He points an index finger out to the center of the lake to our left. "There."

A large black dot bobs on the water. Perhaps it has caught our scent on the winds. It lifts, its wings hardly flapping, and skims the water for several yards. Then its wings fall to its sides. It emits another wail then glides away, becoming smaller by the second. "Quiet," Bob cautions. "Listen. There's another one."

We hear the wail . . . not quite a tremolo . . . of a second loon. We can't spot it, but its cry comes from our right.

Very slowly, we slip the canoe into the water, climb aboard, and push off with the help of a paddle. Directly to our right, not fifty yards away, is another loon—not a black dot this time.

The first loon we spotted—perhaps a female—is moving away. But the second—we believe it to be a male—is paddling closer to the canoe. We move quickly out into the lake. The male paddles faster, directly toward our canoe. We float, our raised paddles dripping teardrops.

The gentle current seems to push the canoe toward the loon. Forces bring us together. He is now a mere twenty feet off, now fifteen, as together we ride farther out onto the pond. The female is moving toward us. She wails, attracts our attention, then flies off the surface, scans the lapping waters, alights again, and awaits our cue.

She wails once more, beating her wings to catch our focus. The male is closer to us still. Bob paddles sluggishly, steering us off the natural course created by a breeze on the water.

The ripples. Something is causing the lake to buckle. It is a fledgling, a young loon from this year's hatch. It dives playfully, abandons care, fearless. Quickly it surfaces, dives once more for a moment, then reappears, bobbing on the surface.

The male floats closer to the active young bird. It does not wail. There is no tremolo, no yodel, no hoot, no sound of throttled fear, danger, distress. Its red eye, its severe gaze, is focused on the canoe, all its senses intent on our movements, our breathing. We are now eight feet from it.

Farther out, the other loon is flapping wings against the water, splashing hard, making great disturbance, calling out loud wails in her attempt to draw our sight away from the male and the chick. She rises up, flaps the water. The fledgling must be in trouble, great trouble. Yet it bobs on the surface, diving, surfacing, seeming to enjoy its outing on the lake.

We and the male are now maybe six feet apart. We have a profile view. Its eye's curt glance cuts us to the quick. "Know thy friend," it seems to say, and we are probably not its friend. If we were, we would paddle off and leave this bird family in peace to deal with the fledgling's problem in its own manner, its own natural way. We have created an extra strain upon the parents, caused more stress than what this family should bear.

It has been said that if a loon is in extreme danger from a predator—and we humans are predators—the powerful stress can cause a massive fatal heart attack.

We humans, Bob and myself, we're the cause of the anxiety. Though the adult male appears calm, in charge of the situation, relaxed and fearless, we know it suffers an agony only the terrified can know.

"Bob, let's shove off," I suggest. "We'd better paddle away from here."

He agrees, and reluctantly, in the very heat of a first and probably last experience such as this, we lower the paddles into the water and move swiftly away from the loon.

We do not have a camera. That day we would have given our right arms, our bank accounts, to have had a camera with us. Yet nothing can capture the moment at hand, the black of the wing and the white of the collar, the tilt of the head or rise to the light.

We were alone on that pond with one male adult loon, one female adult and a chick. The male we could have touched with our paddle, or possibly our hand, as its life and the life of its offspring rested in our minds—our judgment—in that fleeting experience.

I am thankful Bob is a gentle and caring human being, that he made the crucial decision to paddle away from the loon and the chick, knowing the frightful danger in which we had placed the birds.

"Why didn't it fly off when we came so close? Why didn't it encourage the chick to fly off?"

We continue asking this question over and over on our way home. Was it the adult who was sick? It didn't appear to have a broken wing. We couldn't see signs of a bullet or fish hook wound. It appeared healthy. We were sure it was the chick who was in trouble. And yet it, too, appeared healthy, bobbing up and down.

What was wrong? We have no idea. Why didn't it wail or give a tremolo? We have no idea. Some questions invite no answers.

Why is the loon sixty million years on this earth on Turtle's back? Why did it aid Sky Woman in her fall from the Iroquois Spirit World? Why does it nest each year in the same spot on its return from southern seas? Why does it call its mate each year after separation? How has it survived so many millions of years?

That is the mystery and the magic of nature, the gift of the Creator, the Great Spirit.

Monday. Town. Downtown: gift shops, windows in the hotel, posters in the frame store, reprint photos in the bank. Loons. Loons all over town: postcards, posters, t-shirts, sweatshirts, wood pins, plaster replicas, ties, bolas, hand-painted coffee mugs, plastic plates, china plates, canvas paintings, tote bags, books and books and books, poems, essays all about the mysterious, private loon.

There is indeed something very special about being born and raised in Northern New York, especially in the foothills of the Adirondack Mountains. On a good night you can hear the song of the old coyote on the mountain or the tremolo of the loon passing overhead at twilight.

I, too, am considered a tourist, someone passing through. I wasn't born inside the "Blue Line." Northwest of the mountains were my natural waters/earth, although I felt attachment to the hills and woods, the lands I had abandoned for so many years. The lands I've come home to before it is too late to see the herons, cranes, mallards and kingfisher, hear the cry, the song of the loon—not as a visitor, but as someone who has a natural identity, a natural need to be apart of the North.

It was my people, my Sky woman whom loon helped to descend safely onto Turtle's back. I have a right to the North. I have a right to my home. I have a right to hear the song of crow, the growl of bear, wind in white pine, loon.

Memories from the Shadow of Mt. Baker

Carolyn Boggs

THE MOUNTAIN, THE RIVER, AND THE TOURISTS

I grew up just outside the village of Saranac Lake, across the road from the Saranac River. On the other side of the river was Mt. Baker, an easily climbed, wooded peak with blueberries growing on top and breathtaking views of the surrounding mountains and lakes below.

I climbed it many times, first with my older brothers, later with my twin sister and younger neighbors. Once we brought back enough wild blueberries to make two pies. Once my sister and I camped overnight on top, surprised at how cold and dark a mountaintop can get on a summer night.

The Saranac River is ideal for canoes. My sister and I kept a canoe hidden in the underbrush on the bank, and spent many summer days with paddles in hand. Drifting silently downstream was perfect for birdwatching and nature photography, each bend of the river revealing new subjects for binoculars and camera. A mallard duck with yellow ducklings swimming behind her made a splendid photo, and my sister was thrilled to spot a grebe, which demonstrated its remarkable diving abilities for us.

For more physical thrills, we paddled (or waded) upstream against a swift current that would threaten to smash us against rocks as we "shot the rapids" coming back. Swimming was tempting on hot days, but the bloodsucking leaches that bred in the mucky river bottom generally kept us out.

My first inkling that not everyone lived in such a setting came on the day my father rescued the lost hikers. A couple of tourists, wearing Bermuda shorts rarely seen on locals, had climbed Mt. Baker and lost their bearings at the top. They headed down the back side, which has few trails and connects with miles of wilderness. By the time they reached the river, they had panicked and run through blackberry thickets or some other thorny vegetation, covering their bare legs with deep scratches.

My father had taken us fishing in a rowboat with a small outboard motor, and they hailed us from the shore. He refused the money they offered him, and we children were frightened by the blood-stained bills they tried to thrust into our hands as we ferried them back to civilization.

The following summer, my mother signed up with the Fresh Air Fund to provide a two-week vacation to a child from the city. The boy who came to stay with us had never been fishing, climbed a mountain, or gone swimming in a lake. Everything we did with him was new and wonderful, and through his eyes, I began to appreciate our surroundings. That didn't stop me from leaving to pursue an education and a career, but eventually I found my way back, with my own child, so that she too could enjoy the peaceful beauty of nature's playground.

FARMING IN FRANKLIN FALLS

My father was one of twelve children raised on a farm near Franklin Falls, a few miles from Whiteface Mountain. The growing season there is about sixty days, from the last frost of spring to the first frost of fall, and Dad remembers it snowing (once) in July. Snow covers the ground at least six months of the year, and temperatures in the teens and twenties below zero are common.

The ground is stony—better for pasture than planting, and the mountain-fed streams run cold all summer.

Survival required hard work and ingenuity. In winter, trees were harvested to sell, or for the next year's firewood. Teams of horses were used to drag the logs from the deep woods. Ice was harvested from the nearest lake, sawed into blocks, and loaded onto horse-drawn sleds. It was stored until summer, when it was used to keep food from spoiling or to make ice cream.

Early spring was for sugaring, collecting the sweet maple sap in wooden buckets and boiling it down to make soft sugar, kept in barrels for topping pancakes. The pancakes were made of buckwheat, the only grain besides oats that would ripen in the short growing season.

After spring planting came haying, filling the barn loft with the fragrant food that kept the cows alive all winter. Swarms of tiny, biting blackflies that crawled into our eyes and ears made the warmth of our early-summer visits seem less of a blessing. The second haying, in late summer, would be accompanied by the much larger deerflies or horseflies, attracted by perspiration. Blackfly bites itch, but deerflies hurt. My father suffered from hay fever, adding itching eyes and sneezing to the fun of pitching forkfuls of hay from field to wagon and wagon to barn.

While Grandpa and his six sons pitched hay, six daughters helped Grandma with the inside chores. Bread was baked daily, before breakfast, and served with bacon, eggs, pancakes, oatmeal, and potatoes. Breakfast followed morning chores, so appetites were large. Two dinners were served during hay season—late-morning and late-afternoon—and with the extra help they needed in the fields, there might be thirty people to feed. Supper was a light meal—often just bread and milk, eaten at bedtime.

In addition to crops such as potatoes, yellow turnips (rutabagas), green peas and beans, carrots and parsnips, they ate wild berries and greens such as those of dandelion and lamb's quarter. Cows were kept for milk, chickens for eggs, and pigs and sheep for meat. The meat was normally sold to the grocer in Bloomingdale, six miles away. He kept the choicer cuts and sold back the less tender meat, which was then salted or canned.

If the winter diet of salt pork (mostly fat) and boiled potatoes grew tiresome, the men and boys went hunting. Dozens of antlers hanging on the side of the barn attested to their appetite for venison. As a teenager, my father was sometimes hired as a hunting guide, helping well-heeled out-of-towners find and kill a whitetail buck. The visitor was shown where to stand, and the local hunters located a deer and chased it toward him. Sometimes they had to shoot it for him as well.

Dad was twelve in 1929, when the stock market crashed and the Great Depression began. A lifestyle in which cash played a minor role had its advantages; no one went hungry who had land and could work it. Flour and sugar came from the store; the cloth flour bags were used to make clothing. Shoes were necessary only during the school year; they were stored over the summer, and in the fall, each child got whichever pair would fit. A traveling shoemaker made replacements to fit as they became necessary.

Education was a priority; chores were done before and after school hours. A one-room grade school served the local children, who did indeed walk several miles through deep snow to get there. When my father's leg was broken and in a cast, he was pulled to school on a sled. The high school was in Bloomingdale. The girls boarded with families in town, but the boys were needed for chores at home and had to go in a horse-drawn sled to the main road, where the car was left.

Despite the obstacles, seven of my father's siblings went on to college. Four became teachers, one a nurse.

My father liked working with his hands. He maintained the gas-powered washing machine and kept the windmill that pumped the water for the farm working. He became a machinist in a munitions factory, and then in the Army. After the war, he found work as a carpenter and later as a building contractor. One uncle stayed on the farm, kept a herd of dairy cows, and looked after my grandparents. After they died, he stayed on, selling the cows when he could no longer milk them.

We visited the farm from Saranac Lake every Sunday when we were children and my grandparents were alive. In the winter, we played with the toboggan on a wind-swept hillside until the cold forced us in. The smell of woolen snowpants drying on a rack above the woodstove blended with my grandfather's pipe as we snacked on homemade bread and fresh raw milk.

In summer, there was a brook to fish for trout, and puddles that bred tadpoles. A huge rock in the middle of the field, a local landmark with a tall white pine tree growing through a crack in the middle, served as a playhouse. We slept on a bed of soft green moss, and used the branches of the tree for stairs from one level to the other.

Spring was for petting baby animals and counting the eggs in the swallows' nests in the barn rafters. A rope that hung from the roof made a fine swing—until my brother landed in the hay and got barbed porcupine quills stuck in his knee. Fall was for hunting by groups of men and teenage boys. Getting a hunting license was a rite of passage for my brothers, along with learning to play pinochle well enough to play with the men.

I hunted with my father once, although I brought a camera instead of a gun. I got some good photos, and he got his buck. I saw him shoot it, helped him track it and gut it, and together we dragged it several miles back to the car. I never went again.

I got my turn at pinochle also, after my brothers went off to college. In my first game, I made the mistake of bidding against my grandfather, who was not an aggressive player and gave in easily. This violated a tacit agreement the men had to let him win whenever he got a good hand. Another time my aunt and I took on my father and uncle (the only time I remember any of the other women playing) and trounced them soundly.

The farmhouse still stands. It was the site of a recent family reunion that drew relatives from as far as California. Like dozens of previous such gatherings, the crowd overflowed into the yard, where the food was set out on long tables. This time a sudden downpour interrupted the festivities, sending attendees scurrying for cover.

If life is change, learning to cope with Adirondack weather is good preparation.

GRANDFATHER'S FUNERAL

My grandfather died in his eighties, after collapsing while digging fence post holes on the farm he had owned for some sixty years. It was hard manual labor for an old man with a bad heart, and not work he had to do. Perhaps it was his way of choosing not to outlive his usefulness.

He and my grandmother had argued—in their quiet way—about which of them would die first. Neither wanted to be left behind. She endured several years of failing health after he died; I wonder if he would have lasted as long without her.

After his funeral, we all gathered at the old farmhouse where twelve children had been born and raised. Worn linoleum covered the creaking wooden floors, and the walls bore many layers of faded wallpaper. It was summer, and the cast iron wood-burning cookstove was cold. My father sat on a wooden stool beside it, and my grandmother in her rocking chair beside him wept softly.

Aunts, uncles, cousins, and neighbors sat in straight-backed chairs behind the round wooden table in the kitchen, or overflowed into the living room, where family pictures hanging on the wall competed with the stuffed and mounted antlered head of a white-tailed buck. Younger children played in the dusty, seldom-used front room, with the out-of-tune piano no one had touched since Uncle Edgar died twenty-five years earlier.

I found a seat on one of a row of mismatched wooden chairs along the outer wall of the kitchen. West-facing windows let in the golden late-afternoon sunshine and the quiet green of the sugar maples and distant tree-covered mountains that surrounded the farm. Even in summer, the isolation of a house from which no other houses could be seen felt desolate to me. The long, bitter winters, with their endless snow and wind, were the land's true owners, only lending their fields for a brief season of hay and strawberries. Uncle Frank sat down beside me, his work-calloused hands contrasting with his Sunday suit. The oldest of my father's siblings, now nearly bald, he had never outgrown the habit of teasing and annoying others for his own amusement. At fifteen, with three older brothers of my own, I had little patience for his game of reaching behind my back to yank on my braids. I was about to move to another seat when a different solution occurred to me.

Smiling innocently, I turned to Frank and commented, "It really is amazing how much you and my father look alike." Their profiles are nearly identical, although the differences in their dispositions clearly show in their coloring and expressions.

"Yup," Frank replied, "Couple of handsome devils, aren't we?"

"I suppose so," I stalled, preparing to spring the trap. "But what I don't understand is why Grandma would make the same mistake twice."

The room was suddenly silent, as Frank's face became even angrier and redder than usual and I realized that our conversation had been overheard by most of the group. Then the room exploded with laughter, and I looked up to see my father laughing so hard he could barely keep his balance on the wobbly old stool. Even my grandmother stopped crying and began to chuckle.

It was payback time for Uncle Frank, completing the circle of cause and effect, just as death completes the circle of life.

ALBERT

Albert was my father's younger brother, the one who stayed on the farm and took over when Grandpa got too old to work it. The cows he fed and milked and cared for were like his children, and there were always puppies or kittens or some other animals in his life long after the cows were sold. He took care of Grandma after Grandpa died, and then lived alone with his animals in the isolated old farmhouse until his final illness.

The family stories include one about Albert leaning over my crib when I was very small, and me grabbing him and kissing him and refusing to let go. When I was a chubby, self-conscious pre-teen, my grandmother told me Uncle Albert thought I was pretty. I asked my mother why he never married, and she said that he had been a high-spirited young man, but the war had changed him.

Decades of smoking cigarettes had changed him too, leaving

him short of breath from emphysema. After years of oxygen tanks, bouts of pneumonia, and a constant struggle to breathe, he finally lost the battle.

The funeral home overflowed with his siblings (six of the original twelve survived him), their children and grandchildren, and a few family friends. It felt to me like a joyful occasion, a celebration of his release from a long ordeal. I struggled to keep my jubilation in check, in deference to those who preferred to weep.

I also struggled with the service, which felt heavy and mournful and full of guilt over our human imperfections. I wanted to stand up and shout something, or maybe sing, but we weren't brought up that way, and besides, the minister was my brother. So I shut my eyes and tried to drown out the sermon by singing a love song to God in my mind. I was sure I could feel Albert's presence, and that he was rejoicing in his new freedom.

When the service ended, I opened my eyes and turned to my thirteen-year-old daughter beside me. She was obviously upset, which puzzled me, since she had not known her great-uncle well. I wondered if she was embarrassed by my lack of sorrow. When we got to the car to drive to the graveyard, she said to me tearfully, "I thought people were supposed to be sad at their own funeral." At first I thought I had misunderstood her, that she was scolding me, but then she explained.

During the service she had noticed a man walking around the room, waving his hand in people's faces and getting no reaction. Then he looked at her and smiled, realizing she could see him just as she realized he was the same man whose body lay in the open coffin at the front of the room. He began to clown around for her benefit, complaining about the makeup on his corpse, trying to rub it off, saying, "Why did they do this? I never wore makeup!" As my brother the minister delivered the eulogy, Albert was making "rabbit ears" behind his head and telling him to "cut the crap!" At one point, Albert moved among the crowd, hugging his siblings, including my father. He looked up and saw my daughter starting to cry, so he began to polish the top of my father's bald head.

In an empty corner of the room, my daughter went on, she saw an elderly woman who could only have been my grandmother, who had died long before my daughter was born. Later, she noticed that Albert's form had begun to shimmer; when he put a hand on her shoulder, he left a glowing handprint behind. She wiped it off onto the chair, and left a glowing stain no one else could see.

I assured my daughter that it was not required of the deceased that he show respect for his own corpse; I felt that my uncle was entitled to turn cartwheels in the aisles if he wanted. I was delighted to hear that the transition had not changed his irreverent sense of humor. And I was impressed by her ability to see what I could only dimly sense; like my sister, she has a gift, whether she wants it or not.

The tiny cemetery was on top of a steep hill overlooking a wooded valley and the mountains beyond it. Late spring sunshine poured down from a clear blue sky, and birds sang from atop the tall, asymmetrical white pines surrounding the site. A dog barked in the distance. The joy I had felt at the funeral continued, like the Easter mornings of my childhood: the certainty of resurrection, the triumph over death. Uncle Albert and my grandmother were there, though only my daughter saw them.

She last saw Albert sitting on the branch of a tall white pine, high above the cemetery, like a high-spirited boy just released from school. And that is how I choose to remember him.

John W. Van de Water:
A North Country Gentleman Farmer

John W. and Peter Van de Water

John W. Van de Water was to have written an essay for this book, but he died when the essay was in progress. The selections from John's writings which follow center on Jonsalvania, his Canton farm. They are introduced in italics, by his son, Peter.

In 1969 my father retired as chairman of the Liberal Arts division at Jefferson Community College. The following excerpt from Chichee's Trunk *reveals his excitement at finding the retirement farm of his dreams.*

At Watertown, we lived in a beautiful old stone house near the college. But our roots were in the soil, and we talked more and more of a retirement farm. So in 1969, after seven happy years at Jefferson Community College, we began the search which ended here at Jonsalvania Farm in Canton.

It took us over a year, and most of our looking was in the Canton area. We wanted to be in the Northeast near our children and their families. We wanted to be near a college town where we could enjoy libraries, plays, concerts, lectures, athletic events. Sally wanted another old stone colonial house she could furnish accordingly. I wanted woods, pastures, pond sites, garden space, an orchard, an area to plant Christmas trees, a good cattle barn. It seemed like a large order, and as we looked and looked in vain, we began to feel we would have to compromise.

One Saturday we went to Canton, where popular auctioneer and real estate agent Roger Huntley showed us an old stone house with 12 acres on the Grasse River. We were tempted, but it was not large enough to suit the restless urges that keep me out of doors whenever possible. The next morning before daybreak the phone rang, and I answered, still half asleep. Sally says this was my part of the conversation:

"You're kidding."

"You're kidding."

"You're kidding."

"You're kidding."

"You're not kidding? We'll come right up."

It was Peter, reporting that he had met Roger Huntley the previous evening, and that Roger reported a brand new listing exactly to our specifications.

It was perfect. Owners Millard and Marion Poole wanted to sell quickly. She didn't like the "gloomy old house," and after a lifetime of daily milking, he had had his fill of farming. They wanted to retire to a little trailer on an eighth of an acre, and we wanted to retire to a farm on 180 acres.

The 1820 stone house, one of the first in the area, was solid. The broke-gabled, Dutch-knuckled barn was good, both serviceable and picturesque. The Pooles were not agri-business farmers and had used no poisons or chemicals on the soil. There were seven plausible sites for ponds. There were 75 acres of woods.

It was located on Little River south of Canton, just where the flat valley of the St. Lawrence River begins to rise into the rocky foothills of the Adirondacks. A sweeping view extended to the spires of Gunnison Chapel on the St. Lawrence University campus to the north, and historic old Brick Chapel Church to the east. We would be well watched over. A discreet check indicated that the nearby farmers would make the best of neighbors.

We were ecstatic. I would start a herd of Hereford cattle, build two ponds and a wildlife marsh, plant 70,000 trees, have big organic gardens and orchards. We would have our own organic fruit, vegetables, fish, meat, milk, butter, eggs, poultry. The freezers and cellar and barn would store a winter's supply of food for us and for the cattle. The house was big enough to accommodate any of our children and their growing families. It would be a perfect place for the grandchildren to visit. Sally could renovate and furnish the house, have a big flower garden, and a steady flow of organic foods to her kitchen.

We bought it on the spot and christened it for ourselves: Jon-Sal-Van-ia.

The Pooles, the couple my parents replaced, fit a familiar mold. The farm had been in Millard Poole's family for generations. He was born and grew up here. A small farm as far as tillable land, it could sustain no more than thirty milking cows. This had been adequate for Millard's father, but was increasingly inadequate for him as methods changed. His wife Marion taught school to make ends meet. One by one, their children left for the city, not loving the farm enough to commit to the continuous struggle necessary to ensure its survival.

Millard was like many North Country men who instantly gain your trust when first you meet them. There is something in the speech: slow, measured, laconic, unostentatious, and colloquial. In the face is something of gentleness mixed with firmness. The gentleness shows in a twinkle about the eyes, the firmness in a set to the jaw. Such men wear an air of calmness and serenity, as though they are at peace with themselves and their world.

Millard's love of all living things was revealed in his affection for his trees. While we walked through his woods of many acres, it was obvious that Millard was personally acquainted with every tree. He was aware of a branch newly broken here, an elm tree showing signs of disease there. At the front of his house were nine large maples that afforded shade against the hot days of summer. They had, in fact, grown together to form too tight a canopy, rendering the living room a bit dark and gloomy.

"I think I will take this one out to give the house more light," I said in the thoughtless manner of a new buyer eager to make the place his own, oblivious to the feelings of the old owner. A shade crossed his eyes.

"My wife said the same thing," he said. "But I couldn't do it. Those maples have been there a long time. But it's yours now; I guess you can do what you want." I changed the subject.

What different things men see, though they look at the same trees, the same forests.

I feel better, thinking about this man and his farm and his trees, to know that I have planted far more trees—more than 70,000—on his farm than I have taken down. Maybe enough to call it my farm now.

In 1976, my wife Becky and I built a stone house just south of the old 1820 stone house. My father wrote "The Barn" to dedicate the new stone house.

THE BARN

Snug-set against the hillside
the barn stands on stone foundation—
stone taken from those very fields
whose hays and grains it wintered thru the years.
Broke-gabled roof, unique among its peers
guards what's beneath with impartiality,
kitten and pigeon claiming equality
with cattle that the farmer shelters there.
No gleaming paint now mars the siding of this barn,
but faintly can be seen
a trace of red-stained buttermilk
applied now decades gone
and buried deep into the wood.
Beside the barn in silent partnership
the stone house stands as it has stood
these many moons and will stand.

And now, just south, another house,
this too of granite stone from off this farm,
has sprung full-statured, bold.
Eyes facing north, it sees the old
and sees connecting them a link, a path,
which wends its well-worn way—will wend—
thru open gates, from old to new, and new to old.

Between the old stone house and the new stone house sits a weathered. grey frame house, originally attached to the old stone house—probably to provide for extended family—but since moved across a broad lawn to cover its own cellar hole. A series of short-term renters occupied "the tenant house"; those my father liked best were willing converts to country ways.

Bob Johnson was New York City bred and raised. He and Joan were newly married and had just rented our tenant house. Bob had his first teaching job at Knox Memorial Central School in the little Adirondack foothills village of Russell.

They had not been with us long before it was plain that Bob, in spite of his background, was an organic farmer at heart. He was interested in all the activities at Jonsalvania Farm: the organic fruit and vegetable gardens, the food preserving, the Hereford cattle, the composting, the Christmas trees, the wood lot, the fish ponds, the chickens, the maple syrup, the cider, the bees and the birds.

So I was not surprised one day when Bob said, "You have just about everything else here. Why don't you keep a milk cow?"

"Well, I can get all the milk we need at $1.25 a gallon from the Sibbitts Farm. And a milk cow requires attention night and morning. And Sally and I couldn't begin to take care of all the milk she would give. We used to keep a Jersey cow when all the kids were home though," I added.

Bob had all the answers. "The milk you are buying is agribusiness milk," he accused. "It doesn't fit in with the rest of your food and lifestyle."

"True," I acknowledged.

Bob was getting to be as organic-minded as I.

"So suppose you buy the cow and I'll milk her for you if I keep half the milk? We could make butter and yogurt. Feed the extra to the chickens."

"Maybe," I said doubtfully. "I'll think it over."

The very next week an auction notice caught my eye—a Jersey auction at a nearby farm. And the auctioneer was Roger Huntley, my favorite caller and the man who had sold me my retirement farm. I knew I could trust Roger.

I strode over to Bob's house.

"Jersey auction coming up Saturday," I said. "Want to go down with me at milking time and have a look?"

Bob needed no persuading, so that evening we drove off to the farm near the little village of Hermon. As we rode along, I told Bob what I knew about buying a family cow and what we would look for when we got there.

We arrived at the clean and neat dairy barn during milking time. While the owner was busy with the machines, we strode up and down behind the cows, inspecting each one. I spotted one I liked the looks of.

"When's this one due?" I asked the owner.

He unbent, spat, and consulted a chart. "April 14," he said.

I wanted a cow to freshen in early spring, so it was just right for my needs.

"Mind if I try her?"

"Go right ahead."

I approached her cautiously, rubbed her udder gently, and milked her right front teat. It was long, filling my hand perfectly, and the milk flowed quickly, easily, and abundantly. Aha! She would be a good, easy milker. And she was calm and gentle, having shown no sign of nervousness with me, a stranger. My hand explored the rest of the udder to find her left front quarter was slack.

"She's a three-titter," I muttered to Bob. "Maybe a bad sign and maybe not. Anyway, she'll sure go cheaper for it."

I spoke again to the owner. "How'd she lose her front quarter?"

"Got it stepped on. Second lactation. Couldn't save it."

It was the answer I was hoping for, if true.

"No mastitis, ever?"

"No, she's been clean. It's a good clean herd all around." I looked at him carefully, but his voice had a ring of pride and conviction. They did all look good to me—healthy and alert. I decided he was telling the truth.

"How old is she?"

"She's eight this spring."

I went back to Bob. "She's an older cow as well as a three-titter. Won't go too high at the auction."

I called again to the owner. "Mind if we look at them up front?"

Bob and I went around to the front of her row, and twenty brown heads swung around in unison to give the strangers the once-over. But none of them showed the least sign of nervousness.

"They've been well handled, Bob," I said. "Jerseys can be a bit high strung; and if they were mistreated at all, they wouldn't be acting so calm."

I took a closer look at my choice's head. It may surprise some people to hear that all cows *don't* look alike. Even all brown Jerseys don't look alike. Some have wild and mean expressions while others look docile and gentle. The secret is in the face. Some look intelligent, some stupid. Some bold, some shy. Bessie (I had already named her in my mind) was beautiful. Soft, gentle, limpid, brown eyes. An intelligent and sensitive face with that typical Jersey dip and with a head coloring darker than the rest of her.

I pointed these features out to Bob as we drove home.

The next day when I saw Bob I said, "Still think you want to milk a cow every day?"

But now he sounded doubtful. "I don't know. Joan and I have been talking it over. Not sure I can handle it. I've never milked a cow—and I have to be at school at eight every morning. Suppose I get sick?"

"You're never sick," I said. "Anyway, if you are or if you

have to go away, I'll take care of her. Talk it over with Joan some more." It was then I realized that I wanted to own Bessie. If Bob backed out, I would probably try to buy her anyway.

The next morning, the day of the auction, Bob was still dubious and wavering. It was a big step for a man brought up on the sidewalks of New York.

"Let's go to the auction anyway," I said.

On the way Bob asked, "How much should she go for?"

"Well, she's a beauty and in her younger days, with four good quarters, she should bring between five and six hundred. But at her age, and a three-titter, and nearly ready to dry off, probably not over $200."

When it came Bessie's turn to be driven in the ring, I was amazed at the bidding. The highest Jersey so far had sold for $575. For Bessie, the bidding started at $350 and quickly climbed to $450 while I stood open-mouthed and silent. At that point, I called to the auctioneer. "Roger, do you know she's a three-titter?"

Roger was visibly embarrassed. "Wait, she's a three-titter, folks. Sorry I didn't notice that. We'll have to start the bidding over. Who'll say two hundred?"

Nobody bid. "One hundred-fifty dollars," I said, trying to look disinterested.

One other bid came in at $155. I quickly raised it to $160; and before I knew it Bessie and I owned each other, and I was looking up Rich Rowen, the trucker.

Bob quickly learned to milk and take care of her. Not only that; he, too, fell in love with her, and on frosty fall days I often woke to hear him happily whistling his way to the barn, milk pail in hand, for his daily morning rendezvous.

It was good to have the day's milk set on my doorstep every morning, to have raw skimmed milk to drink, not to mention butter, buttermilk, and yogurt.

"Much better than the artificial, additive-laden stuff you get at the supermarket," Sally said.

But Tom, my oldest grandson, had never tasted raw milk. The first time he tasted it he said, "Yuk, Grandpa, this tastes artificial."

Bob and Joan fell so in love with our way of life at Jonsalvania Farm that they went looking for a farm of their own nearer to Bob's teaching job in Russell. With mixed feelings I helped them look, and the next spring we found it. Good house and barn, 75 acres, streams, pasture, haylot, woodlot, sugarbush. Bob and Joan would have all they wanted, and in a beautiful spot to bring up their family.

My happiness for Bob and Joan, and now little Carrie, was tempered by sadness in seeing them leave. They had been good tenants.

> *My father reveled in the realities of rural living. Dirt under his nails, scratches on his hands, mud and manure on his boots proved his affinity for the natural world. Yet in many ways he remained a "country gentleman," a college French major who wrote poetry, and a devotee of croquet. Some North Country styles and speech patterns would never be his, but he found them intriguing anyway.*

Red DeLorme, one of my horseshoe pitching buddies, lives down toward Pyrites. Jonsalvania Farm is halfway between Pyrites and Canton. Both villages are on the Grass River, but there the resemblance ends. Canton is a thriving village with an excellent private university and a state college. Pyrites is an old mill town nestled in a lovely rural setting. One day I had occasion to call on Red, who was to be my doubles partner in a tournament at Pulaski the following week. I knew he lived somewhere near Pyrites, so I should have no trouble finding him.

We drove down Pink Schoolhouse Road and passed a neat looking church and a red brick schoolhouse. All the windows in the school were shattered. "Looks like they think more of religion than education in Pyrites," Sally said.

We entered the village, and I stopped to ask the first fellow I saw where Red's house was.

"Jesus Christ," he said. The church influence is strong here, I thought. Aloud I said, "I'm John Van de Water."

"Jesus Christ," he said. "I know you. You drove Troop 47 up to Boy Scout camp two years ago."

"That's right," I said. I was a Troop Committeeman. "Now about Red . . ."

"Hell, it's easy to get to Red's place. You come in from Canton?"

"Yeah, over Pink Schoolhouse Road."

"Jesus Christ, you came right by it. Didn't you see that big white house at the bottom of the hill? That's Red's place. Biggest house in Pyrites, by God."

I thanked him and drove back, taking a more thoughtful look at the lovely church and dilapidated school. Nobody was home at Red's place, so we came back to town. There was a softball game in progress behind the school. I stopped and asked another young fellow if Red was around. He spat. Fortunately I was upwind, so was unscathed. He spat again, eyeing me furtively and moving toward the diamond. I moved with him, keeping upwind and avoiding the next three spits. Finally he spoke.

"Jesus Christ," he said. "Follow me. Red's over there." He pointed to a spot just beyond third base.

My first informant then appeared. "Jesus Christ," he said. "You asked me how to get to Red's house. You didn't say you wanted to find Red."

The two escorted me to Red's car, where he and his wife were enjoying the softball rivalry between Pyrites and neighboring Hermon. Red is a local hero, and had been the Babe Ruth of the area in his heyday.

I had just finished my business with Red when I noticed a man belligerently push through the crowd and start toward us.

"God damn you, you red-headed bastard!" he shouted.

Red is about six feet tall and weighs about 250. I would never have considered addressing him with anything but a respectful "Hi, Red." And the guy coming on was skinnier than I.

I looked around for an ambulance or a police car. None in sight. The man came on. I glanced at Red's wife. She was still sitting there with a broad smile on her face. Evidently she enjoyed mayhem, or was confident in the considerable strength and athletic prowess of her mate.

Red rolled out of his car, spat a large stream of tobacco juice, and rushed to meet his assailant. "Jesus Christ," Red roared. "God damn you, where in Hell you been?" They were pounding each other, and it dawned on me this was the normal affectionate greeting of long-separated Pyrites pals.

I left them embracing each other and decided to watch the ball game for awhile. The vocabulary was consistently and enthusiastically church-oriented and totally good-natured.

There was one beautiful and sedate looking young lady. She seemed to be a friend of one of the Pyrites heroes, and when he came to bat, she began shouting encouragement. He popped one up foul near the third base line, and the Hermon hot-sacker made a hard run and a spectacular diving catch right in front of the beautiful young lady. "Jesus Christ," she shrilled. "You rotten bastard! Why don't you go on back to Hermon where you belong?"

I had been raised in a family where "thunder" could be a forbidden curse word, and I mused on this as we drove home in the gathering dusk. I was not sorry I had been brought up never to take the name of the Lord in vain. But I couldn't help feeling that, in this liberated world of today, the good people of Pyrites were in certain aspects more liberated than I. And golly sakes, I found I was envying them just a wee bit, gol darn it!

At my father's memorial service, Max Coots, minister of the Unitarian-Universalist Church of Canton for thirty-four years, said this in his eulogy:

"He's not only followed world events; he translated them into where they really count: into the care and nurture of birds and animals, plants and people and every aspect of the natural world, which is so often sterilized into 'environment.' It was personal to him, a part of him—apples and garden rows, the health of soil and seed and cattle in the field and beaver in the pond. Spiritually and physically, he walked the land like Abraham, feeling his kinship to it and everything that lives, through the soles of his shoes."

Max was right. My father truly loved his land. At dawn or dusk, I often saw him strolling slowly along the winding path that led past the pond; over the "troll bridge," into the big woods, and eventually on toward the cabin he had built there. Yet he loved his land not by owning it—possessing it—but more as the Native American, who held his land in stewardship.

"I husband it," he wrote, "to leave it better than I found it so that future generations may have and enjoy it. I do not own land. Perhaps, rather, it owns me. And that is good."

My father expanded his theme in this poetic passage with which he concluded This Land, These People.

I do not own a bit of earth. I tenant it. The earth is part of all of us, and not an inch belongs to me. Or you. It all belongs to all of us. When I say us, I count all living things upon the earth. All balance and all interact. Without them we could not exist.

I cherish earth—replenish it; renew; recycle it with love. And thank the Lord who put it there. Or call her Manitou, Jehovah, Allah, what you will. The Mother Earth has blessed us well.

Nor do we own the water which we drink. It was put there for all—the baby chick the day he pips the egg; the lion on the plain; the trees on mountainside. All living things depend on it and need it clean and pure, or else they die. Witness the whales upon the beach, the fish in mountain lake, the trees on mountain top. We watch in wonder as our fellow creatures die, and ask ourselves why. Someday we'll know, if we survive.

Nor do we own the air that all must breathe. The leaves of trees and grasses make the air. I guess that's what Isaiah meant, who said "all flesh is grass." We must protect that air all ways we can and not defile it to pollute and kill the very trees that furnish it.

How can a man take up a child into his arms and look it in the eye and not avow that he will do his part to leave the air and sea and land fit for that child to share with all God's creatures everywhere?

We must do that if we survive.

Afterword

Beavers have dammed another stream, flooded a shallow dip in the North Country's characteristic rolling landscape. Grey masts of drowned trees surround their pond; their lodge is a dome of sticks and mud on the far side. In late September, they labor to insulate it against the cold they know will come.

No boundaries separate pond from land: there are no hard edges, no lines, no measured spaces of ending or beginning. Each sphere melds with every other, in cycles that are never done.

Trees across the pond, maples backed by conifers, will soon blaze like rainbows for a moment I cannot keep, then turn grey on evergreen, soon to be touched by winter white, soft yellow-greens of spring, darker summer greens, and rainbows once again. Their cycle is never done; the conifers, meanwhile, never change. And the water will cool, thicken and glaze, freeze and bear snow's weight, soften and sink, and melt and warm. Its cycle is never done.

No boundaries separate the seasons. There are no hard edges, no moments of ending or beginning. One season becomes the next, as coyote joins prey or mate, as pond drains to brook to river to sea to pond. The cycle is never done.

In blending times, wind carries spicy mixes of distant, inscrutable scents. It rips leaves to earth, heralds blizzards, prophesizes warming air that devours rotting snow.

Golden needles of tamarack rain like shattering chandeliers. Shortly, sound will come from icy snow, striking snow and stubborn leaves of beech, from relentless rains of spring and slashing summer storms. Red-wing blackbird voices seasons quickly gone, fiery witch-hopple seasons soon to come. Torn, jaundiced birch leaves fall on black pond water lapping dark thin shores. No boundaries separate the cycles. . . .

Beaver swims, slaps, gnaws, swims, slaps, gnaws. She comprehends more of this than I ever will.

—Neal Burdick

About the Authors

Co-editor Natalia Rachel Singer is an associate professor of English at St. Lawrence University. Her fiction and non-fiction have been published widely, in magazines and journals that include *Ms.*, *Harper's*, *Redbook*, *Creative Nonfiction*, *Prairie Schooner*, *The American Scholar*, and *Shenandoah.* She has won a number of awards, including Second Prize in the Annie Dillard Award of Nonfiction, First Prize in the World's Best Short Short Story contest, and she was a recipient of a grant from the New York State Foundation for the Arts for Nonfiction Literature. She has been the director of St. Lawrence's Writers Series and a workshop leader at the University's annual Young Writers Conference in the Adirondacks.

Co-editor Neal Burdick is a native of Plattsburgh and a graduate of St. Lawrence University. He has been a summer theater technician in Plattsburgh; a high school English, drama and outdoor education teacher in Maine; a railroad worker in New Hampshire; and a wilderness survival instructor in the Adirondacks. He is publications editor at St. Lawrence and co-director of its Young Writers Conference, as well as a freelance writer and editor, having published reviews, essays, articles, poetry, short fiction, chapters and introductions in local, regional and national magazines, journals, newspapers and travel books. He is editor of *Adirondac*, the magazine of the Adirondack Mountain Club, and of the club's series of hiking guides, and a frequent contributor to *Adirondack Life* and *Adirondack Explorer.* He is on the Steering Committee of the Adirondack Center for Writing and has been a New York Foundation for the Arts nonfiction grant panelist.

Heather Allison-Jenkins grew up in New Jersey and Massachusetts. She fell in love with the North Country and especially the Adirondacks while a student at St. Lawrence University. After graduating with a writing major in 1992, she remained in the North Country as a newspaper reporter, freelance writer, and horseback riding instructor. She has been a columnist for *The Horseman's Yankee Pedlar* and, more recently, the public relations coordinator for the Green Mountain Waldorf School in Wolcott, Vermont. She has been living in Vermont with her husband, three children, and cat since 1998.

Chris Angus is a life-long resident of Northern New York. He grew up in Canton, graduated from St. Lawrence University, then obtained a master's degree in park and recreation administration from Central Michigan University. He has been a small businessman, property owner, freelance writer, environmental activist, newspaper columnist, and participant in many North Country groups. He is book review editor of *Adirondac* and the author of *Reflections from Canoe Country—Paddling the Waters of the Adirondacks and Canada.* He has written articles, book reviews and essays for *Adirondac*, *Adirondack Life*, *Adirondack Explorer*, *Canoe*, *American Forests*, the *Albany Times Union*, and the *New York Times.* His forthcoming biography of the noted Adirondack guide, pilot and conservationist Clarence Petty will be published by Syracuse University Press.

Peter J. Bailey is the author of two critical works, *Reading Stanley Elkin* and *The Reluctant Film Art of Woody Allen.* He has taught American literature and fiction writing at St. Lawrence since 1980.

Mary Blake was born in Ogdensburg and spent her early years in Black River and Potsdam and every summer at Oak Point on the St. Lawrence River. She has been book review editor for *Adirondac* magazine, has published articles in *Sewickley Magazine* and *Mid-Atlantic Antique Review,* and had a four-year stint as an American antiques columnist for the *Pittsburgh Post Gazette* newspaper. She is working on children's fiction of the Adirondacks and teaching sixth grade at the Village Charter School in Chapel Hill, North Carolina.

Carolyn Boggs grew up in Saranac Lake, New York, and earned a bachelor's degree in human nutrition and foods from Cornell University. She lives in Ithaca, New York, and is a registered dietitian with a nonprofit community agency. Her previous writing experience includes articles on nutrition for agency newsletters and poems published in her church newsletter.

Lynn Case Ekfelt is a retired archivist and curator of special collections at St. Lawrence University. She holds an M.A. in library science from the University of Denver and an M.A. in folklore from Indiana University. She has published three articles in the St. Lawrence County Historical Association *Quarterly*, a guidebook in German for St. Lawrence students on the university's program in Vienna, and bibliographies of St. Lawrence's collections on Frost, Hawthorne, and E.A. Robinson. She has also been editor of the *Bulletin of the Friends of Owen D. Young Library* at the university. Her book on North Country foodways, *Good Food, Served Right*, was the winner of the 2000 Tabasco Prize.

William Gadway was born in Plattsburgh, New York, and raised in nearby Morrisonville. He has a bachelor's degree in vocational technical education, the initial two years being spent at Canton ATC (now Canton College of Technology) and the final two at the State University of New York at Utica/Rome. This is his first published writing.

Jim Gould taught writing and literature in the environmental studies program at Paul Smith's College for more than a dozen years. A graduate of Columbia University's MFA Writing Program, he lectures and writes frequently on Adirondack topics and issues, and his work has appeared in the *New York Times*, *New York Magazine*, *Outside Magazine*, *Backpacker*, *Adirondack Life*, *The Washington Post*, the Syracuse *Post-Standard*, and other publications. He has also been book review editor of *Adirondac*. An avid hiker, cross-country skier, flatwater paddler and licensed guide, he and his wife own a home near Lake Placid, New York.

Alice Paden Green was born in South Carolina but reared during the 1950s in Witherbee, New York, a small Adirondack mining community. She has a doctorate in criminal justice and has served in high-level state positions in that field. She left her last state position to become executive director of the Center for Law and Justice, a community criminal justice program which she founded in 1985, in Albany, New York. In 1999, she co-authored *Law Never Here, A Social History of African American Responses to Issues of Crime and Justice* with Frankie Y. Bailey. She also has established The Paden Institute and Retreat for Writers of Color in Essex, New York. Actively involved in a number of race and criminal justice issues, she spends part of her summers in Essex and also spends time in Witherbee, where she owns her childhood home, She and her husband, Charles Touhey, have two adult children.

Randall T.G. Hill is an associate professor of speech and theatre at St. Lawrence University, His research interests include performance ethnography, Native American studies, and rhetoric, and he has published articles on Native American ritual work and appropriation, methods of reading Native texts, and teaching performance-centered approaches to the rhetoric of social movements. Professor Hill, a member of the Lumbee tribe, is conducting fieldwork among the Lumbee people of southeastern North Carolina in an effort to gather, edit, and introduce some of these peoples' personal narratives in a collection titled *Lumbee Talk: Telling Our Lives.*

Elizabeth Inness-Brown, a native of New York's North Country, graduated from St. Lawrence University in 1976 and earned her master's degree in creative writing from Columbia. She has taught writing at the University of Southern Mississippi, St. Lawrence, Purdue, the University of Hartford, Vermont College, and St. Michael's College, where she is director of the Writing Center and an English professor, She has also led workshops at St. Lawrence's International Young Writers Conference. Her first collection of stories, *Satin Palms* (1981), won her a fellowship from the National Endowment for the Arts, a Pushcart Prize, an Associated Writing Programs award, and other recognition, Her stories have appeared in the *New Yorker*, *North American Review*, and *Glimmer Train.* Her second story collection, *Here*, was published by the Louisiana State University Press in 1994. Her novel, *Burning Marguerite*, is forthcoming from Knopf in winter 2002.

Constance Jenkins is a native of Ogdensburg, New York, who graduated from St. Lawrence University and then spent fourteen years as a journalist in New Hampshire before reconnecting with the North Country. Currently city editor of the *Saratogian*, the daily newspaper for Saratoga Springs, New York, she has also had some work published in regional magazines and poetry collections.

Arthur L. Johnson, a native of Massachusetts, received his B.A. from Kenyon College and his M.A. and Ph. D. in American history from the University of Maine. He has been a faculty member in history at the State University of New York at Potsdam since 1968. He is a member of the Adirondack Mountain Club, the Adirondack Forty-Sixers, the Massachusetts Bay Railroad Enthusiasts, and the Railway and Locomotive Historical Society.

Karen M. Johnson-Weiner has degrees from Hope College, Michigan State, and McGill University. She has been studying the Amish and Mennonites for seventeen years and has published articles in several journals on Amish education, language, and culture. Her research has been supported by grants from the National Endowment for the Humanities and Potsdam College's Research and Creative Endeavors Program. Dr. Johnson-Weiner is a member of the anthropology department at SUNY Potsdam, where she teaches linguistics and linguistic anthropology.

Maurice Kenny, a Mohawk and the author of twenty-four collections of poetry and two of fiction, has been hailed by *World Literature Today* magazine as the dean of Native American poetry. His poetry has been published in thirteen countries and translated into nine languages. He has received the American Book Award, a New York State Council on the Arts fellowship and residency, and a Corporation for Public Broadcasting award. He has read his poetry several times on National Public Radio, and his poems, stories and essays appear in over 150 anthologies and textbooks. He has been published in more than 200 magazines and journals ranging from the *New York Times* and *Adirondack Life* to *Mid-America Review* and *Open Places.* Among his collections are *The Mama Poems*, *Between Two Rivers*, *Rain & Other Fictions*, *North: Poems of Home*, *Tekonwatonti: Molly Brant*, *Poems of War*, *On Second Thought*, and *Backward to Forward: Essays.* An editor, publisher, arts council panelist, and member of the board of directors of the Coordinating Council of Literary Magazines, he has been a visiting professor/poet-in-residence at the University of Oklahoma, the University of Victoria at Penticton (British Columbia), North Country Community College, and Paul Smith's College. Poetry editor of *Adirondac* magazine, he has been a workshop leader at St. Lawrence's Young Writers Conference since its inception. He teaches at SUNY Potsdam.

Ken Lawless grew up in Saranac Lake, New York. He was an Andrew Mellon Fellow at the University of Pittsburgh and taught at Michigan State, City College of New York, and Baruch College. He helped launch the North Country Arts in Education program and the Prop Trunk Players and has published many books of trade paperback humor, most recently *Bluff Your Way in New York.* His articles have appeared in *Adirondack Life*, *American Heritage*, *Antioch Review*, *People's Almanac*, and other places. Two books of fables and three of poems were issued by small presses. He now concentrates on poetry and performance art with over 120 titles in a repertoire he calls The Liberal Arts Performance Series.

Jonathan Mairs is a native of Geneva, New York, and a 1994 graduate of St. Lawrence University, where he majored in writing and was a member of the English honorary society. His essay on the Canton fair won the first-ever North Country Studies Award from the Friends of the Owen D. Young Library at St. Lawrence in 1992. Jon's interest in writing and storytelling grew largely out of his experiences as a canoe-tripping guide in northern Ontario. A 1990 graduate of Phillips Exeter Academy, he currently lives in New York City.

Shirley McFerson recently retired after twenty years of service to the Caldwell-Lake George Library in Lake George, New York. After growing up in Lake George and Glens Falls, she earned bachelor's and master's degrees at Albany State. She was a teacher and librarian in Lockport and Peekskill and worked for the New York Public Library before returning to the North Country to care for her parents. She has been active in community theater, has taken writing and playwriting workshops, and still lives in Lake George, performing as a storyteller by the name of Sweet Mama String Bean.

Bill McKibben is an author and environmentalist whose writings have appeared in newspapers and periodicals ranging from the *New York Times* and *Natural History* to *The Atlantic* and *Rolling Stone.* A former staff writer and author of hundreds of articles for *The New Yorker*, his first book was *The End of Nature*, a best-seller that dealt with environmental problems and was translated into sixteen languages. This was followed by *The Age of Missing Information*, which examined mass media and environmental degradation. He has also written *The Comforting Whirlwind*, about religion and nature; and *Hope, Human and Wild*, an account of places around the world where people live more lightly on the planet. His book *Maybe One: A Personal and Environmental Argument for Single-Child Families* was published in 1998, and *Long Distance: A Year of Living Strenuously* came out in 2000. He lives with his wife, writer Sue Halpern, and their daughter, Sophie, in the south-central Adirondacks.

Homer Mitchell's poetry, fiction, and non-fiction have appeared in numerous publications including *Southern Review*, *Small Pond*, *Comstock Review*, *Plastic Tower*, *Adirondac*, and *Blueline.* As an adjunct instructor he has taught literature, composition, and poetry writing for several colleges in upstate New York and Vermont. He is currently visiting instructor at SUNY Cortland. Mitchell has edited four chapbooks of poems by students in North Country prisons and community colleges, including *Burger of a Whale*.

Roger Mitchell attended Saranac Lake High School and graduated from Northwood School in Lake Placid. He is the author of six books of poetry and one of non-fiction. Two of these concern the history of the Adirondacks: *Adirondack*, a volume of poems; and *Clear Pond: The Reconstruction of a Life*, a work of non-fiction about a pioneer mill-wright in the Elk Lake area. Before retiring, he taught in the creative writing program at Indiana University. He is an honorary citizen of the town of North Hudson, New York.

Tam Lin Neville's poetry has been published in *Mademoiselle, American Poetry Review, Ironwood, Crazyhorse, The Massachusetts Review*, and others, as well as in a number of anthologies. Her essays and reviews have appeared in *The Threepenny Review, The Hungry Mind Review, American Poetry Review*, and others. Her book, *Journey Cake*, was published in March 1998.

Peter Owens is a widely published and award-winning journalist, software author, Web publisher, fiction writer, and educator who teaches at the University of Massachusetts Dartmouth. His novel *Rips*, recently published, is also distributed by North Country Books. His software includes *The Research Paper Writer* and The *Classroom Newspaper Workshop* published by Tom Snyder Productions and *Super Scoop* by Queue. He is the founder and former publisher of *KidNews*, one of the first kids' writing sites on the Internet. His fiction has appeared in the *North American Review* and *The Smith*, his journalism in many newspapers and magazines in the U.S. and in *The Guardian* of London. He earned his B.A. at Wesleyan and his master's and doctorate at Harvard. He was born in Utica, grew up in Prospect, lives most of the year with his wife and two children on Cape Cod, and travels several times each year to his island camp on the St. Lawrence River.

Harry W. Paige is a professor emeritus at Clarkson University in Potsdam, New York. Among his publications are *Songs of the Teton Sioux* (1970), the first literary study of the songs of the Plains Indians and a finalist for a Western Writers of America Spur Award for best non-fiction of the year; four young adult novels; *Land of the Spotted Eagle: A Portrait of the Reservation Sioux* (1987), a winner of the Chicago Clinic Award and Best Book Award by the Catholic Press Association of the U.S. and Canada; *Tunes and Testaments*, a book of poems; The *Eye of the Heart* (1990); and numerous short stories, articles, essays, and plays. He won the Spur Award for Short Fiction in 1989 and again for nonfiction in 2001.

Joan Potter has been a professional writer for thirty years, publishing articles in the *New York Times* and various periodicals. She has contributed many pieces to *Adirondack Life* magazine and is a co-author of *The Book of Adirondack Firsts* and author of *African American Firsts.* Both books were published by Pinto Press, a publishing company that she and her husband started in 1992. Among the press's books is *Growing Up Strong: Four North Country Women Recall Their Lives*, a compilation of memoirs written by women from Elizabethtown and Lewis, in the eastern Adirondacks, who attended a writing workshop that she led. She has taught writing classes at the state prison facility in Moriah, New York, and the Northern Westchester Center for the Arts in Mount Kisco, New York, and teaches at the Hudson Valley Writers' Center in Sleepy Hollow, New York. She is co-author of a children's book, *African Americans Who Were First*, published by Dutton.

Betsy Tisdale was born in Indiana and spent her childhood in Connecticut. Her photography, articles, and poetry have been published in several media. Her work has appeared in the Plattsburgh *Press Republican, Adirondack Life*, *The Conservationist*, and *Adirondac*, the magazine of the Adirondack Mountain Club. Author of the first edition of the Adirondack Mountain Club's guidebook *Adirondack Trails: Eastern Region,* she is a quilt dealer and designer, working with the women of an Amish community near her home in Potsdam, New York. Recently she taught English as a second language to adult students from ten countries.

John W. Van de Water was to have written an essay for this book. After retiring from a career in education, he wrote a popular column called "The Canton Gardener" for the *St. Lawrence Plaindealer*, then in 1980 began writing the weekly "Rural Living" column for the *Watertown Daily Times.* These columns and his books *Chichee's Trunk* (1980), an anecdotal autobiography, and *This Land; These People* (1990), a collection of essays about North Country life, earned him a wide readership in Northern New York. He had begun drafting an essay for this book when he suffered a stroke and died in November 1992. The selections from John's writings center on Jonsalvania, his Canton farm.

Peter Van de Water is a graduate of St. Lawrence University and holds a doctorate from the University of Michigan. He was for many years vice president for student affairs at St. Lawrence. He has written articles for *Adirondack Life* and is the author of *Alexander* G. *Ruthven: Biography of a University President.* He produces apples, blueberries and Christmas trees on his farm just south of Canton, New York.

Tom Van de Water grew up in Canton, studied geology and poetry at Middlebury College, and fell under the spell of the Adirondack community of Mineville while interviewing miners for a senior thesis in 1983. He studied for a year in Hokkaido, Japan, on a Watson Fellowship, taught outdoor education and literature at Sterling College in Vermont, and was drawn back to the North Country to build a solar house with his wife, Betsy Kepes. He teaches earth science at Canton High School and works with his family on a fire lookout in Idaho during the summer. He and Betsy published the story of their bicycle journey across the Hidaka Mountains with their young son Lee in the Japanese journal *Northern Lights.*

Credits

Maurice Kenny's essay "Tremolo," although commissioned for this book, was published first, with the editors' permission, in *Iroquois Voices, Iroquois Visions* (Bright Hill Press, 1996) and *Backward to Forward* (White Pine Press, 1997). Portions of Neal Burdick's selections appeared in different form in the Winter 1996 issue of *St. Lawrence*, the magazine of St. Lawrence University. Natalia Rachel Singer's essay "A Girl in Winter" was first published in the January/February 1996 issue of the Adirondack Mountain Club's magazine, *Adirondac*. Jim Gould's contribution also appears in his anthology *Rooted in Rock: New Writing from the Adirondack Mountains* (Syracuse University Press, 2001).